Herstellung: Books on Demand GmbH

ISBN 3-8311-1660-1

To my family

ii

Summary

This work deals with the possibilities of analysing high dimensional categorical data by means of visual tools. *Mosaicplots* here have a central position. Though these plots were introduced back in 1981 by Hartigan & Kleiner, this work for the first time provides a formal definition and description of mosaicplots based on tools known from the mathematical description of contingency tables and modelling processes.

Starting from this formal structure, variations of the mosaics, such as the *Fluctuation Diagram* or the *Same-Bin-Size Representation*, can be described similarly. *Doubledecker plots* are introduced as a new plot type.

The mathematical foundation gives the key to capture and describe the properties of mosaicplots. This leads in a natural way to coefficients of associations such as the χ^2 value or the odds ratio. By means of the odds ratio the connection between mosaicplots and categorical models appears, particularly loglinear models and several specimens of association models. To be able to handle higher dimensions, both in category numbers and in the number of variables, the concept of odds ratios has to be extended to *generalised odds ratios*. This had been suggested by Bhapkar & Koch (1968) but had not been put into practice.

Since mosaicplots are hierarchically constructed, the order, in which the variables occur, is crucial as well as the order of the categories within the variables. Based on the results of the Quine-McCluskey algorithm, a procedure is developed to automatically sort the variables in a way, which is optimal with respect to a binary target variable. This technique has several applications, among them the possibility of grouping cells according to previously unknown patterns or a method of identifying groups of cells. This is an especially interesting application for the interactive querying system.

At the interface between categorical and continuous data there are the *biplots* (Gabriel (1971), Gower & Hand (1996)). Being a dot based rather than an area based representation form, they provide another approach to visual modelling. Starting from the biplot representation a visual tool for mixed linear models is developed, which proves to be a powerful technique when equipped with interactive features.

Applications of mosaicplots in the area of data mining lead on the one hand to a proposal for the visualisation of *association rules*, which enables a visual assessment of the quality of a single rule. On the other hand, the attempt to visualise decision and classification trees makes it necessary to extend the structure of a Mosaic further to a tree-like structure. The resulting plots combine several aspects, which reflect the quality of a tree and gives a possibility of comparing several trees visually.

Literature

This work is based on graphics, so we must not omit the fathers of statistical graphics, William Playfair (1786) and Charles Minard. Interactive graphics is a lot younger, and goes back to the PRIM-9 project by Fisherkeller, Friedman & Tukey (1971) and Becker et al. (1987). Cleveland & McGill (1984) were one of the first to try to answer the question how and when graphics work well.

Especially in the recent past the approaches to formalise graphics and capture, why graphics work, have become more frequent. The monograph "The Grammar of Graphics" by Leland Wilkinson (1999) has to be named as one of the standards for static displays, the work by Wilhelm (2000) on the linking paradigm is its counterpart on the side of interactive graphics. My work has been strongly influenced by Antony Unwin, under whose supervision have been developed various software packages for interactive statistical graphics: Diamond Fast (with Graham Wills), Regard (with John Haslett & Graham Wills), Manet (with George Hawkins, Bernd Siegl & Heike Hofmann), Turner (with Stephan Lauer) and Cassatt (with Sylvia Winkler).

Besides these has also to be named Data Desk, a commercial software package by Velleman (1995).

Chapter 1 and consequently, this thesis as a whole is based on all of these references.

Mosaicplots, the red line through chapter 2, have been introduced by Hartigan & Kleiner (1981). Michael Friendly propagated their relationship to loglinear models (Friendly 1994a). Friendly (1999) proposed ways to visualise residuals by means of mosaicplots. Theus & Lauer (1999) followed this idea at the same time with a slightly different approach.

Sorting and re-ordering in variables is based on an algorithm by one of the founders of logical calculus, the mathematician and philosopher, Quine (1955). .

The mathematical basis of chapter 3 is given by PCA and MCA (Greenacre 1984). Biplots have first been introduced by Gabriel (1971). A recent monograph by Gower & Hand (1996) presents a detailed, clear overview and embeds several variations of biplots in a uniform framework. Interactive features for biplots have been proposed in Hofmann (1998).

Chapter 4 consists of a mixture of techniques with various origins. Association rules were proposed by Agrawal et al. (1993). Especially in the KDD Journal and the proceedings of the KDD conference may be found a lot of work on refinements, pruning mechanisms and, more rarely, applications of them.

Trees have their origin in the field between statistics and machine learning. Breiman (1984) has to be cited as one of the standards. A more recent introduction to the classification part of rules is by Hand (1997). Various algorithms implementing slightly different splitting criteria are on the market, among them, first of all, the C4.5 (Quinlan 1996) and C5.0 (Quinlan 2000). One of the problems while using trees in (commercial) packages is to figure out, which algorithm and splitting criterion exactly is implemented in the software.

Bayesian networks are a special case of graphical models. The most prominent monograph here, still is Steffen Lauritzen's book "Graphical Models" (Lauritzen 1996). Heckerman (1995) gives an introduction to Bayesian models from an application based view, which makes enjoyable reading.

Acknowledgement

At this point I'd like to thank all former and present members of the Rosuda Crew for their help and support during the process of this work.

First and foremost, my thanks go to my supervisor, Antony Unwin, for offering to me that many possibilities and supporting me as much as he did. He managed to find funding ever since three of us came tumbling through his office door, asking to share a programming job he had announced. I would like to thank him for leading me into interactive statistical graphics by putting me in front of a piece of software to program on. It now has a name and mosaicplots. Thanks, also, for blocking my career as programmer heavily by introducing me with one of his favourite phrases:

"schreiben! schreiben! schreiben!"

Thanks for a ready ear and advice in times when I got stuck.

I would also like to thank Adi Wilhelm for getting Typ-B funding for me for the last two years. I am grateful to him for many valuable discussions and advice.

I want to say thanks to John Hartigan for inviting me and having a lot of time for interesting and fruitful discussions.

I would like to thank Arno Siebes for inviting me to the CWI Amsterdam. These two months have been very productive and packed with new ideas ... and Amsterdam is worth a visit, for sure.

I am indebted to Christian, not only for having patience with me, but for spending hours and hours of minute proof-reading of my drafts. The results of his work were not always accepted as gratefully as they should have been. Thanks goes to my family for their love, support and patience.

Heike Hofmann   Augsburg, Oct. 2000

Contents

Chapter 1

Introduction

Welcome back Heike, we have recommendations for you in books, music and DVD & Video (if you're not Heike, click here).

This is the way a well-known online bookstore greets potential buyers when they "enter the shop". When looking at the recommendations, one finds a list of books, which the bookstore hopes you will find interesting enough to buy.

A similar list appears while browsing through the books.

Customers who bought this book also bought:

An interesting question is, how these lists are generated. But other nice features are in the web sites - reviews of books are given, with additional hints on their quality.

12 of 17 people found the following review helpful:

And a possibility of rating it at the end.

Was this review helpful to you? yes/no

This example gives only a glimpse of how easy it is to generate and collect information in all areas of daily life, and not only online. What the data in the example have in common is, that they are categorical: book titles and binary yes/no answers.

Categorical data appear in all areas of data analysis, from social sciences and surveys to data mining. They occur either in the form of nominal variables, such as **amazon**'s recommendations to readers - or in the form of ordered, bestseller lists, for instance, and interval grouped data as in (possibly censored) data of statistical offices. As computers and methods are able to handle ever larger data sets, the importance of analysing categorical data grows accordingly. Approaches are made in this direction, but often enough the analysis remains on the level of merely a listing of numbers: **12 of 17 people ...**

1

Data mining plays an especially large role, since in this field categorical data are not only analysed but also vast amounts of categorical output are produced and have, again, to be analysed in order to obtain interpretable results.

In the field of statistical modelling there are several approaches in dealing with multivariate categorical data - linear and loglinear models, logit and probit models are some of the most common methods. For all of these models it is necessary to check how well the data are fitted. Examining residuals with respect to structural behaviour or irregularities is vital. In the case of continuous data, graphical displays are used for this task. For categorical data graphical displays, also, exist, even for high-dimensional situations. But the connection between the graphical display and the model is far less explored for categorical data than for continuous data. A scatterplot of two (continuous) variables Y vs. X, for example, enables us to draw (rough) conclusions on the correlation coefficient between X and Y and gives information about how well a regression will fit the data. Nothing similar exists for categorical data.

The overall objective of this work is therefore to bring together the graphical display of categorical data and the corresponding models resulting in an approach to visual modelling.

Chapter 1 contains an introduction to the possibilities of visualising categorical data and to the concept of interactive statistical graphics with basic interactive features.

Chapter 2.1 starts with a formal definition of the structure of mosaicplots. This formal basis enables us later on to give precise definitions of the statistical parameters e.g. the odds ratio, which can be read off from mosaicplots. In section 2.6 we show how to visualise and compare odds ratios.

Besides that chapter 2.1 contains a description of several important variations of mosaicplots including the same-bin-size display and the fluctuation diagram, as well as an explanation of their functionality.

The application of mosaicplots for visual modelling forms the last part of the chapter. Among the models discussed are mainly loglinear models and several association models proposed by Goodman (1979).

Chapter 3 is devoted to another approach of visualising categorical data: biplots visualise results from a correlation analysis of the data. The same method also applies to results from regression or variance analysis. This chapter is important especially due to its character of combining both continuous and categorical data in a graphical display.

The exploratory analysis of large data sets is the focus of data mining methods. Using examples of association rules, decision trees and Bayesian networks it is shown in chapter 4, how visualization techniques may help to post-analyse results from these techniques. Quality assessment as well as interpretability of the results are important factors, here. For association rules we further give examples how structural relationships among the results can be made visible.

1.1 Graphical Methods for Categorical Data

There exist various possibilities for visualising a categorical variable - the first known barchart goes back to William Playfair (1786) in "The Commercial and Political Atlas". Graphics, known as "info graphics", in more recent media , show mainly pie charts or - worse - their elliptic 3D counterparts. Pie charts are the more modern plots, but that does not imply that they are better than barcharts - they are just different. At first we will consider four different types of plots: pie charts, barcharts, stacked barcharts and spine plots (Hummel 1996). Examples for all of these displays are given in figure 1.1.

The variety of plots raises the question, whether there is something like a "best display" for categorical values?

It is clear that different views of the same data emphasise different aspects.

But even if the plots do show the same aspects, one plot may be superior to another because the information can be extracted more easily from it. This leads to a crucial question of visualization:

What is easy to compare? Cleveland & McGill (1984), p. 536, gave a list of visual cues corresponding to some basic tasks for visual data analysis, which they ordered according to their "easiness" of decoding from easiest to hardest:

1. positions along a common scale

2. positions along identical, non-aligned scales

3. length, direction, angle

4. areas

5. volume, curvature

6. shading, color saturation

In the list Cleveland & McGill did not, however, distinguish between different shapes of areas. It is obvious, though, that the shape has a crucial influence for comparisons: rectangular areas for example are far easier to compare visually than circles or any irregular shape.

With respect to the above list of tasks the four types of plots for categorical data differ: what all of these plots have in common is that they are *area based* displays, i.e. the area represents the counts of a corresponding frequency table. The shape of the areas, though, is different for pie charts from the other plot types. Here, we have to compare segments of the circle instead of rectangular areas.

One trick to ease the comparison in area based plots is, of course, to reduce the dimension of the area by exploiting equalities. In barcharts and stacked barcharts all bars have the same

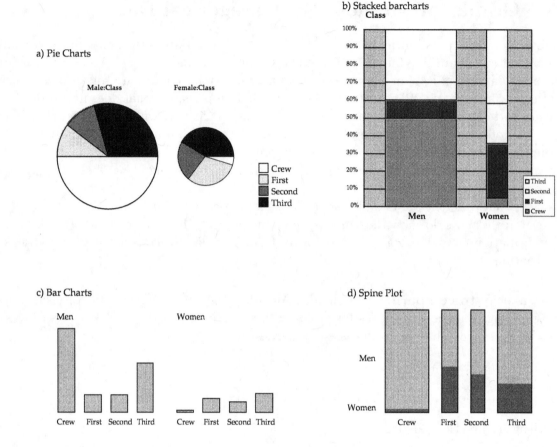

Figure 1.1: *a) Pie charts, b) stacked barcharts, c) barcharts and d) spine plot of the Class by Sex distribution of persons on board the Titanic.*

width, in spine plots all bars have the same height, the slices of a pie chart have the same radius.

According to the rules above this makes barcharts superior to the other plot types for comparing the categories' counts, since a comparison for barcharts only involves positions along a common scale. (Comparisons of category counts in stacked barcharts and spine plots correspond to comparisons of positions along identical, but non-aligned scales, in a pie chart angles need to be compared.)

As noted above, though, different views emphasise different aspects and therefore different comparisons are involved.

Table 1.1 gives an overview, which properties may be compared, for the four plot types.

These comparisons are especially important when not only one plot is of interest, but also

plot	category counts	cumulative counts	speciality	comparison
pie chart	angle (3)	angle (3)	% es, shares	angle (3)
stacked barchart	height (2)	height (2)	cumulative counts	height (2)
barchart	height (1)	-	category counts	height (1)
spine plot	width (2)	-	highlighted proportions	height (1)

Table 1.1: *Comparison of several tasks for different types of plots. In brackets the number of the task as given in the list of tasks may be found.*

comparisons between several plots of the same type. How do we have to modify them so that we are able to compare them directly, i.e. that the area-count ratio is constant. What additional information do we gain from a second plot of the same type?

Figure 1.1 already includes two plots of the same type (except for spine plots, where we do not need a second plot to represent the same information). All plots are modified such that the area-count ratio remains constant within each type of plot.

For high dimensional categorical variables there are many different plot types available, as well. In contrast to the one dimensional plots the higher dimensional ones are more specialised for certain purposes and it is not as easy to compare them.

Friendly (1994b) discusses several plot types and gives an overview of the ones most commonly used.

For two way tables Friendly proposes (cf. figure 1.2) the use of *sieve diagrams* (Riedwyl & Schuepbach 1994), later called *parquet diagrams*, *fourfold displays* for 2×2 tables and *association plots*.

All these plots have the same goal: to show the deviation from total independence in the data, i.e. here already a model assumption is involved; none of the displays show the observed counts.

A different approach to visualising higher dimensional categorical data is the use of *biplots* (Gabriel (1971), Gower & Hand (1996)). Biplots show the (two dimensional) results from a correspondence analysis. In contrast to all other types of plots mentioned so far this plot is *point based* - each combination of the variables, i.e. each cell of the contingency table, corresponds to one point in the display.

Mosaicplots (Hartigan & Kleiner 1981) are the only plots, which show both the counts without any underlying model assumption and are extendible to higher dimensions and arbitrary numbers of categories of the variables. It is this type of plot we therefore want to focus on in the sequel.

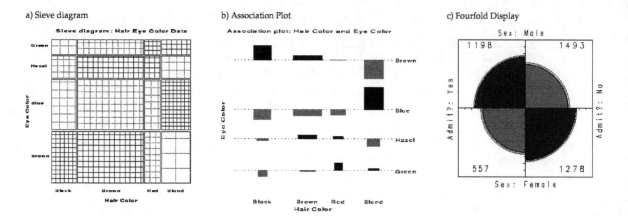

Figure 1.2: *a) Sieve Diagram, b) association plot of the Hair Eye Sex Data and c) Fourfold Display of the Berkeley Admission Data.*

1.2   Basics of Interactive Statistical Graphics

In the past it was difficult to find effective ways of displaying and exploring categorical data graphically. Static methods did not prove successful because they are difficult to interpret and are overloaded by labels, even for a small number of variables. But increasing data availability and modern data exploration methods call for the visualization of categorical data. Larger and larger data sets have to be analysed which cannot be handled with existing tools. Many of the data mining procedures which have been introduced to tackle this problem only work with categorical variables and they often produce results defining groupings of the cases, i.e. yet more categorical variables.

Innovative interactive graphical tools provide a solution to the problem of visualising categorical data just at the time when such analyses are more needed than ever.

As computer power increases, more powerful software is demanded. Existing methods do not only become faster, but have to be more intuitive in usage and supportive to creativity. But what makes software interactive? There is an almost bewildering abundance of applications which go under the heading of *interactive software* - yet there seem to be quite different opinions of what *interactivity* means.

The definition and use of this term is not quite clear even among computational statisticians as a recent survey on this topic by Swayne & Klinke (1999) made clear.

Human-computer interaction, as we understand and use it, is based on the definition proposed by Unwin (1999) as the *direct manipulation of plots and plotting elements in them*. This goes back to one of the first definitions of interactivity made by Becker et al. (1987), p. 2: "dynamic methods have two important properties: direct manipulation and instantaneous change. The data analyst takes an action through manual manipulation of an input device and something happens, virtually instantaneously, on a computer graphics screen". Huber (1988) corrects the term of dynamic graphics to *high-interaction graphics*. *Virtually instantaneously* hereby is often interpreted as real time changes, e.g. by Wills & Eick (1995), with the maximum response time set to 20 ms or equivalently an update speed of 50 frames per second. This, however, looks rather dangerous as it emphasises the role of the underlying hardware and may even lead to different decisions about which methods can be classified as interactive or not. Therefore it is probably better to speak of a *potentially interactive* method, if it fulfills the proposition of being directly manipulative. *Direct manipulation* depends on two conditions:

- **immediacy of place**

  by using a pointing device such as a mouse the analyst can specify visually the areas of the plot, which are meant as a starting point of an action.

- **the immediacy of action**

  the action is triggered by using a clicking device such as a mouse, pressing keys on the keyboard (but not typing in commands) or via some other such input device

Basic interactive features

Becker et al. (1987) proposed in their article 'Dynamic Graphics For Statistics' a list of several methods for interactive graphics. Among those were *"Identification of Labeled Data"*, *"Deletion"*, *"Linking"*, *"Linking, Deleting and Labeling by Brushing"*, *"Scaling"*, *"Rotation"* and *"Parameter Control"*.

All of these methods still exist and have proved to be essential for an interactive system. They are, however, very different in functionality and usage. Rotation for example is a rather specific action, as it is only sensible in case of at least three (continuous) variables while the identification of data is a very basic action, usable and necessary in absolutely every situation.

Another approach on describing the idea of interactivity has been made by Theus (1996). Theus discussed Becker's methods and reduced their number to only four basic methods, namely *Highlighting, Linking, Interactive Querying* and additionally *Warnings*.

Again, though, the methods are rather different in nature: linking, especially, is more of a concept, which may be applied on different levels of abstraction as discussed in Wilhelm (2000), than a method.

In the sequel we will assume an interactive system with the above basic methods and a strong linking mechanism on all levels.

Of course, interactive methods are very much related to computer software. The ideas of this work are not intended to depend on a specific software but describe general tools, which are useful to have while exploring categorical data.

I am strongly influenced, though, by MANET, a software, for which I have the main responsibility. MANET has been developed at the department of computer-oriented statistics in Augsburg university since 1995. It is at the moment the only system that implements mosaicplots in the interactive manner as described above. Most of the figures in this work are created with the help of this software.

Conveying "interactivity" on paper is a rather hard, if not impossible, task. The graphics shown are, of course, robbed of their interactive features. Their explorative nature, though, remains, as they are intended to be cornerstones in an interactive exploration process.

Chapter 2

Mosaic Plots for Categorical Data

2.1   Constructing Mosaicplots

The same data can be displayed in various formats. Tables 2.1 and 2.2 show two different formats, which we will use primarily. In the table on the left, the data is displayed on the basis of individuals, whereas table 2.2 holds the aggregated data.

Both tables show the Titanic Data (see section A.11). In the table on the left, each person on board is displayed in a single line. The identification number (ID) enables us to distinguish between individuals. Additional information for each person, such as their name or continuous variables such as age or weight could also be included if known.

The table on the right hand side shows aggregated data. Each line displays one combination of the variables *Class*, *Age*, *Gender* and *Survived* together with the number of people, who fall under this description. The variable *count* is called a *weight* variable. Weight variables can be used for several purposes. They can be used for summarizing data as shown in table 2.2. Here, 24 lines of data fully describe the information of 2201 lines of data from table 2.1. Another application for weight variables is the comparison of a continuous measurement for different categories, such as total area, population number or population density of different countries. Graphically it is quite naturally to use barcharts in this situation. William Playfair introduced them in his monograph "The Commercial and Political Atlas" (1786) in exactly this way.

In the following section we want to introduce a formal way of working with categories and (multidimensional) categorical data. In order to achieve independence from a specific data format, we will also consider weighting variables.

ID	Class	Age	Gender	Svd
1	First	Adult	Male	Yes
2	First	Adult	Male	Yes
...				
57	First	Adult	Male	Yes
58	First	Adult	Male	No
59	First	Adult	Male	No
...				
157	First	Adult	Male	No
158	First	Adult	Female	Yes
159	First	Adult	Female	Yes
...				
315	First	Adult	Female	Yes
316	First	Adult	Female	No
317	First	Adult	Female	No
318	First	Adult	Female	No
319	First	Adult	Female	No
320	First	Child	Male	Yes
...				
...				
2198	Crew	Adult	Female	Yes
2199	Crew	Adult	Female	No
2200	Crew	Adult	Female	No
2201	Crew	Adult	Female	No

Table 2.1: *Titanic Data on an individual basis.*

Class	Age	Gender	Svd	count
First	Adult	Male	Yes	57
First	Adult	Male	No	118
First	Adult	Female	Yes	140
First	Adult	Female	No	4
...				
Crew	Adult	Female	Yes	20
Crew	Adult	Female	No	3

Table 2.2: *Titanic Data aggregated over all combinations of the variables.*

2.1.1 Structured Multiway Contingency Tables

Multiway contingency tables are a very common method of displaying frequency data of categorical variables. Unlike two-way tables it is not at all clear for multiway tables, in which order the variables should occur in the display. Tables 2.3 and 2.4 show two different arrangements for the same data (Titanic Data). Each of the tables contains the numbers for *Class, Sex* and *Survival (Svd)*. Table 2.3 lays emphasis on the different survival rates of men and women in all classes, whereas the second arrangement in table 2.4 emphasizes that lower survival rates correspond to lower passenger classes for both women and men. This difference between the tables is due to the different order of the variables *Class* and *Gender*.

Class:	First		Second		Third		Crew	
Gender:	Female	Male	Female	Male	Female	Male	Female	Male
Survived: yes	141	62	93	25	90	88	20	192
no	4	118	13	154	106	422	3	670
Survival Rate (in %)	97	34	88	14	46	17	87	22

Table 2.3: *Numbers of Survivors on the Titanic by class affiliation and Gender. Large differences in the survival rates appear between men and women.*

Gender:	Female				Male			
Class:	First	Second	Third	Crew	First	Second	Third	Crew
Survived: yes	141	93	90	20	62	25	88	192
no	4	13	106	3	118	154	422	670
Survival Rate (in %)	97	88	46	87	34	14	17	22

Table 2.4: *Numbers of Survivors on the Titanic by Gender and class. The survival rates decline for lower passenger classes.*

Multiway contingency table are a hierarchical method of displaying information. Different orders and different directions of the variables support comparisons of different combinations. *Mosaicplots* are the graphical equivalents of contingency tables. Since contingency tables depend on the order in which the variables occur, we expect mosaicplots to be also sensitive to the order of the variables. To distinguish between mosaicplots that show the same data but have a different order of variables, we will introduce the concept of the *p-dimensional structure* of variables. This structure contains the meta-information of a set of categorical variables:

- the values that each variable can adopt (the *co-domain* or *image* of a variable),

- the order, in which these values occur,

- and the order and direction, in which the variables appear in the hierarchy.

One-dimensional Structures

Definition 2.1.1 (Image (Co-domain) of a variable)
Let X be a categorical variable with K categories. The *image of X (Co-domain of X)* is the set of all values X can adopt: the set of all categories $c(X)$,

$$c(X) := \{c_1, \ldots, c_K\}.$$

Definition 2.1.2 (Structure of a variable)

Let $c_{(1)}, \ldots, c_{(K)}$ be the order of the categories in variable X.

The *one dimensional structure of* a categorical variable X with K categories is the K dimensional vector of indicator functions

$$s_X : c(X) \rightarrow \{0, 1\}^K,$$
$$s_X(y) = (\mathbb{1}_{\{c_{(1)}\}}(y), \ldots, \mathbb{1}_{\{c_{(K)}\}}(y)).$$

Let X^i be the ith observation of X, then

$$s_X(X^i) = (0 \ldots 0 \underset{\underset{j}{\uparrow}}{1} 0 \ldots 0), \qquad \text{if } X^i = c_{(j)}, 1 \le j \le K.$$

We will denote with $s_X(X)$ the matrix of dummy variables of X:

$$s_X(X) := \sum_{i=1}^{n} e_i s_X(X^i),$$

where $e_i \in \mathbf{R}^n$ is the ith (column) vector of the standard normal basis of R^n.

Let X be for example:

$$X = (Second, Third, Crew, Second, \ldots, Third, Third)^t, \tag{2.1}$$

the image of X then is the set of categories $\{Crew, First, Second, Third\}$.

One possible ordering of the categories is: $(First, Second, Third, Crew)$. This implies the following structure for X:

$$s_X(y) = (\mathbb{1}_{\{First\}}(y), \mathbb{1}_{\{Second\}}(y), \mathbb{1}_{\{Third\}}(y), \mathbb{1}_{\{Crew\}}(y)).$$

With X as given in (2.1) $X^1 = Second$, and

$$s_X(X^1) = s_{Class}(Second) = (0, 1, 0, 0).$$

The matrix of dummy variables can be calculated successively from $s_X(X^i), i = 1, \ldots, 2201$

as

$$s_X(X) = \sum_{i=1}^{2201} e_i s_X(X^i) = e_1 s_X(X^1) + \sum_{i=2}^{2201} e_i s_X(X^i) =$$

$$= \begin{pmatrix} 1 \\ 0 \\ 0 \\ 0 \\ \vdots \\ 0 \\ 0 \end{pmatrix} (\ 0 \ \ 1 \ \ 0 \ \ 0 \ ) + \sum_{i=2}^{2201} e_i s_X(X^i) = \begin{pmatrix} 0 & 1 & 0 & 0 \\ 0 & 0 & 0 & 0 \\ 0 & 0 & 0 & 0 \\ 0 & 0 & 0 & 0 \\ \vdots & & & \vdots \\ 0 & 0 & 0 & 0 \\ 0 & 0 & 0 & 0 \end{pmatrix} + \sum_{i=2}^{2201} e_i s_X(X^i) =$$

$$= \begin{pmatrix} 0 & 1 & 0 & 0 \\ 0 & 0 & 1 & 0 \\ 0 & 0 & 0 & 1 \\ 0 & 1 & 0 & 0 \\ \vdots & & & \vdots \\ 0 & 0 & 1 & 0 \\ 0 & 0 & 1 & 0 \end{pmatrix}.$$

We will now use the concept of structure for defining several other properties of categorical variables in a very simple way:

Definition 2.1.3 (Absolute and relative frequencies)
Let X be a categorical variable with n observations and structure s_X.
The *absolute frequencies* of the categories of X can be written as

$$\sum_{i=1}^{n} s_X(X^i),$$

and its *relative frequencies* accordingly as

$$\frac{1}{n} \sum_{i=1}^{n} s_X(X^i).$$

In the example of the Titanic data, the absolute and relative frequencies for *Class* with structure $(\mathbb{I}_{\{First\}}(y), \mathbb{I}_{\{Second\}}(y), \mathbb{I}_{\{Third\}}(y), \mathbb{I}_{\{Crew\}}(y))$ are:

$$\sum_{i=1}^{2201} s_{Class}(Class^i) = (325, 285, 706, 885)$$

and

$$\frac{1}{2201} \sum_{i=1}^{2201} s_{Class}(Class^i) = (0.15, 0.13, 0.32, 0.40),$$

respectively.

The concept of structures of variables is flexible enough to include weight variables in a natural way. We will show at the example of the one dimensional structure, how the definition may be extended. Afterwards, however, we will not distinguish between a structure or its weighted equivalent.

By extending the definition of structure slightly we are able to include weight variables in the formal context:

Definition 2.1.4 (Structures with Weight Variable)
Let X be a categorical variable with structure s_X and W a weight variable, i.e. the entries in W, W^i, are non-negative real numbers $\forall i$.
The *weighted structure sw* of X and W is defined as

$$sw_{X,W}(y, w) = w \cdot s_X(y).$$

Weighted variants of relative and absolute frequencies are a natural extension of the definition by replacing the unweighted structure with the weighted one.

Multidimensional Structures

Starting from the one-dimensional structures of the variables , we want to combine several of them. For this, we find the *Kronecker Product* most useful.

Definition 2.1.5 (Kronecker product)
Let A and B be $n \times k$ and $m \times r$ matrices. The product $C = A \otimes B$ is the *Kronecker product of A and B.*

$$C = \begin{pmatrix} a_{11}B & a_{12}B & \dots & a_{1k}B \\ a_{21}B & a_{22}B & \dots & a_{2k}B \\ \vdots & \vdots & \ddots & \vdots \\ a_{n1}B & a_{n2}B & \dots & a_{nk}B \end{pmatrix}$$

C is an $nm \times kr$ matrix.

In the following the Kronecker product is used in a form $v \otimes A$, where A is a matrix but v is a (row or column) vector only. In this case, the Kronecker product simplifies to:

$$v \bigotimes A = \begin{pmatrix} v_1 A \\ v_2 A \\ \vdots \\ v_n A \end{pmatrix} \qquad w \bigotimes A = (w_1 A, w_2 A, \dots, w_n A),$$

for $v, w^t \in \mathbf{R}^n$. Using the Kronecker product, we can now build structures of an arbitrary dimension from the one-dimensional structures:

Definition 2.1.6 (Structure of p variables)
Let $X_1, \dots, X_p$ be p categorical variables and $X_{(1)}, \dots, X_{(p)}$ be one order of them. The *structure* of $X_1, \dots, X_p$ is an expression S of the following form:

$$S(y_1, \dots, y_p) = h_1(y_1) \bigotimes h_2(y_2) \bigotimes \dots \bigotimes h_p(y_p),$$

where $h_j = s_{X_{(j)}}$ or $h_j = s_{X_{(j)}}^t$, $1 \le j \le p$.
The *set $\mathcal{S}$ of all p dimensional structures* of $X_1, \dots, X_p$ consists of all possible expressions S as above.

The product of two variables

There are basically two possibilities of "multiplying" the structures of two categorical variables X and Z:

$$s_X(x) \bigotimes s_Z(z)^t \text{ and } s_X(x) \bigotimes s_Z(z)$$

To understand the results of a Kronecker multiplication better, we will have a short look into both.

What is $s_X(x) \bigotimes s_Z(z)^t$? In the Kronecker product of two one-dimensional structures, the product of indicator functions appears at each entry of the result. Since any product of indicator functions, however, can be written as another (higher-dimensional) indicator function, the result again is a vector or matrix of indicator functions. The product of two one-dimensional indicator functions gives a new indicator function, where the condition results from combining the two old conditions with a logical "and".
Let X and Z be categorical variables with images $c(X) = \{c_1, \dots, c_p\}$ and $c(Z) = \{d_1, \dots, d_q\}$ respectively.
The product $s_X(x) \bigotimes s_Z(z)^t$ yields a **matrix of indicator functions**. The (i, j)th entry of this matrix has the form:

$$\mathbb{I}_{\{c_{(i)}\}}(x) \cdot \mathbb{I}_{\{d_{(j)}\}}(z) = \mathbb{I}_{\{c_{(i)}, d_{(j)}\}}(x, z)$$

and

$$s_X(x) \bigotimes s_Z(z)^t =$$

$$= \begin{pmatrix} \mathbb{1}_{\{c_{(1)},d_{(1)}\}}(x,z) & \mathbb{1}_{\{c_{(1)},d_{(2)}\}}(x,z) & \cdots & \mathbb{1}_{\{c_{(1)},d_{(q)}\}}(x,z) \\ \mathbb{1}_{\{c_{(2)},d_{(1)}\}}(x,z) & \mathbb{1}_{\{c_{(2)},d_{(2)}\}}(x,z) & \cdots & \mathbb{1}_{\{c_{(2)},d_{(q)}\}}(x,z) \\ \vdots & \vdots & \ddots & \vdots \\ \mathbb{1}_{\{c_{(p)},d_{(1)}\}}(x,z) & \mathbb{1}_{\{c_{(p)},d_{(2)}\}}(x,z) & \cdots & \mathbb{1}_{\{c_{(p)},d_{(q)}\}}(x,z) \end{pmatrix} \in \{0,1\}^{p \times q}$$

What is $s_X(x) \bigotimes s_Z(z)$? As before, the product of indicator functions in X and Z builds another indicator function. The form, however, is different. The expression $s_X(x) \bigotimes s_Z(z)$ results in a **vector** of indicator functions. If X and Z have the same structure as above, the product of their structures is

$$s_X(x) \bigotimes s_Z(z) = \begin{pmatrix} \mathbb{1}_{\{c_{(1)},d_{(1)}\}}(x,z) \\ \mathbb{1}_{\{c_{(1)},d_{(2)}\}}(x,z) \\ \vdots \\ \mathbb{1}_{\{c_{(1)},d_{(q)}\}}(x,z) \\ \mathbb{1}_{\{c_{(2)},d_{(1)}\}}(x,z) \\ \vdots \\ \mathbb{1}_{\{c_{(p)},d_{(q)}\}}(x,z) \end{pmatrix} \in \{0,1\}^{qp}.$$

Therefore we can regard the result from multiplying the structures in this way as a new variable with $p \times q$ categories. This variable is called the *cross-product* of X and Z.

Definition 2.1.7 (Structured Contingency Table)
A *(structured) p-way contingency table* consists of p categorical variables $X_1, \ldots, X_p$ and a structure S.
If the variables have n observations, the contingency table is written as

$$\sum_{i=1}^{n} S(X_{(1)}^i, \ldots, X_{(p)}^i).$$

If W is a weight variable, the corresponding *weighted contingency table* can be written as

$$\sum_{i=1}^{n} W^i S(X_{(1)}^i, \ldots, X_{(p)}^i).$$

accordingly.

Example 2.1.8 *Titanic Data*
*The variable **Class** of the Titanic Data has image*

$$c(Class) = \{crew, 1st \ (passenger \ class), 2nd, 3rd\},$$

*one possible structure of **Class** is $s_{Class}(y) = \left(\mathbb{1}_{\{1st\}}(y), \mathbb{1}_{\{2nd\}}(y), \mathbb{1}_{\{3rd\}}(y), \mathbb{1}_{\{Crew\}}(y) \right)$, variable **Sex** has image $c(Sex) = \{f, m\}$ and we will set the structure to*

$$s_{Sex}(y) = \left(\mathbb{1}_{\{f\}}(y), \mathbb{1}_{\{m\}}(y) \right).$$

*There are several different options for two-dimensional structures of **Class** and **Sex**. Each of these structures will lead to a different visual display (see figures in example 2.1.11):*

- $S_1(y_1, y_2) = s_{Class}(y_1) \otimes s_{Sex}(y_2)^t$:

$$S_1(y_1, y_2) = \left(\mathbb{1}_{\{1st\}}(y_1), \mathbb{1}_{\{2nd\}}(y_1), \mathbb{1}_{\{3rd\}}(y_1), \mathbb{1}_{\{Crew\}}(y_1) \right) \otimes \left(\begin{array}{c} \mathbb{1}_{\{f\}}(y_2) \\ \mathbb{1}_{\{m\}}(y_2) \end{array} \right) =$$

$$= \left(\begin{array}{cccc} \mathbb{1}_{\{1st,f\}}(y_1, y_2) & \mathbb{1}_{\{2nd,f\}}(y_1, y_2) & \mathbb{1}_{\{3rd,f\}}(y_1, y_2) & \mathbb{1}_{\{Crew,f\}}(y_1, y_2) \\ \mathbb{1}_{\{1st,m\}}(y_1, y_2) & \mathbb{1}_{\{2nd,m\}}(y_1, y_2) & \mathbb{1}_{\{3rd,m\}}(y_1, y_2) & \mathbb{1}_{\{Crew,m\}}(y_1, y_2) \end{array} \right)$$

- $S_2(y_1, y_2) = s_{Class}(y_1)^t \otimes s_{Sex}(y_2) = S_1(y_1, y_2)^t$

- $S_3(y_1, y_2) = s_{Class}(y_1)^t \otimes s_{Sex}(y_2)^t$:

$$S_3(y_1, y_2) = \left(\begin{array}{c} \mathbb{1}_{\{1st,f\}}(y_1, y_2) \\ \mathbb{1}_{\{1st,m\}}(y_1, y_2) \\ \mathbb{1}_{\{2nd,f\}}(y_1, y_2) \\ \mathbb{1}_{\{2nd,m\}}(y_1, y_2) \\ \mathbb{1}_{\{3rd,f\}}(y_1, y_2) \\ \mathbb{1}_{\{3rd,m\}}(y_1, y_2) \\ \mathbb{1}_{\{Crew,f\}}(y_1, y_2) \\ \mathbb{1}_{\{Crew,m\}}(y_1, y_2) \end{array} \right)$$

The corresponding contingency tables are

- $S_1 = s_{Class} \otimes s_{Sex}^t$:

		Class			
		1st	*2nd*	*3rd*	*Crew*
Sex	*f*	*145*	*106*	*196*	*23*
	m	*180*	*179*	*510*	*862*

- $S_2 = s^t_{Class} \otimes s_{Sex}$:

		Sex	
		f	m
Class	1st	145	180
	2nd	106	179
	3rd	196	510
	Crew	23	862

- and $S_3 = s^t_{Class} \otimes s^t_{Sex}$:

Class	Sex	
1st	f	145
	m	180
2nd	f	106
	m	179
3rd	f	196
	m	510
Crew	f	23
	m	862

The structure of p variables $X_1, X_2, \ldots, X_p$ is a matrix of indicator functions, the number of rows and columns is given by the numbers of row and column vectors in the expression. If S is constructed as described and s_{X_j}, $j \in J \subset \{1, \ldots, p\}$, are the column vectors in the expression, the number of columns of S is given as the product of their categories: $\prod_{j \in J} |c_{X_j}|$ (analogous for the number of rows).

2.1.2   Formal Definition of Mosaicplots

A *mosaicplot* of $X_1, \ldots, X_p$ is a function, which takes a structured multiway contingency table as argument and produces a graphical output according to the following rules of construction:

Procedure 2.1.9 (Construction of a mosaicplot)
Let $S = h_1 \otimes h_2 \otimes \ldots \otimes h_p$ be the structure of $X_1, \ldots, X_p$,

(i) Starting point is a rectangular area with width w and height h. This area is named bin, there is at first no condition for the values of $X_1, \ldots, X_p$ to fall into this bin.

Set $k = 1$ and proceed with (ii).

(ii) If $k = p + 1$ stop.

For variable $X_{(k)}$ calculate the size and proportion of a new set of bins from the dimensions of the old bin:

If h_k is a row vector, the old bin is divided horizontally, otherwise it is divided vertically.

Let h_k be a row vector.

Extract from the sub-structure $h_1 \otimes h_2 \otimes \ldots \otimes h_k$ of S the vector of indicator functions, which fulfill the condition of the old bin. This results in a row vector of dimension K, if $X_{(k)}$ has K categories.

Extract from the contingency table given by the structure $h_1 \otimes h_2 \otimes \ldots \otimes h_k$ the cells corresponding to the vector of indicator functions above. Let the cells be $n_{(1)}, \ldots, n_{(K)}$.

The position p_j (top-left corner) and size of the bin corresponding to the jth category of $X_{(k)}$ then is calculated as follows:

- y-value of $p_j = y$-value of the top-left corner of the old bin,
  x-value of $p_j = $ sum of the widths of the $j - 1$ previous bins corresponding to the $j - 1$ previous categories.

- The **height** of the new bin is the height of the old bin,
  the **width** of the new bin is given by:

$$\text{new width} = \text{old width} \cdot \frac{n_{(j)}}{\sum_{i=1}^{K} n_i}.$$

Increase k by 1.

For each category $c_{(j)}$ of $X_{(k)}$ restrict the old condition with the further condition $y_k = c_{(j)}$. Take the new condition and the bin corresponding to category $c_{(j)}$, and proceed with step (ii).

$\square$

Remark 2.1.10
In the above procedure no space for gaps between bins was taken into account. Gaps between bins are indispensable. Without any gaps empty cells e.g. could not be visualised and we were not able to decide graphically, *which* combinations were empty and which were not.
In practice, we will therefore always leave gaps between the bins. The width of the gaps is calculated from the level on which they appear - the deeper down gaps appear in the hierarchy the smaller they are.

Example 2.1.11 *Titanic Data*
Let us take the structure S_1 and contingency table from example 2.1.8:
$S_1 = s_{Class} \otimes s_{Sex}^t,$

		Class			
		1st	*2nd*	*3rd*	*Crew*
Sex	*f*	*145*	*106*	*196*	*23*
	m	*180*	*179*	*510*	*862*

Figure 2.1 shows the construction of a mosaic plot for structure S_1 according to the steps given in procedure 2.1.9.

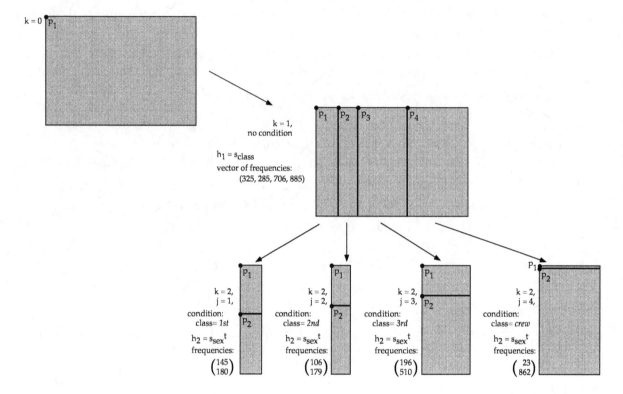

Figure 2.1: *Step-wise construction of the mosaicplot of structure S_1 according to procedure 2.1.9.*

Figure 2.2 gives an overview of all mosaicplots corresponding to the structures S_1, S_2 and S_3 from example 2.1.8.

Remark 2.1.12

(i)   Hartigan & Kleiner (1981) introduced mosaicplots with a structure consisting of alternating row and column vectors.

     By changing this default we are also able to take cross-products of variables into consideration, which allow us to visualise high-order interaction terms of loglinear models

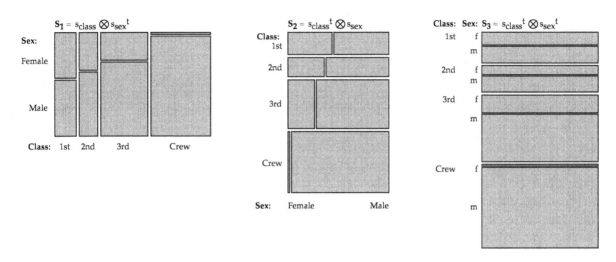

Figure 2.2: *Mosaics corresponding to the structures from example 2.1.8.*

later on (see section 2.7.1).

(ii)   For more than two variables the order in which the variables occur in S is crucial.

As we have seen with multiway contingency tables, different orders of the variables support different comparisons. We will have to examine in more detail, which orders of variables support exactly which comparisons.

(iii) Up to now, we have dealt with static displays only. Yet, mosaicplots gain a lot by adding interactive features. Some very useful features are the interactive labelling and querying system, the linkage of mosaics with other displays, which allows highlighting, as well as the possibility to reduce dimensions interactively. This helps immensely to understand the inner structure of a mosaic.

2.1.3   Interactive Features

Highlighting in Mosaicplots

Highlighting is based on the concept of linked views. The corresponding linkage is the linking of displays on basis of the observations. We may code the highlighted values in a dynamic variable H with two categories: one for "value is highlighted" and a second for "value is not highlighted".

Highlighting then works like adding a new variable to a mosaicplot: it will split the existing bins once more. The direction of the split, however, is fixed to be orthogonal with respect to the last direction. Additionally, the bins corresponding to the highlighted values are filled with the highlighting colour just as in the other displays in order to further emphasize highlighting visually.

Formally we can denote the addition of highlighting to a mosaicplot with a change of the underlying structure S to

- $S \bigotimes s_H$, if S ends with a vertical direction s_X, or

- $S \bigotimes s_H^t$, if S ends with a horizontal direction s_X^t,

where s_H is the structure of the (binary) highlighting variable.

Example 2.1.13 *Titanic Data*
*Figure 2.3 shows two three-dimensional mosaicplots of **Class**, **Sex** and **Survival**. By chang-*

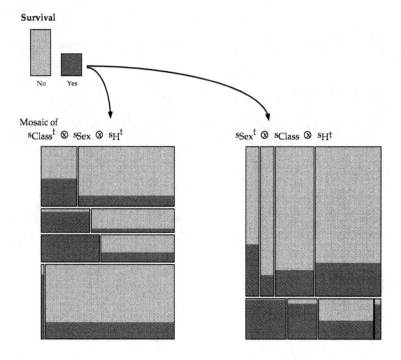

Figure 2.3: *Three-dimensional mosaicplots with exchanged order of variables. Highlighting shows the survivors.*

ing the order of the variables different aspects of the data are emphasized. Highlighting is the same for both mosaicplots, it shows the survivors.
On the left highlighting shows the differences in survival rates between women and men for all classes. The mosaic on the right shows the survival rates within the different classes (first, second, third and crew) for men and women.

Editing the structure

Categories of a variable are part of the structure underlying a mosaic plot. Whenever this structure is changed, the mosaic display should react to this change. There are several possibilities to change the structure of a single categorical variable. Some of them are:

- re-ordering the categories

- grouping categories together

- or splitting categories

The software MANET provides the possibility of performing all of these actions on the bins of corresponding bar charts. These changes get promoted to the mosaicplot. Figures 2.4 and 2.5 give examples for the actions mentioned above.

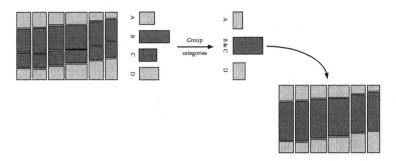

Figure 2.4: *Grouping categories of a variable within a barchart causes a change of the mosaic display.*

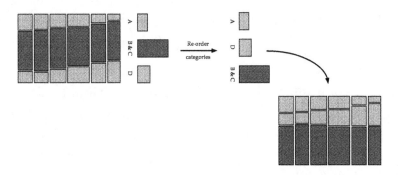

Figure 2.5: *Re-ordering categories of a variable within a barchart causes a change of the mosaic display.*

Another way to change the structure of a mosaicplot is to reduce or increase the number of variables. This kind of changes fits in very well with the hierarchical structure of mosaics. We now want to have a closer look at the influence of a specific order of the variables in a structure. For this, we want to answer the question, which statistical measures can be read from one mosaicplot and which can not.

2.1.4 Properties of Mosaicplots

From the list of basic tasks - as given in the introduction on page 3 - we will look at the following four:

- positions along a common scale

- positions along identical, non-aligned scales

- length

- areas

more closely in the case of mosaicplots. Each of these comparisons enables us to draw different conclusions, i.e. in order to get information about specific aspects of the data, we will have to look at different properties of a mosaicplot.

Comparing areas: visualising a multinomial distribution

From the construction of a mosaicplot it should be clear that the area of a tile is proportional to the size of the cell of a corresponding contingency table. The factor of proportionality is given by the total area of the mosaicplot. A mosaicplot therefore shows an estimate of the common distribution of all the variables involved. This gives a nice starting point for the other comparison methods.

Figure 2.6 shows a mosaicplot of the Rochdale Data together with a histogram of the corresponding cell sizes. A prominent feature of this data set is the high number of empty or small cells. Cells containing less than 7 households are highlighted in the display. They represent more than 90% of all the cells.

Positions along a common scale: visualising a conditional distribution

in the following we will use the concept of *cross-products* between variables frequently. For convenience of notation we will therefore denote a cross-product of variables in the same way as a simple variable (with structure and image adjusted as necessary).

Any structure S contains sequences of the form:

$$s_1 = s_X^t \bigotimes s_Y \bigotimes s_Z^t \qquad \text{or} \qquad s_2 = s_X \bigotimes s_Y^t \bigotimes s_Z, \qquad (2.2)$$

8 dimensional mosaic plot

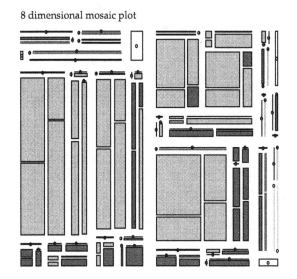

histogram of the cell sizes

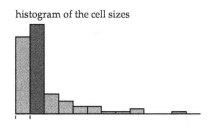

Figure 2.6: *Mosaicplot of the Rochdale Data; on the right a histogram of the corresponding cell sizes. Highlighted are bins with a cell size less than 7 households.*

where X, Y and Z are arbitrary cross-products of categorical variables. Furthermore, it is easy to verify that any structure is built up from sequences s_1 and s_2 alternatively. Very short structures, such as those from the *Double Decker Plots* (see 2.2) can also be included in this scheme by allowing one of the s_i elements as in (2.2) within the structure to be empty. The structure of a Double Decker plot therefore can be written as

$$s_X \qquad \text{or} \qquad s_X^t$$

without highlighting and

$$s_X \bigotimes s_H^t \qquad \text{or} \qquad s_X^t \bigotimes s_H$$

considering also a highlighting variable H.
We will have to show therefore, what exactly we can derive visually from these sequences. Let us examine first structures ending with a sequence as above:

Proposition 2.1.14
Let X and Y be any cross-product of categorical variables (including the empty product) with the restriction that Y may not be empty, if X is not empty. Let Z be any non-empty cross-product of categorical variables.
Let S be a structure ending with s_1 or s_2 (see eqn. (2.2)), i.e.:

$$S = \ldots s_X^t \bigotimes s_Y \bigotimes s_Z^t \qquad \text{or} \qquad S = \ldots s_X \bigotimes s_Y^t \bigotimes s_Z,$$

where the dots indicate possible further variables (without any restrictions).
Then the following statement holds:

The **heights** (the **widths** respectively, if $S = \ldots \otimes s_2$) of the bins in a mosaicplot corresponding to structure S are the ML-estimates of the conditional distribution of Z given Y for fixed levels of X (and any other variable, which may appear in the structure before X).

For a proof we have to consider, which bins and proportions are compared - see figure 2.7. Wlog let the number of categories in Z be 2:

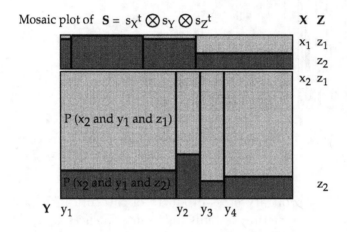

Figure 2.7: *Mosaicplot corresponding to structure* $S = s_W \otimes s_X^t \otimes s_Y \otimes s_Z^t$.

Remember that the tiles of a mosaicplot are by construction proportional to the cells of the corresponding contingency table. We may therefore use the areas of the tiles as ML-estimates of the common distribution of the variables involved.

We will prove the above statement by induction over the structure S.

For the simplest case of $S = s_Z$ or $S = s_Z^t$ the statement is trivial (due to the construction of a mosaicplot).

Now assume that $S = \ldots \otimes s_1$:

Let S' be a beginning sequence of S, i.e. $\exists \tilde{S}$, such that $S = S' \otimes \tilde{S}$.

The induction hypothesis then is that the statement holds for all mosaicplots with structure S'.

Consider two tiles t_1 and t_2 from the mosaicplot of structure S corresponding to the conditions $X = x_{(i)}, Y = y_{(j)}, Z = z_{(1)}$ and $X = x_{(i)}, Y = y_{(j)}, Z = z_{(2)}$ (for some valid i, j) as for instance the two tiles framed in figure 2.7.

Since the tiles t_1 and t_2 are proportional to $P(X = x_{(i)}, Y = y_{(j)}, Z = z_{(1)})$ and $P(X = x_{(i)}, Y = y_{(j)}, Z = z_{(2)})$ respectively, the sum of their areas is proportional to $P(X = x_{(i)}, Y = y_{(j)})$.

By assumption, the statement holds for $S' = \ldots \otimes s_X^t \otimes s_Y$. Therefore the width of the union of t_1 and t_2 shows the conditional probability $P(Y = y_{(j)} \mid X = x_{(i)})$ and the heights of t_1 and t_2 are calculated as fraction of each tile's area and width:

$$\text{height } (t_1) \quad \propto \quad \frac{P(X = x_{(i)}, Y = y_{(j)}, Z = z_{(1)})}{P(Y = y_{(j)} \mid X = x_{(i)})} =$$

$$= \quad P(Z = z_{(1)} \mid X = x_{(i)}, Y = y_{(j)}) P(X = x_{(i)}) =$$

$$= \quad P(Z = z_{(1)} \mid Y = y_{(j)}) \text{ for } X = x_{(i)},$$

$$\text{height } (t_2) \quad \propto \quad P(Z = z_{(2)} \mid Y = y_{(j)}) \text{ for } X = x_{(i)}.$$

Similarly for $S = \ldots \otimes s_2$. $\qquad\qquad\qquad\qquad\qquad\qquad\qquad\qquad\qquad\qquad\qquad\square$

We have shown, that the heights of all bins (the widths respectively) show a conditional distribution of the variables. But we can do even better than that:

Since the construction of mosaics is strictly hierarchical, the mosaicplot of structure S also contains (visually) all beginning structures S' of S, where $S = S' \otimes \ldots$.

Corollary 2.1.15

Let S be a structure of the form

$$s_{X_1} \otimes s_{X_2}^t \otimes \cdots \otimes s_{X_i} \otimes \cdots \otimes s_{X_p},$$

where $X_1, \ldots, X_p$ are any cross-product of categorical variables. Then the corresponding mosaicplot shows for all i, $1 \leq i \leq p$ the conditional distribution

$$X_i \mid X_{i-1} \text{ for fixed levels of } X_{i-2}, \ldots, X_1 \text{ collapsed over } X_{i+1}, \ldots, X_p.$$

Figures 2.8 to 2.10 show a series of pictures of the same mosaicplot, where all conditional distributions within it are emphasized one after the other by suitable highlighting. The mosaic corresponds to the structure $S = s_W \otimes s_X^t \otimes s_Y \otimes s_Z^t$ of the four binary variables W, X, Y and Z. Figure 2.8 highlights the four conditional distributions of $Z \mid Y$ for fixed levels of W and X. Figure 2.9 concentrates on the lower-dimensional mosaicplot with structure $S = s_W \otimes s_X^t \otimes s_Y$. Because of the hierarchical construction, there is no need to draw another mosaicplot. Reducing the structure can be done visually by "ignoring" the last step in constructing the higher-dimensional mosaicplot. The corresponding action in a contingency table is to collapse over the last variable Z.

The last figure in the sequence shows the distribution of $X \mid W$ collapsed over Z and Y. Here, only the structure $s_W \otimes s_X^t$ is of relevance for the conditional distribution.

Conclusion: With the means of the easiest of all possible visual cues, the comparison of positions along a common scale, we are able to "look" at the conditional distribution of any categorical variables. Re-ordering categories ensures that this comparison is in fact all we need (see figure 2.11).

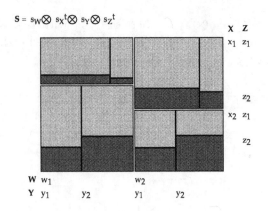

Figure 2.8: *Four conditional distributions of* $Z \mid Y$ *for fixed levels of* W *and* X. *An interesting pattern among the distributions appears: while the probabilities of* $z_1 \mid X, Y$ *are higher than the probabilities of* $z_2 \mid X, Y$ *in the upper row (for* $X = x_1$*), this effect is reversed for the probabilities in the bottom row.*

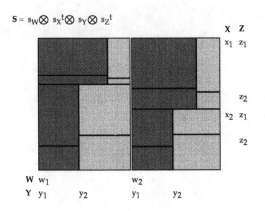

Figure 2.9: *Two conditional distributions of* $Y \mid X$ *for fixed levels of* W *collapsed over* Z.

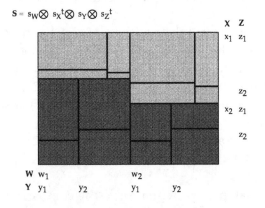

Figure 2.10: *Conditional distribution of* $X \mid W$ *collapsed over* Z *and* Y.

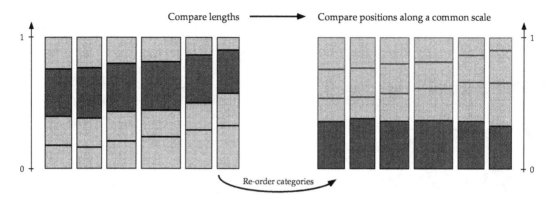

Figure 2.11: *Re-ordering categories of the variables in a mosaicplot reduces the difficulty of the visual task from comparing lengths to comparing positions along a common scale.*

Application: Statistical Dependencies between Variables Since we are able to estimate the conditional distributions between two categorical variables visually, we may also estimate statistics, which are based on the conditional probabilities.

One of these statistics is the *statistical dependency* between variables:

Let X and Y be two categorical variables with I and J categories respectively.

These variables are said to be *statistically independent*, iff π_{ij}, the probability of cell ij in the corresponding contingency table, can be written as product of row and column probabilities:

$$\pi_{ij} = \pi_{i.} \cdot \pi_{.j} \quad \forall 1 \leq i \leq I, 1 \leq j \leq J. \tag{2.3}$$

Dividing by $P(X_i) = \pi_{i.}$ reformulates eqn. (2.3) in terms of conditional probabilities to:

$$P(Y_j|X_i) = P(Y_j) \qquad \forall 1 \leq i \leq I, 1 \leq j \leq J.$$

Independence between two variables therefore is equivalent to constant conditional proba-

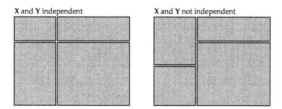

Figure 2.12: *Mosaicplots corresponding to statistical independence and dependence of two variables X and Y (Theus & Lauer 1999).*

bilities for all j within each level of X. As the conditional probabilities show up as widths (heights) of the bins in a mosaicplot, statistical independence corresponds to a lattice-like appearance of the bins (see figure 2.12). Statistical dependencies and associations among variables is discussed in more detail in section 2.6.

Example 2.1.16 *Rochdale Data*

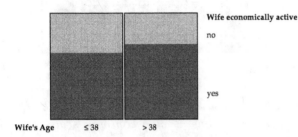

Figure 2.13: *Mosaic of **Wife's Age**. Highlighted are households, where the wife is economically active. Wives are more likely to be economically active, if they are older than 38.*

Figures 2.13 to 2.15 show a series of three mosaicplots of the Rochdale Data. Highlighted in each of them are households with an economically active wife. The first mosaic (fig. 2.13) shows the conditional probabilities for the wife being economically active given her age: the rate of economically active women above 38 is higher than the rate for younger women.

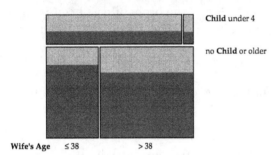

Figure 2.14: *Mosaic of **Child** and **Wife's Age**. Highlighted are households, where the wife is economically active. In households with small children, the age of the wife has no impact on her economic activity, without children or children older than 4, wives younger than 38 are more likely to be economically active.*

*After adding another explanatory variable as done in figure 2.14, however, this turns out to be an example of Simpson's paradox. Regarding, whether a child under the age of four is in the household or not, alters the ratios of the probabilities for an active economy: If there is a child under the age of four in the household, the age of the wife has no impact on her economic activity. The economic activity is **partially independent** of the wife's age. If there is no child in the household or all children are older than 4, the rate of economically active wives is higher for younger women. The inverse effect of what we obtained before.*
This conclusion is yet intensified by taking into consideration whether a household is of Asian origin or not (cf. figure 2.15). There are only few Asian households in the data set, the number of economically active wives among them is even less. For non-Asian households,

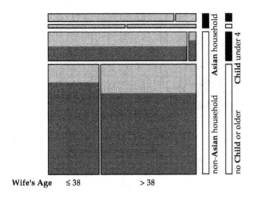

Figure 2.15: *Mosaic of **Asian**, **Child** and **Wife's Age**. Highlighted are households, where the wife is economically active. There are only few Asian households, the number of economically active wives among them is yet smaller. For non-Asian households the probabilities for an active economy of the wife are correlated to the variables Child and Age.*

*we make the same observation as before. If there is no child in the household, the rate of economically active wives is higher for women under 38. But now we see a corresponding effect in households with a child under the age of four. Here, the rate of economically active wives is higher, if the wife is older than 38. This hints at a three way interaction between the variables **Wife's Age**, **Child** and **Economy**, which we will further examine in section 2.6.*

Positions along non-aligned scales: comparing conditional distributions

From the conditional probabilities we can read from a mosaicplot, we are able to get "impressions" on how the conditional distributions look. By means of these impressions we are able to compare different conditional distributions.

More specifically, the conditional distributions we can estimate visually from a mosaic are of the form

$$Z \mid Y \text{ for fixed values of } X.$$

The goal is to find something two or more conditional distributions have in common for different values of X. An "impression" we may get for a fixed level of X can of course only be a very prominent feature, such as

- (partial) independence of variables or

- a trend over the categories or

- a common "behaviour" among the probabilities of the categories, such as a common ordering for example.

Let us consider a mosaicplot with structure $s_X \otimes s_Y^t \otimes s_H$, where X is a binary variable and Y has four categories. H denotes the highlighted cases as usual. Figure 2.16 shows the

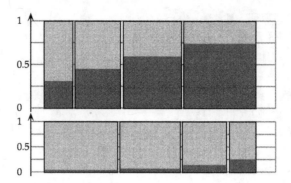

Figure 2.16: *Mosaicplot with trend in the highlighting proportions. Two conditional distributions are visible and can be compared with the help of the underlying scale.*

corresponding graphic. Detecting the trend between Y and the highlighted proportions for both categories of X is easy, as well as the fact, that in both cases we deal with a **positive** trend. To consider more specific results such as to compare the trends in greater accuracy is graphically a much harder task to tackle, since we deal not only with non-aligned scales but also with different accuracies of the same range. In order to compare the highlighting proportions of the two rightmost bins of the mosaicplot in figure 2.16 we have to compare the factors between the highlighted and non-highlighted areas of each of the bins, which is approximately 3:1 in the upper bin and 1:3 in the lower bin.

We will show later on representations of the data, which are better suited for this kind of problems.

Example 2.1.17 *College Plans*
*Figure 2.17 shows a two-way trend among the highlighted cases in the College Plans Data (see A.3). The mosaic has structure $s_{IQ} \otimes s_{SES}^t$, where **SES** is the socioeconomic status of the parents. Highlighted are pupils with college plans "yes". The increase of highlighted cases with higher social standard of the parents is obvious for all four categories of the **IQ**. A second trend is present, though, not as easy to detect as the first: the numbers of highlighted cases also increase with the **IQ** for all of the social classes. This, however, is based on a comparison of areas, a graphically harder task. Furthermore the mosaic contains even a third trend, independently from the **College Plans**. If we concentrate on the mosaic itself, we can see that the number of pupils with high **intelligence quotient** is positively correlated to the **socio-economic status** of their parents. The largest bins represent pupils with low IQ, whose parents have also a low SES, and pupils with high IQ and a high parental SES. The smallest bins are those, where the opposite effects have been recorded.*

Example 2.1.18 *Letter Recognition Data*
Figure 2.18 gives an example of the Letter Recognition Data. Highlighted are cases with

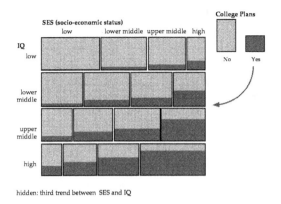

Figure 2.17: *Mosaicplot for a two-way trend.*

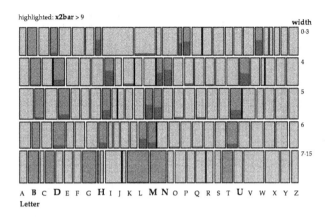

Figure 2.18: *Mosaicplot with pattern among the highlighted cases.*

*a value for **x2bar** of at least 10, the mosaic shows all letters from left to right classified according to five different classes of **width**. The upper four rows all show the same pattern for the highlighted cases; the conditional probabilities are increased for the five letters **D**, **H**, **M**, **N** and **U**. In two of the rows also **B** shows increased highlighting proportions.*

There are two things, which have not been solved satisfactorily in the previous example. The first is, that the described second trend in figure 2.17a) is difficult to see. Secondly, the pattern of highlighted cases in figure 2.17b) is rather hard to detect because of the changing position of the bins corresponding to each letter.

Both problems, however, are not of a structural nature but only depend on the choice of the graphical display, especially on the shape and the position of the mosaic bins. In the following we will introduce two major variations of the mosaic, the *Same-Bin-Size Display* (2.1.5) and the *Fluctuation Diagram* (2.1.5), which are more suited for the graphical representation of data as above.

Further comparisons

Besides the basic information of proportions highlighted vs. proportions unhighlighted, we also gain insight to the structure of a problem by comparing highlighted proportions between several categories.

From the differences in the heights of highlighted areas we will later on be able to draw conclusions about the odds ratios between variables (see section 2.6). This only involves comparisons of the **lengths of objects**.

2.1.5   Variations of the Display

Size, shape and location of a bin in a mosaicplot have until now been determined in the mosaic's hierarchical construction process (see 2.1.9). Variations of these features are, of course, possible, and are very useful for exploring the data, as each of them tends to emphasize different aspects of the data. In the following two of the main variations are discussed: the *Same-Bin-Size display* and the *Fluctuation Diagram*.

Same-Bin-Size

As the name suggests, the *Same-Bin-Size* variation of a mosaicplot defines all bins to be of equal size. This makes the *Same-Bin-Size* display a mosaicplot with a special form of weight variable: W^i, the weight of observation i, is chosen to be proportional to the inverse of the number of cases in the cell, into which observation i falls. Without any additional information this plot has by definition to be a rather boring one. Where are the advantages of it?

There are mainly two different areas, where *Same-Bin-Size* displays have proved to be very useful. One application is the **comparison of conditional distributions**, visualised by highlighting heights, another application is the search for **patterns** among the data, e.g. the empty-bin pattern in sparse data cubes.

Additional Highlighting   We have seen the necessity of comparing highlighting heights, the estimators of the conditional probabilities, for **all** combinations within one mosaicplot in the discussion of examples 2.1.17 and 2.1.18. Figure 2.19 shows the change from a default mosaicplot to the *Same-Bin-Size* variation. With it a change of the scale is connected. For a comparison of highlighting heights between upper and lower row as mentioned already in the previous section we need to compare only positions on identical, though non-aligned scales in the *Same-Bin-Size* display.

Example 2.1.19 *Letters Recognition Data*
Figure 2.20 contains a mosaicplot with the same data and structure as in example 2.1.18 but with a Same-Bin-Size display. Now the pattern of highlighted values is absolutely obvious.

Sparse Data Cubes   The second application of the *Same-Bin-Size* variation does not exactly deal with additional information, but rather with missing one. If we have a sparse data cube we can exploit the fact, whether a cell contains any data at all. The goal now is to provide methods to first get a quick overview of the empty cells of the data set, and in a second step to gain insight to the empty-bin-pattern within a dataset and help to answer questions like:
How many empty bins are there? Where do they occur? Is a structural behaviour recognisable or are they completely random?

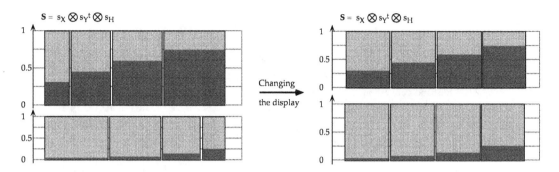

Figure 2.19: *Changing from a default mosaicplot to a Same-Bin-Size variation. The comparison of highlighting heights between upper and lower row changes from calculating fractions to comparing positions along identical scales.*

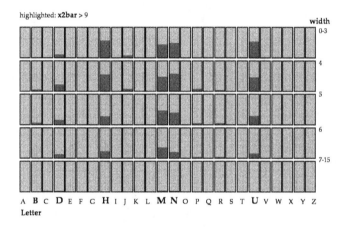

Figure 2.20: *Two-dimensional mosaicplot of the Letter Recognition Data. Due to the Same-Bin-Size representation the pattern within the highlighted cases is very clearly visible.*

Especially when looking for patterns and groups of combinations the order of variables is important. Reordering the variables and collapsing over empty combinations provide additional help.

Example 2.1.20 *Rochdale Data*
In the Rochdale Data only 91 from a total of 256 combinations of the variables are filled. Figure 2.21 shows the empty cells pattern. Re-ordering the variables in a suitable way as in figure 2.22 emphasizes the pattern of empty cells.

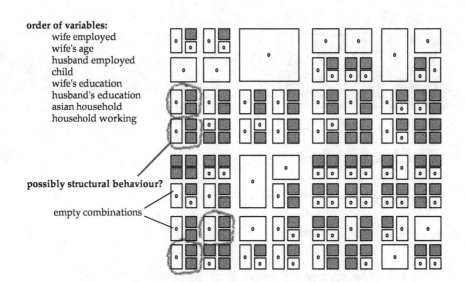

Figure 2.21: *Mosaicplot of the Rochdale Data in Same-Bin-Size Mode. Cells marked with a circle are empty, the curls mark locations, where the same pattern of empty/filled cells occurs.*

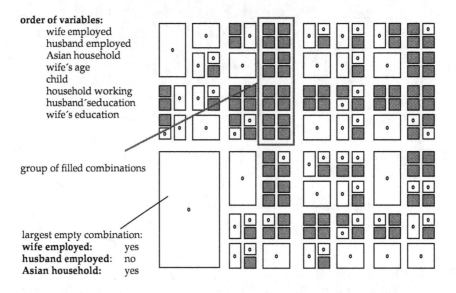

Figure 2.22: *Mosaicplot of the Rochdale Data. Variables have been re-ordered to get better insight into empty/filled cell patterns. The framed group of filled cells contains all of the cells marked by curls in fig. A.9, the large empty cell at the bottom shows, that in none of the Asian households the wife was working while the man was not employed.*

As the example shows, the "right" choice of the order of the variables is crucial. This choice has to be automatized, since there are exponentially many different orderings possible. We will develop an algorithm for high dimensional sorting, which provides a solution for several optimization criteria (see section 2.3).

Fluctuation Diagram

In *Fluctuation diagrams* the area of each rectangle represents the number of cases, but the position of the bottom right corner of a bin is fixed on a grid. The display is useful for emphasising large bins, while small or empty bins simply vanish. Another area, where fluctuation diagrams have proved to be very useful, is the visualisation of matrices. This is discussed in more detail in section 2.5.

Fluctuation diagrams are constructed as follows:

Starting from a Same-Bin-Size representation of a mosaicplot, the information on the cell sizes is included again, by shrinking both height and width of each bin equally such, that the remaining area is proportional to the cell size. If the original display is quadratic, the height and the width of a bin end up being proportional to the square root of the cell size. This makes comparisons of widths and heights of the bins possible at the same time.

Example 2.1.21 *College Plans*
*Figure 2.23 shows the same mosaic as in example 2.1.17 of the College Plans Data. Again, the **intelligence quotient** is plotted versus the **socio-economic status** of the parents and the highlighting shows all pupils with the intention of going to a college. In this representation*

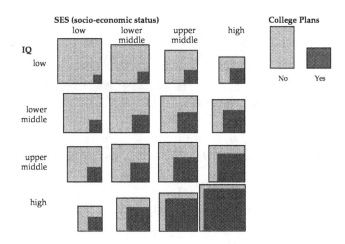

Figure 2.23: *Two-dimensional mosaicplot in fluctuation mode. Highlighting shows pupils who have the intention to go to a college. In contrast to fig.2.17 all three trends are easy to recognize.*

we are able to detect all three trends graphically without the need of calculating one. Let us first consider the highlighted values. The highlighted areas grow both from left to right and from top to bottom. This form of highlighting is necessary to see both of the following trends at once: firstly, socially better constituted pupils are more likely to go to a college and secondly, the percentage of college goers also increases with the IQ.

Besides these two trends the connection between social status of the parents and the pupils' IQ is visible: with increasing social status also the IQ increase and vice versa.

2.2 Doubledecker Plots

Doubledecker plots are a special case of Mosaic plots. Instead of splitting the bins alternately in horizontal and vertical direction as in a default Mosaic plot all bins are split horizontally in a doubledecker plot. All bins of a doubledecker plot are equally high and are drawn side by side. Doubledecker plots of p variables $X_1, \ldots, X_p$ therefore have the structure $s_{X_1} \otimes s_{X_2} \otimes \ldots \otimes s_{X_p}$. Highlighted areas appear orthogonal to the bins. Thus highlighting heights in a p dimensional mosaic plot of variables $X_1, \ldots, X_p$ show the conditional probabilities $P(h \mid X_1, \ldots, X_p)$.

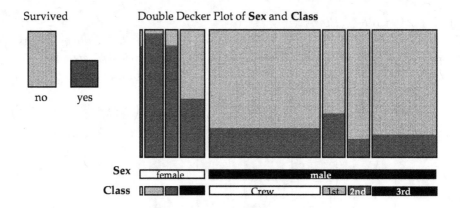

Figure 2.24: *Doubledecker plot of the Titanic Data. Survivors are highlighted. The highest survival rates appear among women in the Crew and in the first or second class.*

One thing that distinguishes doubledecker plots from standard Mosaics is that they may easily be labelled. This is done by drawing a striped bar below the graphic for each of the variables. The stripes show different shades of grey, each colour representing one category of the corresponding variable. The stripes' widths are determined by the widths of the bins in the Double Decker plot.

The exact combination a bin represents can be read from these labels by drawing (a virtual) vertical line from a bin through the bars below. The colours, which this line hits, give the exact combination of the bin.

The first bin of the doubledecker plots in figure 2.24 therefore is the combination of **Sex** = female ∩ **Class** = Crew, the second bin shows all female passengers in the first class, and so on.

The value of doubledecker plots will become apparent both in the visual modelling process in section 2.6 as well as for visualising association rules in section 4.1.

2.3 High Dimensional Sorting

The strictly hierarchical construction of a mosaicplot attaches huge importance to the order in which the variables occur. Even more so, if we additionally want to find patterns within the cells of the resulting display or put together "similar" cells. As we have seen in the previous sections, the order of the variables, i.e. the structure underlying a mosaicplot, has an immense impact on what is easy to see in the display. An "optimal" ordering of the variables, of course, depends strongly on the question we want to answer in the first place.

Since there are factorial many possibilities for the order of the variables, the need exists for an automatized solution to this problem.

Depending on the kind of representation, emphasis is laid on different aspects of a plot. If e.g. all bins in the Mosaic have the same size, the pattern of empty/filled cells is of special interest. Empty cells are aggregated (cf. figure 2.25), since it would not provide any additional information, if an empty cell was split according to further variables. The number of visible empty cells therefore depends on the order of the variables.

We will treat cells from other definitions of "target cells" in this way. This ensures that all representations have in common that the number of target cells depends on the order of the variables. With that comes the ability of detecting the existence of a pattern. Detecting a common property of several cells is a lot harder than viewing only one cell, which automatically combines cells with the same properties. The following example shows this for the empty-bin pattern of only four variables:

Example 2.3.1

Let V, W, X and Y be four binary variables and let the events X and Y be mutually exclusive. This facts shows up in a mosaicplot of all four variables as either four different empty combinations as in fig. 2.25a) or in one combination of four empty cells as in fig. 2.25b), dependent on the order of the variables.

The overall goal is to summarise cells, which belong to the same group, by re-ordering the variables in the display. By this, we hope to detect patterns, which will help to identify and describe this group of cells. For simplification we will assume at first that we may decide uniquely, whether a cell belongs to a specific group or not, i.e. that the group is represented by a boolean function, which assigns a cell the value **true**, if the cells belongs

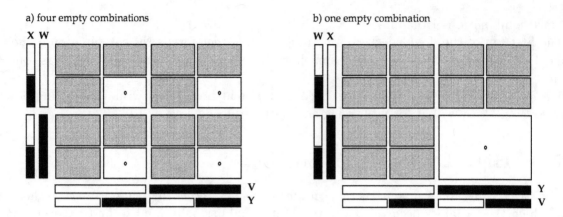

Figure 2.25: *Two four dimensional mosaic plots in Same-Bin-Size representation. Re-ordering the variables summarises the empty cells of figure a) to only one combination as in fig. b).*

to the group, and **false** otherwise. Functions like this are called **truth functions**. Quine (1955) introduced a method of simplifying such truth functions. Based on the results of this algorithm a data driven method is developed in the following to minimize the number of cell combinations in a Mosaic. Several variations of the method open the way to a wider field of graphical analysis of categorical data.

The strategy we want to employ is as follows: based on a truth function f, which describes the group of cells we want to summarise, the algorithm of Quine (1955) provides us with a new description of f, which consists of logical expressions in the variables. These expressions are as short as possible, e.g. $X \cap Y$ in the example above.

By choosing expressions from this set in a suitable way, an optimal ordering of the variables can be derived from it.

2.3.1   Truth functions

The truth function f associated with a group of cells, such as for instance all empty cells, is defined on the set of all cells in a mosaicplot. Since the cells are uniquely given by the cross-product of all categories of the variables within the mosaicplot, we can write a truth function of p variables as

$$f : c(X_1) \times \ldots \times c(X_p) \to \{\textbf{true}, \textbf{false}\}, \text{ where}$$

$$f(x_1, \ldots, x_p) = \textbf{true} \iff \text{ the cell } (x_1, \ldots, x_p) \text{ belongs to the group of interest.}$$

f can be written in *disjunctive normal form*, i.e. it is constructed from a series of expressions of the form

$$X_1 = c_{i_1}^{X_1} \wedge X_2 = c_{i_2}^{X_2} \wedge \ldots \wedge X_1 = c_{i_p}^{X_p} \qquad \text{if the cell belongs to the group}$$
$$\neg \left(X_1 = c_{i_1}^{X_1} \wedge X_2 = c_{i_2}^{X_2} \wedge \ldots \wedge X_1 = c_{i_p}^{X_p} \right) \qquad \text{otherwise,}$$

where $c_{i_j}^{X_j} \in c(X_j) \; \forall i_j, j = 1, \ldots, p$. If the meaning is unique, we may also write $c_{i_1}^{X_1} \wedge c_{i_2}^{X_2} \wedge \ldots \wedge c_{i_p}^{X_p}$ instead of $X_1 = c_{i_1}^{X_1} \wedge X_2 = c_{i_2}^{X_2} \wedge \ldots \wedge X_1 = c_{i_p}^{X_p}$ for short.

These expressions are called *monoms* or *implicants*. Implicants can be distinguished in *positive* and *negative* implicants, where positive implicants describe groups of cells, which belong to the target group, and negative implicants describe groups of cells, which do not belong to the target group.

Usually, only the positive implicants are listed in a truth function.

2.3.2 The extended Quine-McCluskey Algorithm

Example 2.3.2

For the variables of example 2.3.1 a truth function for the empty-bin pattern is (we will denote with v the event $v = \mathbf{true}$ and with $\neg v$ the event $v = \mathbf{false}$):

$$f(v, w, x, y) \text{ is } \mathbf{true} \quad \Longleftrightarrow \quad \begin{array}{l} v \wedge w \wedge x \wedge y \wedge \vee \\ v \wedge \neg w \wedge x \wedge y \wedge \vee \\ \neg v \wedge w \wedge x \wedge y \wedge \vee \\ \neg v \wedge \neg w \wedge x \wedge y \wedge \end{array} \quad \text{is } \mathbf{true}$$

This function can be simplified to

$$
\begin{aligned}
f(v, w, x, y) \quad &= \quad (v \wedge \mathbf{true} \wedge x \wedge y) \vee (\neg v \wedge \mathbf{true} \wedge x \wedge y) \\
&= \quad \mathbf{true} \wedge \mathbf{true} \wedge x \wedge y \\
&= \quad x \wedge y.
\end{aligned}
$$

If the variables in the mosaicplot are binary, the function can be simplified to a form, where the implicants are as short as possible, as shown in the example. Implicants of a function f which can not be shortened further are called the *prime implicants* of f. The Quine-McCluskey algorithm (Quine 1955) provides the set of all prime implicants of a function. Theus & Wilhelm (1996) have shown that this algorithm can be extended to variables with an arbitrary number of categories in a natural way.

Example 2.3.3 *Titanic*

Simplifying the function f, which describes all empty cells in the data, by means of the extended Quine-McCluskey algorithm results for the Titanic Data in a set of three prime implicants:

$$PI(f) = \{Crew \wedge Child, First \wedge Child \wedge No, Second \wedge Child \wedge No\}$$

*The variable **Age** appears in all three implicants, Crew ∧ Child is the shortest. One sensible ordering with respect to the empty bin pattern therefore is (Age, Class, Survival, Sex), see figure 2.26.*

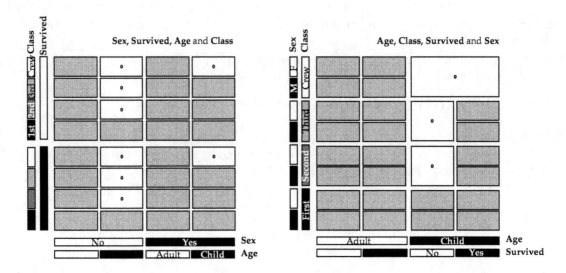

Figure 2.26: *Mosaicplots of the Titanic Data in Same-Bin-Size mode. Different orders of the variables show different representations of the empty-bin pattern.*

From a graphical point of view the shortening of implicants means the exclusion of variables, which are not needed for the display of the group's pattern. The more important a variable is for the description of a group, the more often it remains in the implicants of the function's description. These variables therefore have to be put at the head of the hierarchy in a mosaicplot. Still, there is a high number of possibilities for ordering the variables in a mosaicplot.

2.3.3   Pre-considerations for the Algorithm

Each prime implicant m is assigned an additional number $W(m)$ as a measure of the importance of this implicant for the group the truth functions describes. In the simplest case, each combination of the original (un-compressed) truth function has the same weight and a prime implicant is assigned the number of cells it describes. This number is calculated from the categories of the variables, which are **not** considered by m:

$$W_0(m) = \prod_{\substack{X_i \in \mathcal{X} \\ X_i \notin m}} |c(X_i)|, \tag{2.4}$$

where X is the set of all variables considered.

Remark 2.3.4
The more combinations a prime implicant covers, the further to the front the variables it contains have to be put in the hierarchy.

Example 2.3.5 *Titanic*
Let us consider again the empty cells of the Titanic Data. The set of prime implicants has already been given in the previous example. Now we are interested in the number of combinations each prime implicant covers:

PI	$Crew \wedge Child$	$First \wedge Child \wedge No$	$Second \wedge Child \wedge No$
$W_0(PI)$	4	2	2

*The number of covered cells again suggests that the two variables **Class** and **Age** are important for the description of empty cells. The variable **Survived** has to be put on the third place in the order and **Sex** is put on the last position.*

However, the number of covered cells alone is not enough to determine an optimal ordering of the variables. Consider the following example.

Example 2.3.6
Let f be the function, which describes the set of empty cells between the binary variables A, B, C and D. The function is given in a tabular form:

A	0	0	0	0	0	0	0	0	1	1	1	1	1	1	1	1
B	0	0	0	0	1	1	1	1	0	0	0	0	1	1	1	1
C	0	0	1	1	0	0	1	1	0	0	1	1	0	0	1	1
D	0	1	0	1	0	1	0	1	0	1	0	1	0	1	0	1
f	0	1	0	0	0	1	1	1	0	1	0	0	1	1	1	1

A short description of f is given by

$$
\begin{aligned}
f(a,b,c,d) = \quad & (a = 1 \wedge b = 1) \\
\vee \quad & (b = 1 \wedge c = 1) \\
\vee \quad & (c = 0 \wedge d = 1).
\end{aligned}
$$

All prime implicants cover the same number of cells, namely 4. Therefore any order of the variables should give the same number of empty combinations, if the number of covered cells alone would be sufficient for ordering the variables. However, if a mosaicplots starts with variables A and B, the display contains at least five empty combinations, whereas it minimally contains only four empty combinations, e.g. with the order (C, D, B, A). Where is the difference?

*In contrast to the previous example, the prime implicants here do not describe disjoint sets of cells but have **non-empty intersections**, i.e. the prime implicants $a = 1 \wedge b = 1$ and $b = 1 \wedge c = 1$ have two cells in common, namely $a = 1 \wedge b = 1 \wedge c = 1 \wedge d = 0$ and $a = 1 \wedge b = 1 \wedge c = 1 \wedge d = 1$.*

With an order (A, B, C, D) only two of the four empty combinations, which the prime implicant $b = 1 \wedge c = 1$ describes, are new combinations. The others are already visible in the display.

This leads us to a further criterion we have to include in an algorithm for high-dimensional sorting:

Remark 2.3.7

The number of new combinations a prime implicant covers is affected by previously chosen variables, since non-trivial intersections with other prime implicants may occur.

Remark 2.3.8

The relationship between prime implicants has to be studied, not only because of intersections among them, but also because different prime implicants may contain the same variables, such as $c = 1 \wedge d = 1$ and $c = 0 \wedge d = 0$.

Putting together the three remarks 2.3.4 to 2.3.8 leads us to the necessity of evaluating the order of variables each time we pick a new variable. One criterion to do this is given by the rate of visible cell combinations and the number of cells covered by the currently regarded variables. Let us consider this in a more substantial example:

Example 2.3.9

Let the variables A, B, C, D, E, F, G and H be eight binary variables. Denote the categories of A with a and $\neg a$, the categories of B with b and $\neg b$ and so on.

The truth function f describes the empty bin pattern of these variables and is written as

$$f(x) = 1 \iff$$

$$(b \wedge e \wedge g) \vee (b \wedge d \wedge h) \vee (a \wedge c \wedge g) \vee$$

$$(a \wedge \neg d \wedge f \wedge g) \vee (\neg a \wedge \neg c \wedge d \wedge h) \vee$$

$$(\neg e \wedge f \wedge g \wedge h) \vee (a \wedge d \wedge \neg f \wedge g) \vee$$

$$(d \wedge \neg e \wedge f \wedge h) \vee (b \wedge c \wedge d \wedge \neg g) \vee$$

$$(\neg d \wedge e \wedge \neg f \wedge g) \vee (\neg b \wedge c \wedge \neg d \wedge h) \vee$$

$$(d \wedge e \wedge \neg f \wedge h) \vee (\neg a \wedge c \wedge e \wedge h) \vee$$

$$(a \wedge b \wedge g \wedge \neg h) \vee (a \wedge b \wedge d \wedge \neg f) \vee$$

$$(\neg a \wedge b \wedge d \wedge f) \vee (a \wedge c \wedge d \wedge f) \vee$$

$$(a \wedge c \wedge d \wedge e) \vee$$

$$(\neg a \wedge \neg b \wedge e \wedge f \wedge h) \vee$$

$$(\neg c \wedge \neg d \wedge \neg e \wedge f \wedge g) \vee$$

$$(a \wedge \neg b \wedge \neg f \wedge g \wedge h) \vee$$

$$(\neg b \wedge c \wedge e \wedge f \wedge \neg g) \vee$$

$$(a \wedge b \wedge c \wedge e \wedge \neg f \wedge \neg h) \vee$$

$$(\neg a \wedge \neg b \wedge c \wedge \neg d \wedge e \wedge \neg g) \vee$$

$$(\neg a \wedge \neg b \wedge c \wedge \neg d \wedge \neg e \wedge f) \vee$$

$$(\neg a \wedge \neg b \wedge \neg e \wedge \neg f \wedge \neg g \wedge h) \vee$$

$$(\neg a \wedge b \wedge \neg c \wedge \neg d \wedge e \wedge \neg f \wedge \neg h)$$

Since all variables are binary, the number of combinations each prime implicant covers, may be calculated from its size. The prime implicant $b \wedge e \wedge g$ covers 2^5 combinations as do all implicants consisting of exactly three variables, the implicant $a \wedge \neg d \wedge f \wedge g$ covers 2^4 combinations, accordingly.

For an overview of the following considerations regarding an optimal ordering of the variables see figure 2.27. Starting with the number of combinations a prime implicant covers, we have three different choices of variables in the beginning, namely $\{B, E, G\}$, $\{B, D, H\}$ or $\{A, C, G\}$. Each ordering of the variables has the same proportion, $1 : 1$, of visible combinations vs. total number of empty cells at this stage. The strategy for an optimal ordering is now the following: we try to increase the total number of empty cells as far as possible, while at the same time the number of empty cell-combinations has to be minimized. When trying to find a suitable fourth variable, it becomes obvious that the choice of variables $\{B, D, H\}$ is the best, since only in the case of $(\{B, D, H\}, C)$ another empty cell appears. This lets the other two paths become dead ends. The chosen order of $(\{B, D, H\}, C)$ has rate $2 : 3$.

At this point we have three equivalent choices for a fifth variable. All three paths lead straight

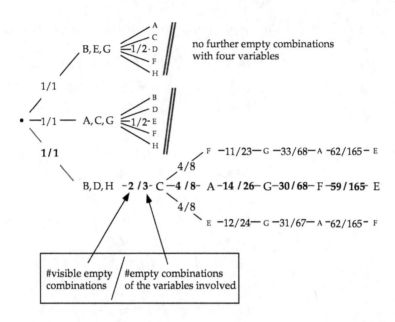

Figure 2.27:   *Overview of the search for an optimal ordering of the variables* *A, B, C, D, E, F, G and H with respect to the truth function given in example 2.3.9.*

to a local minimum for the rate. The global minimum in this example is the middle path as shown in figure 2.27 representing the order $(\{B, D, H\}, C, A, G, F, E)$ of the variables.

2.3.4   An Algorithm for High-Dimensional Sorting

Let f be a truth function with domain $\mathcal{X} = \{X_1, \dots, X_k\}$, the set of variables, which are to be ordered.

Input: the set of all prime implicants Π of f

Output: an order $\mathcal{S}$ of the variables $X_1, \dots, X_k$, which is optimal with respect to the number of visible target cells in the corresponding mosaicplot.

Procedure:

1. Initialize
   the sequence of ordered variables $\mathcal{S}$ with the empty sequence $\mathcal{S} := ()$.

2. Calculate the set of candidate variables $\mathcal{C} \subset \mathcal{X} \setminus \mathcal{S}$, the set of variables with maximal cover with respect to order $\mathcal{S}$.

3. If the set $\mathcal{C}$ has only one element X,

- choose this variable, i.e.

$$S := \text{concat } (S, X),$$

If $\mathcal{X} \backslash S$ is not empty go to step 2, otherwise stop.

- otherwise calculate for each candidate variable X in $\mathcal{C}$ the number of visible cells of X with respect to order S. Let $\mathcal{C}'$ be the set of variables in $\mathcal{C}$ with maximal number of visible cells.

  For each variable X' in $\mathcal{C}'$ do:

  (i) $S := \text{concat } (S, X')$,

  (ii) if $\mathcal{X} \backslash S$ is not empty, proceed with step 2.

  Choose that order, which minimizes the number of visible cells.

Exact definitions of cover and visible cells as well as further considerations on the algorithm may be found in section C in the appendix.

2.4 Applications

2.4.1 Empty (Small) Bin Patterns

Finding patterns among the empty cells of a mosaicplot is one of the applications of the algorithm for high dimensional sorting. The truth function f is defined as

$$f(c) = \begin{cases} true & \text{cell } c \text{ is empty} \\ false & \text{otherwise} \end{cases}$$

We have already seen one example of sorting according to the empty cells in a data set in section 2.1.5 at the Rochdale Data. Here, only 91 out of a total of 256 possible combinations are filled. Figure 2.22 on page 36 shows the mosaicplot with a small number of visible empty cells - 61 from 165. The minimal ordering has only 59 empty cells, the variables then have to be ordered as follows: **household working, wife's age, child, husband employed?, wife economically active, Asian, husband's education** and **wife's education**.

Example 2.4.1 *Exams Data*
*Figure 2.28 shows a mosaicplot of eight variables from the Exams Data. The variables **Question 1 selected?**, ... , **Question 8 selected?** are ordered with respect to visible empty cells. The total of 206 empty cells has been summarized to only 62 as shown in the figure. The largest empty bin is visible in the top left corner of the diagram. It corresponds to the cell "question 4 not selected and question 7 not selected" - that this cell is empty means, that every student in the exam did take at least one of the two questions. The next two*

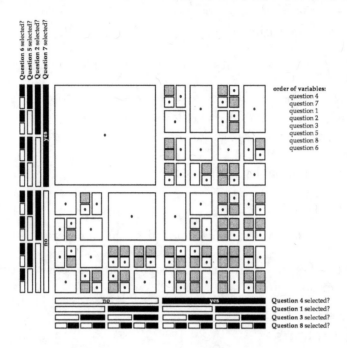

Figure 2.28: *Mosaicplot of the Exams Data. The number of visible empty cells is minimized (62 out of 206).*

questions, questions 1 and 2, were also very popular. Almost half of the students (54 from 110) tried to answer these four questions. The total numbers of students, however, are not plotted in the same-bin-size representation of the mosaic in figure 2.28. For this, a fluctuation diagram as in figure 2.29 is better suited. The highlighting in it corresponds to students who passed the exam. Several "safe" combinations of questions appear, i.e. combinations in which almost all students passed the exam. Such successful combinations of questions were: $\{Qu4, Qu7, Qu1, Qu2, Qu3\}$, $\{Qu4, Qu7, Qu1, Qu2, Qu8\}$, $\{Qu4, Qu7, Qu1, Qu2, Qu6\}$ or $\{Qu4, Qu7, Qu1, Qu2, Qu5\}$

2.4.2   Identification of Groups

The truth function f in this case is not defined statically but dynamically via highlighting. The goal is to find a summarized representation for the selected values. This is especially interesting, if we select subgroups of the data such as may appear visually as clusters in an MCA. Each point in a biplot (cf. section 3) based on an MCA of the data represents one combination of the variables, i.e. exactly one cell in a corresponding contingency table or a mosaicplot. Therefore we may regard the selection of a group of points in a biplot as the

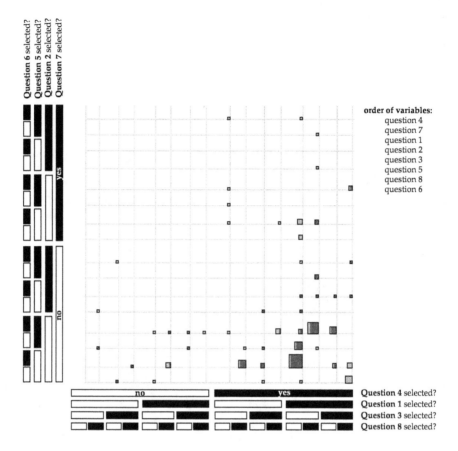

Figure 2.29: *Mosaicplot of the Exams Data with the same order as previously in fig. 2.28. The size of each cell represents the number of students in it. Marked via highlighting are students who passed the exam.*

dynamic definition of a truth function f, with

$$f(c) = \begin{cases} \textit{true} & \text{cell } c \text{ is highlighted } (= \text{element of the group}) \\ \textit{false} & \text{otherwise} \end{cases}$$

In order to identify the whole group of cells we may use the algorithm for high-dimensional sorting.

Below, two different examples are introduced. One has its background in the area of classification and discrimination: we show a graphical way of separating between poisonous and edible mushrooms in the Mushroom Data.

The other example considers an aspect of statistical modelling. We want to examine the residuals for a given loglinear model and try to find patterns. Just as scatter plots reveal structural deficiencies for models with continuous data, strong patterns in a mosaicplot indicate possibly missing interactions and by sorting residuals, we are also able to give a hint as to which interaction is missing.

Identifying Groups in the Classification Process

Example 2.4.2 *Mushroom Data*
Figure 2.30 shows a biplot of a correspondence analysis taking all of the descriptive variables

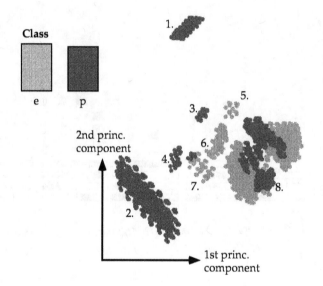

Figure 2.30: *Biplot of an MCA of all of the mushrooms variables. Highlighted are poisonous mushrooms. Some distinct clusters appear (marked by the numbers).*

into account. Several clearly distinguished groups appear in the plane spanned by the first and second principal component axis. These clusters are marked by numbers in the graphic. Using a Mosaicplot of all the descriptive variables, we want to find descriptions (as short as possible) for these groups. Table 2.5 gives a short summary of our results.

Zooming into the display is equivalent to hierarchical clustering via MCA. The seventh group splits up into a group of 8 poisonous mushrooms, which have stalk color y (below and above the ring). Figure 2.31 shows a zoom into the largest cluster, cluster 8. Several more groups show up in the projection plane:

Group	Count	Class	Description
1	1296	poisonous	ring type = I
2	1728	poisonous	gill type: b
3	36	poisonous	stalk color above ring: c (or ring type: n)
4	32	poisonous	stalk surface below ring:y population: v
5	16	edible	stalk surface above ring:y stalk color above ring:n
6	120	edible	ring-type:f or
			ring-type = p, stalk surface: k (below and above ring)
7	56	mixed	48 edible, composited from two groups:
			gill spacing: w, stalk color below ring: n
			gill spacing: w, stalk color below ring: y
8	4840	mixed	4024 edible

Table 2.5: *Clusters in the Mushroom Data after two steps of visual pca clustering.*

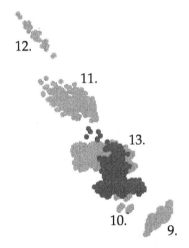

Figure 2.31: *Zoom into group 8 of fig. 2.30, highlighted are poisonous mushrooms.*

Group	Count	Class	Description
9	1726	edible	odor: n, habitat: d, (gill size: b)
10	48	edible	gill spacing: w, bruises: t, cap surface: f
11	408	edible	ring number: t, population: c,n or s
12	192	edible	gill attachment: a
13	2464	mixed	several groups:
			stalk root: c,e, or r
			stalk root: b, stalk shape: e
			stalk root: b, stalk shape: t, cap surface: s

All of the descriptions are only valid for the zoomed data (i.e. with logical "and" of the description for group 8 above).

As long as an MCA of the subgroup is well-defined, we may proceed in the way described in the example to classify the data and at the same time to identify subgroups.

Identifying Structural Behaviour among Residuals   Let us assume a given loglinear model. The goal is to decide from the residuals of the models, whether we have to include a further interaction or whether we may stop at this point with the modelling process, i.e. the question is, whether we are able to detect some structural behaviour or patterns among the residuals or not.

In terms of a truth function this means a definition depending on the (absolute) values of the residuals, e.g.:

$$f(c) = \begin{cases} true & \text{cell } c \text{ has residual } > q \\ false & \text{otherwise} \end{cases}$$

for a fixed value of q.

Of course, other definitions are possible, let $r(c)$ be a residual of cell c, then

a) $f(c) = true \iff r(c) < -q$,

b) $f(c) = true \iff |r(c)| > q$,

for a fixed value of q.

Here, two problems become apparent: first of all, it is very easy to define any truth function interactively via highlighting as described before, but it is not at all clear, which one will be the "right one". Different choices yield, of course, different results and, as the examples will show, the results turn out to be rather different from each other.

Another point to note is that we did not give an exact definition for the residual value of a cell, since there again are different possibilities. However, this has not the same impact on the results as the choice of the truth function f.

Example 2.4.3 *College Plans*
Let us consider for the College Plans Data a loglinear model of the main effects only. Figure 2.32 shows the model (total independence) of the data together with the residuals. Each bin is shaded according to the strength and direction of its residual; bins with positive residuals are shaded orange, with negative residuals they are shaded blue. Here, the residuals of each bin are given as the square root of their χ^2 contribution, i.e. for an expected and observed value of a cell, e_c resp. o_c, the residual is given as $r(c) = (e_c - o_c)/\sqrt{e_c}$.

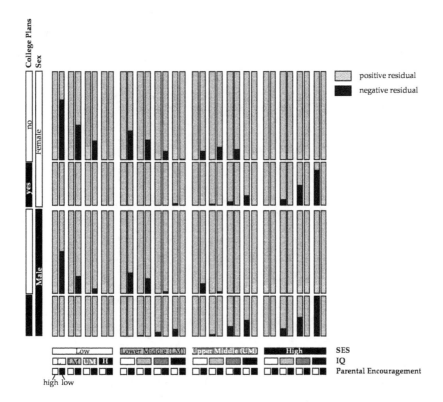

Figure 2.32: *Mosaicplot of all variables in the College Plans Data. Each bin is coloured according to its residual blue or orange.*

To re-order the variables of the mosaicplot according to the residuals, a truth function is defined as

$$f(c) = true \iff r(c) < -20$$

*via highlighting. Sorting gives a mosaic as shown in figure 2.33. The cross-like structure with negative residuals only in the upper left and lower right of the display indicates that the interaction between **College Plans** and **Parental Encouragement** has the most influence in this example. But several other features are of interest also: firstly, we can see horizontal trends among the negative residuals, which are decreasing on the left hand side and increase on the right hand side. The negative trend on the left hand side is a group of pupils, who do not intend to go to college and are not encouraged by their parents either. With increasing socio-economic status of the parents the residuals become less negative. Interestingly, there is also a gender effect in the data: female pupils appear in the residuals between their male counterparts and the male pupils of a lower socio-economic class. Also with increasing IQ the negative residuals become less in this group.*

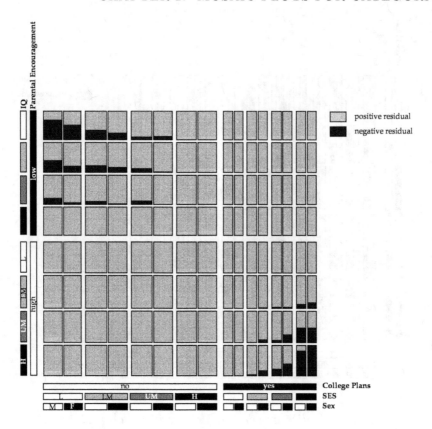

Figure 2.33: *Mosaicplot of the variables in the College Plans Data. The variables are sorted according to the bins' residuals. The variables **Parental Encouragement** and **College Plans** are of most importance.*

*Quite the opposite is true for pupils, who want to go to the college and are highly encouraged to do so by their parents. Here, the residuals become more negative with decreasing socioeconomic class and an increase of IQ. Yet, the same gender effect shows up. Again, female pupils can be found between their male counterparts and male pupils of a lower social class. These linear trends, however, can not be described within a standard loglinear model of the data. Fienberg (1979) proposed a model consisting of a four way interaction between **socioeconomic status, IQ, sex** and **parental encouragement** together with several two and three way interactions with **college plans**. We will show later on, how we may fit a model regarding the trends with association models (see section 2.7.3) with a higher degree of freedom and similar goodness of fit statistics.*

One of the problems while sorting the variables according to the residuals is of course the binary truth function itself. The residuals are continuous, yet we consider for the sorting process only the fact, whether they fulfill the truth function's criterion or not. More sensible would be to regard the residuals directly. It is not possible to extend the algorithm of Quine-McCluskey to a continuous target function, however. Another approach to get a solution in this case could be a weighting of the prime implicants, which then is considered in the sorting process.

2.5 Matrices & Fluctuation Diagrams

One application of mosaicplots, where the weighted form has proven to be especially useful, is the visualization of matrices.

Definition 2.5.1
If the rows of a matrix represent objects and the columns attributes, this objects-by-variables matrix is called a *two-mode matrix*.

One of the goals is to find groups within the data. Basically we want to form groups within the data in such a way, that two objects in the same group are similar to each other, whereas objects in different groups are as dissimilar as possible. In order to be able to speak of "similar" objects, distances between objects have to be defined. A matrix, which contains these distances is called a *similarity* or *proximity matrix* (analogously *dissimilarity matrix*).

2.5.1 Visualisation of Matrices

Usually, we have a data table in a cases-by-variable matrix (Spreadsheet Format). The idea is to visualise such matrices with the help of mosaic plots - how can this be done?
Since mosaic plots take categorical data as input, and fit each tile according to the number of cases within each combination, we can only visualise whole numbers. Therefore, we have to extend the concept of mosaics, again, to **weighted mosaic plots**. Instead of counting the number of cases within each combination of the variables, we additionally use *weights* for each case and sum those. The size of a tile then is given by the total sum of weights for the cases of each combination. Plots like these are sometimes also called *permutation matrices* (Bertin 1967) or *Bertin plots* (Falguerolles et al 1997).
For case-by-variables matrices, we therefore use column labels and row labels as two categorical variables and the entries of the matrix give us the weights.

Example 2.5.2 *Mammals Milk*
*For the Mammals' Milk Data A.6, we have a variable **Mammal**, consisting of a list of the Mammals' names: HORSE, ORANGUTAN, MONKEY, DONKEY, HIPPO, CAMEL, BISON, ... and a second variable **Ingredients** with categories Ash, Fat, Lactose, Protein and Water. As weights in the mosaic plot we use the percentages of the ingredients of the milks for each animal. Figure 2.34 shows two weighted mosaics in fluctuation mode for the*

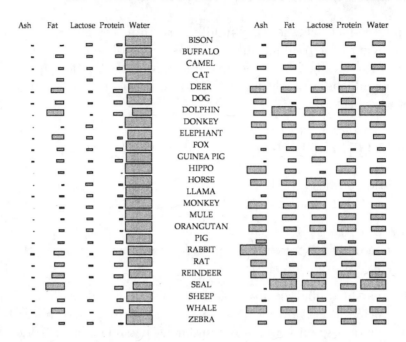

Figure 2.34: *(Weighted) Mosaic plots of the Mammals Data. On the left the raw data is shown, on the right the values are standardized.*

Mammals Milk Data. The cases are sorted according to the mammals' names. On the left side, the raw data are shown - we see, that all of the milks consist mostly of water. DOLPHIN and SEAL show up as outliers, since they have the lowest percentages of Water, and highest percentages of Fat.

The allocation to the different ingredients is rather inhomogeneous, standardized values help us here to detect more detailed patterns between each two mammals. On the right side of figure A.6 are standardized values (via $X \rightarrow X/\sigma_X$) used as weights. Again it is obvious that DOLPHIN and SEAL behave similarly, but now we further detect that DEER and REIN-DEER also are very close. Surprisingly, BISON and BUFFALO seem to be very different.

Our next goal is to find groups of mammals. Using clustering techniques like Complete Linkage gives us results as shown in figure 2.35. The rows of the data table are sorted according to the hierarchical clustering scheme. Now we can check the results of the clustering algorithm graphically by comparing the rows of the mosaic plot. This enables us to choose the number of clusters by graphical means, which, of course, is a soft and very subjective criterion, but can also quickly respond to different situations. Here, we'd probably decide to split the clusters a bit further, take the HIPPO out of cluster 1, split cluster 2 into CAMEL-LLAMA and BUFFALO-SHEEP, take out the ELEPHANT from cluster 2 and the RABBIT from cluster 4. The most questionable cluster is the remaining one, cluster 3 - here we find

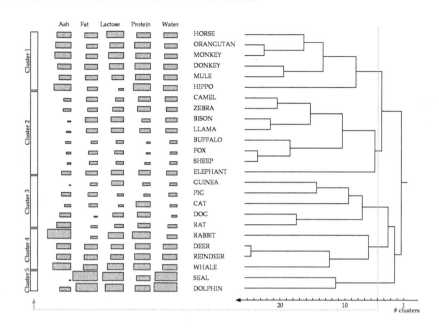

Figure 2.35: *(Weighted) Mosaic plot and dendrogram of the Mammals Data clustered via complete linkage.*

the largest differences graphically. These (graphically found) new clusters basically correspond to a vertical cut in the dendrogram with 11 clusters (see fig. 2.35).

Of course, comparisons of different rows are a lot easier to make, if the rows are not far from each other. For the clustering algorithm, on the other hand, the order of observations in the same cluster is not at all relevant. Shifting whole clusters gives us the possibility to compare distances between them.

Another technique for checking the clustering results would be a principal component analysis of the data. Figure 2.36 shows the results a principal component analysis of the Mammals' Milk Data. The first two principal components carry 95% of the total variation within the data, i.e. the two dimensional distances between data points (each one represents one mammal) reflect the true distances rather well, affirming the especially close relationship between Dolphins and Seals, as well as the isolated status of the Elephant. On the other hand, the graphic shows, that it is almost impossible to actually distinguish between the first three clusters. Finding three clusters could have been a feature of the specific clustering technique we have used - complete linkage tends to find small round clusters. Using another technique, such as single linkage, would have found only one wormlike cluster instead of the three.

Figure 2.37 shows the matrix of Euclidean distances between the percentages of ingredients in a fluctuation diagram. Small rectangles appear between mammals whose milk is similar. Again, DOLPHIN and SEAL show up as closely related.

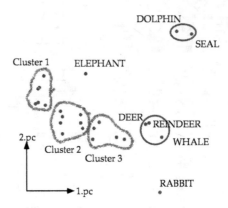

Figure 2.36: *Biplot of the Mammals' Milk Data. The observations are projected into the space of the first two principal components ($R^2 = 0.95$).*

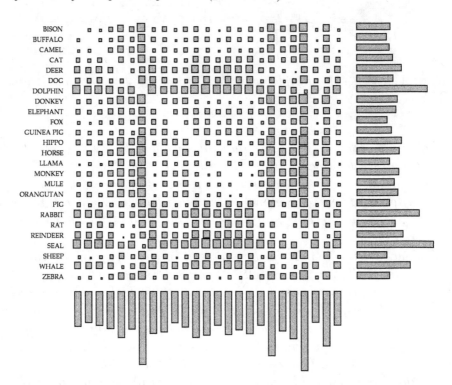

Figure 2.37: *Fluctuation diagram of the distance matrix.*

After re-ordering the clusters of similar milks appear more prominent as in figure 2.38.

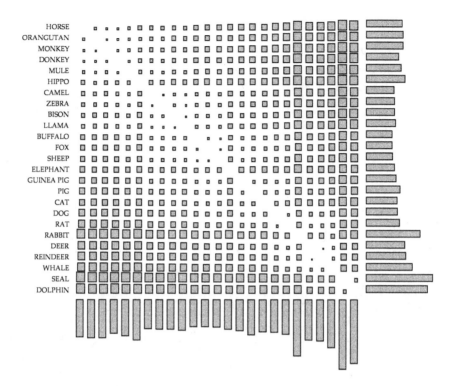

Figure 2.38: *Fluctuation diagram of the distance matrix sorted according to the clustering result as in fig. 2.34.*

2.5.2 Sorting & Re-ordering of Matrices

From example 2.5.2 we have seen that the ordering of rows and columns is important for drawing conclusions visually, since similarities between objects become far more obvious, if these objects are close together. Therefore, methods for re-ordering and sorting rows and columns have to be provided.

Bertin (1967), p. 36, proposes ordering the categories of a matrix "suitably" to visualise clusters in the data.

Falguerolles et al (1997) formalised Bertin's idea by introducing a *purity function* to measure the "simplicity" of a Bertin plot. Optimal orderings correspond to a minimum in the purity function.

Depending on the data and the exact definition of the purity function there are, of course, arbitrarily many possibilities to re-order the categories: For row and column scores and a purity function, which counts the number of pairs in "correct" order, re-ordering according to the purity function means a sorting by the scores.

We will describe some of the re-ordering strategies in more detail:

- **interactive techniques**

    Interactive methods of re-ordering are based on the linking of variables' scales. Re-ordering columns in barcharts affects the order of categories within corresponding mosaicplots as described in section 2.1.3.

    The example below shows an application of re-ordering rows and columns of a fluctuation diagram representing a correlation matrix.

Example 2.5.3 *Gray-scale Image*
For the analysis of ultrasonic pictures results from ca. 150 variables of gray-value statistics are used. Among these variables are minimal and maximal gray-value (gray values are coded in 64 integers), averages and rates of gray-values for example.

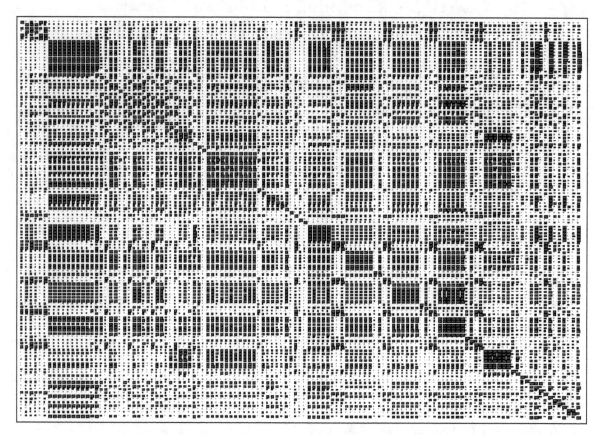

Figure 2.39: *Fluctuation diagram of a correlation matrix of 122 gray-scale variables.*

Figure 2.39 shows the correlation matrix of these variables. For reasons of convenience, the aspect ratio of the display was not chosen to be 1:1 and therefore the matrix does not

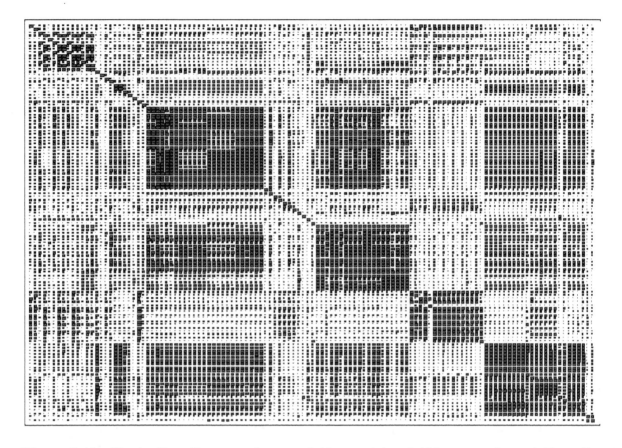

Figure 2.40: *Fluctuation diagram of a correlation matrix of 122 gray-scale variables. Re-ordering the bins makes approx. 5 large clusters of similar variables apparent as well as a number of independent variables.*

appear to be symmetric, though it is of course. In the diagonal of the graphic large tiles indicate the presence of correlation "1". Several similar looking rows become apparent. Re-ordering and grouping these together (in rows and columns) yields a graphic as shown in fig. 2.40. Five large clusters of variables appear in the data, the three largest of them could be grouped further into only one cluster.

- **sorting mechanisms**

  There is, of course, any number of sorting procedures of rows and columns available, depending on the goal of the analysis. For all of these approaches holds that the order of the rows resp. the columns resembles the estimated distances between the objects - the closer two objects are, the more similar to each other they are supposed to be.

Two different methods are introduced in this context:

Sorting according to the results of a clustering algorithm as shown in fig. 2.35 groups clusters of rows together. If additionally a dendrogram of the clustering output is drawn, we are able to estimate distances between rows visually.

Another approach is principal component analysis. Here, the data points are sorted in both vertical and horizontal directions at the same time.

An Example: Sorting with PCA

Given are two (unordered) categorical variables X and Y with r resp. c categories (let $r \geq c$). Goal is to find an order of the categories, which minimizes the distances between adjacent objects. For this, we have to define distances between objects.

We want to display the data in a mosaic plot with structure $Y^t \otimes X$ in fluctuation mode. Let W be the corresponding matrix, where w_{ij} either represents one value of a weight variable or an estimate for the joint probability of X and Y.

The *distance between the rows* D_r is given as

$$(D_r)^2_{kh} = \sum_{i=1}^{c}(w_{ki} - w_{hi})^2, \text{ for } 1 \leq k, h \leq r,$$

similarly, the *distance between the columns* D_c is defined as

$$(D_c)^2_{kh} = \sum_{i=1}^{r}(w_{ik} - w_{ih})^2, \text{ for } 1 \leq k, h \leq c.$$

A singular value decomposition of W gives

$$W = U\Sigma V^t,$$

with U, V orthogonal matrices with rank r resp c and $\Sigma = \begin{pmatrix} D \\ 0 \end{pmatrix}$, D a diagonal matrix of the (descending) singular values $\sigma_1, \ldots, \sigma_c$.

Let $u_1 := Ue_1$ and $v_1 := Ve_1$.

$\sigma_1 u_1$ then contains the first coordinates of X_i in the new coordinate system, v_1 contains the first coordinates of Y_i.

Sorting the categories of X and Y according to the entries within the two vectors u_1 resp. v_1 gives an optimal ordering with respect to the distances between rows and columns.

2.6 Visualising Association and Interaction Terms

"With a powerful conceptual model, a graph can also become a tool for thinking"
Michael Friendly (1995), p.160

Visualising interactions in categorical data has been a problem for a long time, various plots have been introduced to solve it. Yet, none of them could be extended to $I \times J$ tables and beyond.

Among these plots are the fourfold displays (Friendly 1994b) or a version of the stem and leaf plot by Hoaglin et al. (1991).

Friendly (1994b) propagated the use of fourfold displays in order to visualise interactions in $2 \times 2(\times k)$ tables. Figure 2.41 shows the example of a fourfold display of the Berkeley Admission data (Friendly 1994b).

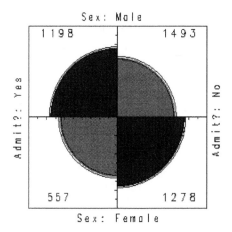

Figure 2.41: *Fourfold Display of the Berkeley Admission Data.*

Fourfold displays are constructed from the frequencies in a corresponding 2×2 table by drawing a quarter circle for each cell. The radius is chosen to be proportional to the square root of the cell frequency, which makes the area of the quarter circle proportional to the frequency. In figure 2.41 the underlying numbers are adjusted to have equated margins. This means the display shows the deviance of expected and observed numbers rather than the raw frequencies.

In the fourfold display of the Berkeley Data the different sizes of the quarter circles show an imbalance between admission and gender, males are by far more likely in this sample to be admitted than females (a further analysis of the data shows, however, that this first impression is the result of a Simpson's paradox and Berkeley can not be accused of discrimination against women based on these data).

Figure 2.42: *Stem-and-leaf plot of the Hardness of Gold.*

One of the obvious problems of this display is that it is not at all clear, how a third variable should be included into this concept or how the plot could be extended to display more than two categories per variable.

Another approach which allows the representation of more than two variables is a version of the stem and leaf plot. Figure 2.42 shows an example of this stem and leaf plot with the Hardness of Gold data (Hoaglin et al. 1991). Five dentists $(D1, D2, \ldots, D5)$ used three different methods $(1, 2, 3)$ on two alloys $(A1, A2)$ to harden gold. The harder the result was, the better. All dentists seemed to achieve better results with alloy $A2$. Furthermore, methods 1 and 2 look slightly superior to method 3. This becomes especially apparent for dentists $D4$ and $D5$. These two facts together correspond to a four way interaction among variables. The drawback of this approach is, however that the order, in which the variables are plotted, is crucial for detecting an interaction - and the four way interaction becomes not even very clear in this "optimal" representation.

Even Hoaglin et al. (1991) admit that using these plots for more than two variables "seems almost certain to lead to (graphical) catastrophe" (p.11).

The goal of the following section is to show, how mosaicplots provide a method for visualising high-dimensional interactions among variables with arbitrary numbers of categories.

Mosaicplots are the graphical equivalent of multi-way contingency tables - therefore they are an appropriate tool to visualise dependencies between categorical variables. Friendly (1992), Theus (1996), Theus & Lauer (1999) used Mosaicplots for visualising the residuals of corresponding loglinear models. To visualise associations between variables directly has been proposed by Theus (1996), yet, he limited this to a maximum of 2-way associations at most. With slight modifications to the concept of mosaics we will show that 2-way associations are not a boundary. In fact, visually there is no boundary at all except for interpreting the results. Practical limits are, as usual, the size of the display and resolution of the screen. On the theoretical side, of course, with increasing numbers of dimensions and cells, the number of different models and interaction terms increases exponentially. The occurrence of empty cells becomes more likely as well, affecting both the asymptotic behaviour of G^2 (Agresti (1984), p.43) and the existence of odds ratios.

2.6.1 Preliminaries

Associations and Interactions

Definition 2.6.1

(i) Variables are said to be *associated (related)* if their values systematically correspond to each other for these observations. There are several ways to "measure" the strength of an association: correlation, χ^2 statistic, Yule's Q, $\ldots$

(ii) An effect of *interaction* occurs when a relation between (at least) two variables is modified by (at least one) other variable. In other words, the strength or the sign (direction) of a relation between (at least) two variables is different depending on the value (level) of some other variable(s).

Statistical Dependencies Independence of two variables X, Y is equivalent to constant conditional probabilities for all levels j of Y within each level of X, i.e.

$$P(Y_j \cap X_i) = P(Y_j) \cdot P(X_i) \iff P(Y_j \mid X_i) = P(Y_j) \quad \forall i, j.$$

A corresponding mosaic plot of X and Y shows a lattice like structure (cf section 2.1.4, Method 1: see fig. 2.43).

This independence can, as well as any other kind of association between X and Y, also be visualised with the use of highlighting: Highlighting the categories of Y one after the other in a bar chart of Y shows up as equally high filled bins of a linked mosaicplot of X (Method 2, cf. fig. 2.44). The following examples describe both of these methods in the example of the Detergent Data.

Example 2.6.2 *Detergent Data*
*Figure 2.43 shows three mosaic plots of **Preference** vs. **M-User**, **Temperature** and*

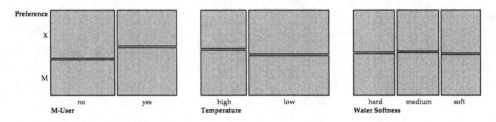

Figure 2.43: *Method 1: mosaicplots of two variables each*
*Mosaicplots of the variable **Preference** vs. variables **M-User**, **Temperature** and **Water Softness**.*

Water Softness. *While **Water Softness** seems to have no association with **Preference**, whereas the association with **M-User** and **Temperature** is fairly strong. Figure 2.44 displays the same information as figure 2.43 with the help of highlighting. Highlighted are persons who preferred brand M. Thus highlighting proportions give a measure for the amount of association between **Preference** and each of the other variables. The strong association between **Preference** and **M-User**, which is in fact the strongest two way association, is particularly interesting, as the study was supposed to be double blind.*

2.6.2 Two-way Associations in multidimensional data

For three variables X, Y and Z with I, J resp. K categories, there are several possibilities for associations among them. Let π_{ijk} be the probabilities of the joint distribution of X, Y and Z, $\pi_{ij.}, \pi_{i.k}, \pi_{.jk}$ the probabilities of the two-way marginal distributions of X, Y and X, Z and Y, Z, etc.:

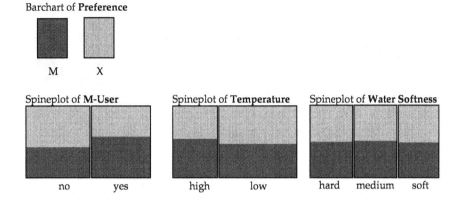

Figure 2.44: *Method 2: Mosaicplot & Highlighting*
*Mosaicplots of the variables **M-User**, **Temperature** and **Water Softness**. Persons pre-*
ferring brand M (after the test) are highlighted.

(i) X, Y and Z are *mutually independent*

$$\pi_{ijk} = \pi_{i..} \cdot \pi_{.j.} \cdot \pi_{..k} \qquad \forall 1 \le i \le I, 1 \le j \le J \text{ and } 1 \le k \le K$$

(ii) Y is *jointly independent* from X and Z

$$\pi_{ijk} = \pi_{.j.} \cdot \pi_{i.k} \qquad \forall 1 \le i \le I, 1 \le j \le J \text{ and } 1 \le k \le K$$

(iii)   a) X and Y are *marginally independent*

$$\pi_{ij.} = \pi_{i..} \cdot \pi_{.j.} \qquad \forall 1 \le i \le I \text{ and } 1 \le j \le J,$$

thus, ignoring the values of Z.

b) X and Y are *conditionally independent* given Z

$$\pi_{ij.} = \pi_{i.k} \cdot \pi_{.jk} \qquad \forall 1 \le i \le I \text{ and } 1 \le j \le J \text{ and for each } k$$

Between these associations the following implications hold (cf. Agresti (1990), pp.133):

$$(i) \Rightarrow (ii) \Rightarrow (iii)$$

The inversion does not hold in general. Marginal and conditional associations of two variables can be quite different. This is known as "Simpson's Paradox" (Yule (1903), Simpson (1951)), see figure 2.45 for an example. In order to avoid this phenomenon conditions are given under which it is "safe" to collapse over one of the variables in a contingency table. The collapsibility condition forms the basis to draw conclusions about the total dependency structure from the conditional distributions. Therefore it is sufficient to study conditional dependencies only.

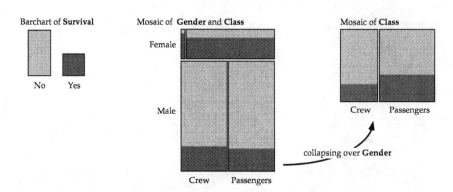

Figure 2.45: *Example of a Simpson's Paradox in the Titanic Data (see section A.11). Highlighted are survivors. Both female and male crew members have better chances of survival than passengers (cf. left mosaic). Collapsing over **Gender** reverses this (cf. mosaic on the right).*

Theorem 2.6.3 *(Collapsibility Condition, Bishop et al. (1975))*
A three dimensional table of X, Y and Z is collapsible over Y, if Y is conditionally independent of at least one of the variables given the other.   (p.39)

Fienberg (1979) gave a collapsibility condition, which is:

Theorem 2.6.4 *(Collapsibility Condition, Fienberg (1979))*
In a three-dimensional table the interaction between two variables may be measured from the table of sums obtained by collapsing over the third variable if the third variable is independent of at least one of the two variables exhibiting the interaction.   (p.49)

Both conditions are sufficient but not necessary.

Recognizing conditional independence between X and Y is done as in the previous section by comparing highlighting heights:

Draw a barchart of Y and a mosaicplot of Z and X (in this order!). If for each level of Z the highlighting of Y_j gives equal highlighting heights for all X_i, X and Y are conditionally independent. Using the collapsibility condition, one now may reduce the mosaic's dimension, by collapsing the table over Y and examine the dependencies between X and Z further.

Example 2.6.5 *Detergent Data*
*Figure 2.46 shows two mosaicplots of the variables **Temperature** and **Preference** resp. **Temperature** alone. Highlighted are cases of soft **Water**. The Mosaicplot on the left shows, that **Preference** and soft **Water** are (partially) conditionally independent. Checking hard and medium **Water Softness** (see figure 2.47) reveals, that **Preference** and **Water Softness** are conditionally independent.*

$$P(\textbf{Water Softness} \,|\, \textbf{Temp.}, \textbf{Pref.}) = P(\textbf{Water Softness} \,|\, \textbf{Temp.}).$$

*The collapsibility condition is fulfilled, therefore collapsing over the variable **Preference** is possible without changing the associations involved.*
*The mosaic on the right of figure 2.46 shows the result of collapsing the table. Since the high-lighting heights in the bins differ, **Water Softness** and **Temperature** are not independent, giving*

$$P(\textbf{Water Softness}) \neq P(\textbf{Water Softness} \mid \textbf{Temp.}).$$

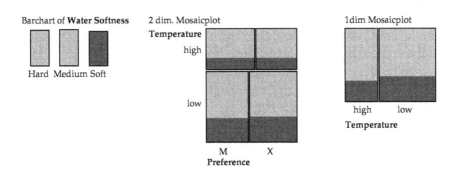

Figure 2.46: *Mosaicplots of the variables **Temperature** and **Preference**. Cases of soft water are highlighted.*

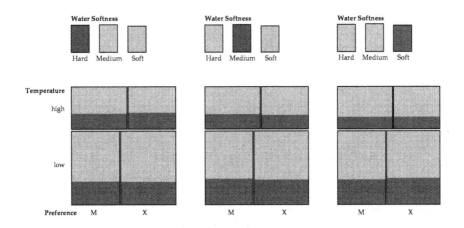

Figure 2.47: *Mosaicplots of the variables **Temperature** and **Preference**. From left to right cases of hard, medium and soft water are highlighted.*

Remark 2.6.6 *For the conclusions drawn throughout this section, it is of no importance whether Z is a single variable or a set of variables.*

2.6.3   Visualising Odds and Odds-Ratios

Preliminaries

One method of measuring the strength of an association between two variables is the *odds ratio* (*cross-product ratio*). E.g. (conditional) independence between two variables corresponds to an odds ratio of 1. The way to visualising higher-order interactions therefore leads to the need for displaying and assessing odds ratios visually.

Definition 2.6.7

The *odds-ratio* (*cross-product ratio*) θ between two binary variables X and Y is defined as

$$\theta = \frac{\pi_{11}\pi_{22}}{\pi_{12}\pi_{21}}.$$

Remark 2.6.8

Odds ratios are symmetric in X and Y.

$\log\theta$ is approximately normally distributed (cf. Agresti (1990) p.17) with an asymptotic standard deviation $\sigma_{\log\theta}$ of

$$\sigma_{\log\theta}^2 = \frac{1}{n_{11}} + \frac{1}{n_{12}} + \frac{1}{n_{21}} + \frac{1}{n_{22}},$$

where n_{11}, n_{12}, n_{21} and n_{22} are the frequencies of the corresponding 2 by 2 table.

There are several possibilities for defining a set of odds ratios $\{\theta_{ij}\}$ between two variables X and Y with I resp. J categories. One is the approach of **local odds ratios**, defined by four corners $\{\pi_{ij}, \pi_{i'j}, \pi_{ij'}, \pi_{i'j'}\}$ of an arbitrary rectangle (see sketch 2.48) within the cells of the contingency table of X and Y.

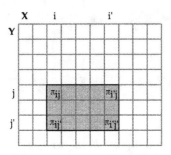

Figure 2.48: *Rectangle of cells in a contingency table of X and Y.*

Definition 2.6.9

The set of *local odds ratios* between two variables X and Y with I resp. J categories is defined as

$$\theta_{iji'j'} = \frac{\pi_{ij}\pi_{i'j'}}{\pi_{ij'}\pi_{i'j}} \quad \text{with} \ \ 1 \leq i < i' \leq I, 1 \leq j < j' \leq J.$$

This defines a set of $I(I-1) \cdot J(J-1)$ different odds ratios. Yet, there exist basis sets of $(I-1) \cdot (J-1)$ odds ratios, from which we can calculate all other odds ratios. The basis set we will use is in the following the set of **adjacent local odds ratios** $\{\theta_{ij}\}$, defined as odds ratios from adjacent cells.

Definition 2.6.10
The *adjacent local odds ratios* $\{\theta_{ij}\}$ between two variables X and Y have the form

$$\theta_{ij} = \frac{\pi_{ij}\pi_{i+1j+1}}{\pi_{i+1j}\pi_{ij+1}} \quad \text{with} \ \ 1 \leq i < I, \ 1 \leq j < J. \tag{2.5}$$

Remark 2.6.11 *The adjacent local odds ratios, indeed, form a basis of all possible local odds ratios, since any odds ratio $\theta_{iji'j'}$ can be expressed as a product of adjacent odds ratios:*

$$\theta_{iji'j'} = \prod_{a=i}^{i'-1}\prod_{b=j}^{j'-1} \theta_{ab}.$$

Definition 2.6.12
Two ordinal variables X and Y are said to be *positive (negative) dependent*, if $\forall i < I, j < J$

$$\log\theta_{ij} \geq 0 \qquad (\log\theta_{ij} \leq 0).$$

Remark 2.6.13 *Note, that the odds ratios depend strongly on the order in which the categories occur - still, odds ratios for different orders can be derived from the basis set as shown above.*

Remark 2.6.14 *The odds ratios of X and Y give a measure of association between these two variables. It holds:*

$$\theta_{ij} = 1 \quad \forall i,j \quad \Longleftrightarrow \quad X \ and \ Y \ are \ independent$$

Proof: "$\Rightarrow$": It has to be shown, that the probability of arbitrary events $A \cap B$ can be written as product of the marginal probabilities of the events A and B. For this, it is sufficient to consider events of single elements, which have the form $X = X_i$ and $Y = Y_j$ (the ith resp. jth category of X and Y).
Since all adjacent odds ratios θ_{ij} are equal to 1, also $\theta_{ijab} = 1$ for $1 \leq i < a \leq I, 1 \leq j < b \leq< J$ and $\pi_{ij}\pi_{ab} = \theta_{ijab} \cdot \pi_{ib}\pi_{aj} = \pi_{ib}\pi_{aj}$.

Let $\pi_{i.} = \sum_{j=1}^{J} \pi_{ij}$ and $\pi_{.j} = \sum_{i=1}^{I} \pi_{ij}$, then

$$\pi_{i.} \cdot \pi_{.j} = \sum_{a=1}^{I} \sum_{b=1}^{J} \pi_{ib} \cdot \pi_{aj} =$$

$$= \sum_{a=1}^{I} \sum_{b=1}^{J} \pi_{ij} \cdot \pi_{ab} = \pi_{ij} \sum_{a=1}^{I} \sum_{b=1}^{J} \pi_{ab} = \pi_{ij}.$$

"$\Leftarrow$": X and Y are stochastically independent. This gives in particular $\forall 1 \le i \le I$ and $1 \le j \le J$: $\pi_{ij} = \pi_{i.}\pi_{.j}$.
With this,

$$\theta_{ij} = \frac{\pi_{ij}\pi_{i+1j+1}}{\pi_{ij+1}\pi_{i+1j}} = \frac{\pi_{i.}\pi_{.j} \cdot \pi_{i+1.}\pi_{.j+1}}{\pi_{i.}\pi_{.j+1} \cdot \pi_{i+1.}\pi_{.j}} = 1.$$

$\square$

Remark 2.6.15 *The notion of positive/negative dependency of variables comes from the analysis of ordinal data. Therefore it strongly depends on the ordering of the categories, whereas odds ratios do not (we will not distinguish between θ and its inverse θ^{-1}). - Since we are only concerned with an analysis of odds ratios, all variables can be considered as nominal and reordering categories is permitted. Reordering the categories may provide sometimes, though not always, a strict dependency (i.e. positive or negative dependency).*

Motivation

Two different aspects are of interest:

- is an interaction present?

- is structural behaviour within an association recognizable?

The first problem corresponds to $\theta_c = 1$, the odds-ratio of the examined interaction. Whether odds-ratios are 1 or not, is answered graphically by the amount of deviation from a lattice structure in a mosaic display. The second problem is more tricky, since an answer of only yes or true is not enough.

Graphical solutions for the second problem are based on the possibility of comparing the items involved.

The following paragraphs will answer these questions. According to this twofold problem, each segment will also have two parts. The first part always deals with the visualization of one quantity and the visual assessment of its size. In the second part two values are compared to each other.

Visualising and Comparing Odds

The *odds* are the ratio of an event to its counterpart event. If a is the event rate for a disease, its counterpart rate is $1 - a$ and its odds are $a/(1 - a)$.

Let X and Y be two binary variables. The probabilities of their joint distribution are given in the following array:

	X_1	X_2
Y_1	a	b
Y_2	c	d

If X denotes the occurrence of a specific disease and Y divides the sample into a treatment-group and a control-group, the odds of getting the disease depending on the group are given by

$$\frac{a}{b} \text{ and } \frac{c}{d}.$$

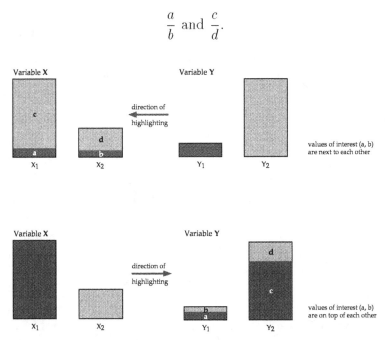

Figure 2.49: *Barcharts of the variables X and Y. Different ways of highlighting re-stacks the corresponding boxes.*

Figure 2.49 shows two ways of highlighting a, b, c and d in the corresponding barcharts of X and Y. According to the highlighting direction either a and c or a and b appear together in the first bin. This provides the basis for two different ways of "reading" the odds graphically. Odds can be visualised with the help of trellis barcharts (Becker et al. 1994): for each level of Y a barchart of the corresponding X values is drawn, see fig. 2.50.

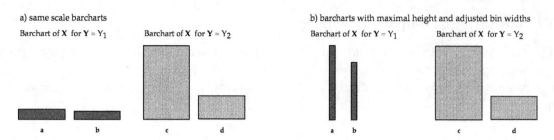

Figure 2.50: *Trellis barcharts of X for all levels of Y. On the left both barcharts have the same scale, on the right the barcharts are drawn with maximal height. The bin widths are adjusted such that the area is proportional to the cell's frequency.*

Figure 2.50b shows trellis barcharts of X, where the highest bins in each barchart have the same height. The widths are adjusted in such a way that the area of the bin is still proportional to the cell's frequency.

The odds a/b and c/d can now be compared by comparing the heights of the bins corresponding to b and d. If the odds were equal, these bins would have the same height. Since the bin for event b is a lot higher than the bin corresponding to d, the odds for group Y_1 are smaller than the odds for Y_2.

There are two drawbacks to this procedure: firstly, the values of the odds can not be estimated visually very well (dividing heights of bins mentally is certainly not one of the basic tasks of a graphical display); secondly, the procedure can not be generalised to tables with dimension $> 2 \times K$.

A more promising approach is given by the direction of highlighting as shown in the lower part of figure 2.49. Barcharts or spineplots of Y as on the right side in figure 2.51 show the values of interest (a, b resp. c, d) on top of each other. The ratio of a and b depends on the height of the area corresponding to a. Since the areas representing a and b have the same width, we may identify the height of the bin representing a with its area and this with a itself.

Then the function for "reading" the odds value from the display is a function in the highlighting height a, odds $(a) = a/(1 - a)$. To assess this value visually without the support of the graph as shown in figure 2.51a is, of course, not possible. For the log odds it is different though. Since this function is symmetric around $a = 0.5$ and fairly linear between $a \in (0.25, 0.75)$, we may read for highlighting values in this range the log odds values according to the log odds scale as sketched on the right most side in figure 2.51b.

2×2 **Tables and the Odds Ratio**

The sketch in figure 2.52 shows a 2 dimensional mosaicplot of the two binary variables A and B. Each of the four areas corresponds to the number of observation within the intersection

Spineplot of **Y,** the values **X** = X₁ are highlighted

a) reading the odds value

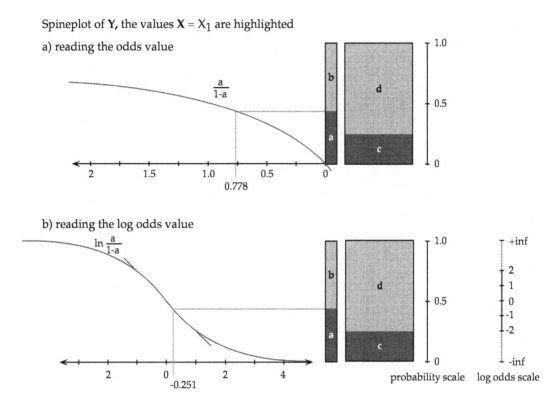

Figure 2.51: *Spineplot of Y, the values X = X₂ are highlighted. From the graphs on the left hand side it becomes clear that the log odds can be read from the spineplot directly for values between -2 and 2.*

of A and B, that is, the areas give an estimate for the joint distribution of A and B.

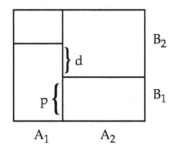

Figure 2.52: *Schematic mosaic plot of A vs. B.*

Let p be the probability of B_1 given A_2, i.e. $p = P(B_1|A_2)$, and let d be the difference in the

conditional probabilities of B given A, $d := P(B_1|A_1) - P(B_1|A_2)$.
The odds-ratio of A and B can be written as

$$\text{odds}(A, B) = \frac{p_{A_1B_1}p_{A_2B_2}}{p_{A_1B_2}p_{A_2B_1}} = \frac{p_{B_1|A_1}p_{B_2|A_2}}{p_{B_2|A_1}p_{B_1|A_2}} =$$

$$= \frac{(p+d)(1-p)}{p(1-p-d)} = 1 + \frac{d}{p(1-p-d)},$$

if $p_{A_1B_2} \neq 0 \neq p_{A_2B_1}$.

Both p and d can be read from the mosaicplot very easily (at least with the help of interactive features such as querying), thus giving the possibility of getting the odds-ratio from the graphical display directly. One may argue, that though reading p and d is very easy, calculating the exact odds ratios from them certainly is not.

But at least one can see that the odds ratio increases with d, the difference between the conditional probabilities of B_1 given A. Another hint on the magnitude of the odds ratio is given by the comparison of $p_{A_1B_1}$ and $p_{A_2B_2}$. If these two values differ a lot, the odds ratio increases as well.

By substituting the denominator with its maximum, one gets an estimate of the odds ratio, which only depends on d:

for $p = (1-d)/2$ the odds ratio between A and B is minimal,

$$\text{odds}(A, B) \geq 1 + 4\frac{d}{(1-d)^2}$$

Using this functional dependency between the odds ratio and d does not, of course, provide a way of obtaining the exact value of the odds ratio from the graphical display. But this is not intended anyway. What the display fulfills very well, though, is to provide a rough estimation of the strength of the association between the variables.

Example 2.6.16 *Rochdale Data*
*Figure 2.53 shows a series of 2 dimensional mosaicplots built up from different variables. The data used is the Rochdale dataset (see section A.9). The first variable in all the graphics is "**wife employed ?**", consisting of the categories yes and no. The aim of the analysis was to examine which factors were associated with whether a wife was employed or not. For this the 2 dimensional relations with the other variables are first of interest. This can be done by putting the variable "**wife employed ?**" at the first position in a mosaic plot and draw each of the other variables as second dimension.*

Comparing Odds-Ratios in 2×2 tables

Definition 2.6.17
For three variables X, Y and Z, the corresponding *(conditional) odds ratios* for fixed levels

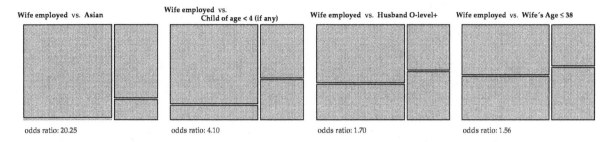

Figure 2.53: *Series of four 2 dimensional mosaicplots of "wife employed ?" vs. four other variables of the Rochdale Data. Comparing the plots we can draw inferences on relative importance of the associations between each pair of variables. The exact odds ratios are given below each mosaic.*

k of Z

$$\theta_{ij(k)} = \frac{\pi_{ij(k)}\pi_{i+1j+1(k)}}{\pi_{i+1j(k)}\pi_{ij+1(k)}}$$

describe the conditional $X - Y$ association.

From the conditional associations we can draw conclusions about higher way associations. There is e.g. no three-way interaction between X, Y and Z is present, if all (conditional) odds ratios of X and Y are equal.

The trick therefore is to compare odds ratios:

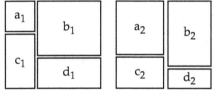

$$\frac{a_1 d_1}{b_1 c_1} = \frac{a_2 d_2}{b_2 c_2}$$

Visual hints The following list gives some necessary, though not sufficient, conditions for the equality of two odds ratios:

1. **trivial case:** If any of the entries is 0 (or 1) on one side, then all corresponding entries on the other side have also to be 0 (or 1).

2. If the heights of c_1 and c_2 coincide, then the heights of d_1 and d_2 also have to coincide.

3. If the height of c_1 is larger than the height of d_1, the same must hold for the heights of c_2 and d_2.

Proof of (3)   Denote with $h(x)$ the height of a rectangle corresponding to value x. Assume $h(c_1) > h(d_1)$, but $h(c_2) \leq h(d_2)$.

This implies $h(b_1) > h(a_1)$ and $h(b_2) \leq h(a_2)$.

As $\frac{h(a_i)}{h(c_i)} = \frac{a_i}{c_i}$ and $\frac{h(d_i)}{h(b_i)} = \frac{d_i}{b_i}$ for $i = 1, 2$, the odds ratios are the same for the heights of the rectangles as well as for their areas:

$$\frac{h(a_i)h(d_i)}{h(b_i)h(c_i)} = \frac{a_i d_i}{b_i c_i}.$$

$$\Rightarrow \frac{h(a_1)h(d_1)}{h(b_1)h(c_1)} = \frac{a_1 d_1}{b_1 c_1} < 1, \text{ but } \frac{a_2 d_2}{b_2 c_2} \geq 1.$$

$\square$

Graphical Solution   The graphical solution is based upon the following observation: whenever two binary variables X and Y have the same odds-ratio, a mosaicplot shows approximately the same difference in the conditional probabilities $X|Y$ (cf. fig. 2.54). This can be

Mosaics of X,Y

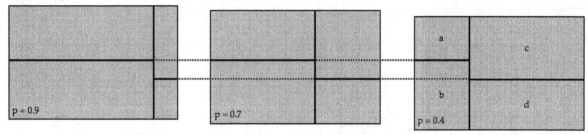

Figure 2.54: *Three mosaicplots of the variables X and Y, the odds ratio, $\theta = \frac{ad}{bc}$, is 0.5 in each case. The mosaics show the same difference ≈ 0.17 between the conditional probabilities.*

read from the display without difficulty.

The difference between the conditional probabilities involved can be written, more formally, as $P(X_0|Y_0) - P(X_0|Y_1) = \frac{b}{a+b} - \frac{d}{c+d}$. The following proposition shows, that this difference indeed only depends on the odds ratio (thus, the difference is constant for constant odds):

Proposition 2.6.18

Let a, b, c, d be the probabilities of a contingency table of two binary variables X and Y, as shown in fig. 2.54.

The difference in the probabilities of X given Y can be expressed in terms of the odds ratio, $\theta = \frac{ad}{bc}$:

$$\frac{b}{a+b} - \frac{d}{c+d} \approx \frac{1-\theta}{1+2\sqrt{\theta}+\theta} \tag{2.6}$$

Proof X, Y are binary variables with $P(Y_0) = a+b$, $P(Y_1) = c+d$, w.l.o.g. let X and Y be negatively dependent, i.e. $a < b$ and $d < c$.
The odds ratio θ, is given as $\theta = \frac{ad}{bc}$ (note, that $\theta < 1$).
The left hand side of equation (2.6) can be transformed by basic calculation,

$$\frac{b}{a+b} - \frac{d}{c+d} = \frac{bc-ad}{(a+b)\cdot(c+d)} = \frac{(1-\theta)bc}{(\frac{a}{b}+\frac{d}{c})bc + (1+\theta)bc} =$$

$$= \frac{1-\theta}{1+(\frac{a}{b}+\frac{d}{c})+\theta}.$$

The rest is done by comparing $\frac{a}{b}+\frac{d}{c}$ with $\theta = \frac{a}{b}\cdot\frac{d}{c}$, that is, comparing the sum of two values $x+y$ with their product $x\cdot y$.
From comparing $(x+y)^2$ and $(x-y)^2$ follows, that

$$x+y = \sqrt{4xy + (x-y)^2}. \tag{2.7}$$

It is clear, that

$$x+y \geq 2\sqrt{\theta}.$$

For an upper boundary, we need the fact, that

$$0 \leq \min(x,y)^2 < \theta < \max(x,y)^2 < 1,$$

which implies that

$$x+y \leq \sqrt{1+3\theta}.$$

This shows both the statement in (2.6) and gives an estimate of the error (cf. fig. 2.55). The error e is maximal for $\theta \to 0$ where at the same time $\min(x,y) \to 0, \max(x,y) \to 1$. In this case, $e = 0.5$, whereas $\theta \to 1 \Rightarrow e \to 0$. $\square$

Example 2.6.19 *Rochdale Data*
Figure 2.56 shows two mosaicplots of the variables "wife employed?", wife's education and husband's education resp. "wife employed ?", husband's education and wife's

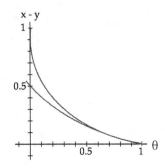

Figure 2.55: *Boundaries of the difference in probabilities*
$X|Y$ *(x − y, as in proof of 2.6.18).*
The upper line shows $\frac{1-\theta}{1+2\sqrt{\theta}+\theta}$, *the lower line* $\frac{1-\theta}{1+\sqrt{3\theta+1}+\theta}$.
The difference between the lines is less than .05 for $\theta > .22$.

age. *Odds ratios can be compared by comparing the corresponding differences in the conditional probabilities. On the left hand side the differences in the conditional probabilities are distinctly different - in terms of odds ratios this corresponds to the existing of a three way interaction between the variables involved ($\theta = 2.55$ resp. $\theta = 6.53$).*
The differences of the conditional probabilities in the mosaic on the right hand side are almost equal, suggesting the absence of a three way interaction between "wife employed ?", husband's education and wife's age ($\theta = 0.72$ resp. $\theta = 0.75$).

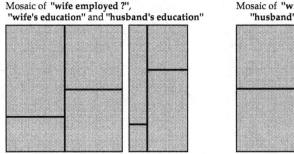

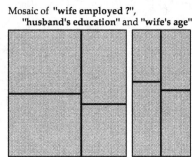

Figure 2.56: *Two mosaicplots of the Rochdale Data.*
On the left hand side a strong three way interaction becomes visible from the large difference in the conditional probabilities. The mosaic on the right, suggests the absence of a three way interaction between the variables "wife employed ?", husband's education and wife's age.

Remark: Where is the approximation good enough?

Denote with $\begin{pmatrix} a & b \\ c & d \end{pmatrix}$ the cell probabilities of a 2×2 table.

If either the difference $\frac{a}{c} - \frac{d}{b}$ or $\frac{a}{b} - \frac{d}{c}$ is small, the approximation works fine, even for $\theta \to 0$

(for proof cf. equation (2.7)). Figure 2.57 gives an example for two different odds ratios. The results together with the exact numbers are listed in table 2.6.

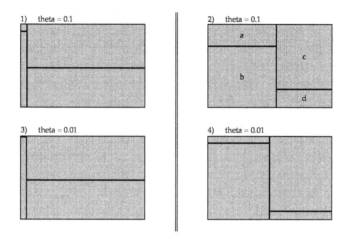

Figure 2.57: *Examples for bad and good approximations. On the left, the differences of the proportions, $\frac{a}{b} - \frac{d}{c}$, are too large for the approximation in prop. 2.6.18, to still work fine. On the right, the approximation holds well. For the exact numbers see table 2.6.*

example	θ	$\frac{b}{a+b} - \frac{d}{c+d}$	approximation	$\left|\frac{a}{b} - \frac{d}{c}\right|$
(1)	0.1	0.42	0.519	0.80
(2)	0.1	0.518	0.519	0.077
(3)	0.01	0.52	0.818	0.89
(4)	0.01	0.818	0.818	0.017

Table 2.6: *List of the odds ratios, conditional probabilities, the value of the approximation and the value of critical difference $\left|\frac{a}{b} - \frac{d}{c}\right|$.*

Remark: Where is the graphical solution good enough? Denote with d the difference between the conditional probabilities, $d := \frac{p_{12}}{p_{1.}} - \frac{p_{22}}{p_{2.}}$, and let D be $D := \frac{p_{11}}{p_{12}} - \frac{p_{22}}{p_{21}}$. The difference in conditional probabilities d can be written in terms of θ and D exactly (see proof to prop. 2.6.18):

$$d = \frac{1 - \theta}{1 + \sqrt{4\theta + D^2} + \theta}$$

Vice versa, θ can be expressed exactly in the difference in conditional probabilities d and D. For $\theta < 1$:

$$\theta = \frac{1 + d^2 - d\sqrt{4 + D^2(1+d)^2}}{(1+d)^2} \tag{2.8}$$

Notice, that the function in (2.8) is strictly monotonic decreasing in $d \in (0, 1)$ for fixed D. So, whenever D is approximately similar for a number of subtables, θ can still be derived from comparing the differences in conditional probabilities (cf. fig. 2.58). For examples (1)

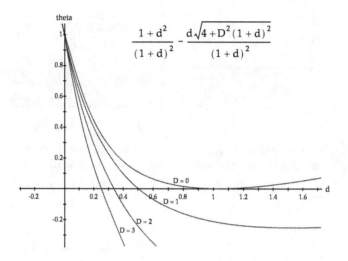

Figure 2.58: *Functional dependency between θ, D and d.*

and (3) in table 2.6 and figure 2.57 therefore still holds (even though the approximation of prop. 2.6.18 does not work), that the odds ratio in (1) is smaller than in (3), because the differences of conditional probabilities are less for (1) than for (3).

Application: Visualisation of Interaction Effects

For two way interactions: the approximation in proposition 2.6.18 shows, that the difference in the conditional probabilities d is approximately

$$d(\theta) \approx \frac{1 - \theta}{1 + 2\sqrt{\theta} + \theta} = \frac{1 - \sqrt{\theta}}{1 + \sqrt{\theta}}.$$

The inverse of this function, $\theta(d)$, is

$$\theta(d) = \left(\frac{1 - d}{1 + d}\right)^2$$

The logarithm of this function is $2\left(\log\left(1-d\right)-\log\left(1+d\right)\right)$, a strictly decreasing function in (0,1) with a pole in 1. A Taylor expansion in 0 gives:

$$\log\theta(d)\approx-4d+0d^2-8d^3+0d^4+\mathcal{O}(d^5).$$

Comparing odds-ratios in $I\times J$ tables

The problem when dealing with $I\times J$ tables is that the four bins involved in an odds ratio θ_{ij} no longer are adjusted and they also can not be adjusted for all $\{\theta_{ij}\}$ at the same time. Figure 2.59 shows a 5×4 table with one possible adjustment of the bins - it becomes obvious, that up to four adjustments are needed to show all different odds ratios and it is not very easy to work with such adjusted displays.

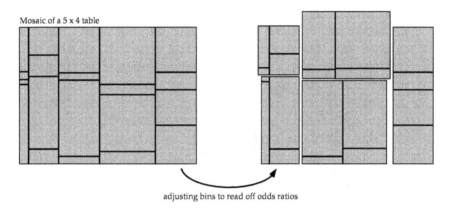

Mosaic of a 5 x 4 table

adjusting bins to read off odds ratios

Figure 2.59: *Mosaicplot of a 5×4 table, on the right is shown one of the possible adjustments of the bins.*

Graphical Solution using interactive techniques

situation: Let X be a variable with $I>2$ categories, whose odds ratios with variable Y are of interest.

strategy: zoom (logically) on each pair of adjacent categories in X within the corresponding mosaic plot.

advantage: this technique is easily applicable, extensible to an arbitrary number of variables and only basic tools of interactive graphics are used (see section 2.7.2 for an application to uniform association models).

disadvantage: $I-1$ steps are needed to get an overall impression of the three way structure.

Example 2.6.20 *Accidents' Victims Data*
Figure 2.60 shows three mosaicplots in hotselection mode. From top to bottom three pairs of **Vehicle** *types are chosen. In the first mosaicplot the odds between pedestrians and bikers are given for different* **Age** *groups and* **Gender**. *A strong dependency between* **Age** *and* **Vehicle** *is obvious: younger people (age ≤ 10) are e.g. far more likely to go by foot than by bike (and to have accidents then). The highest rate of cyclers is among the 10 to 20 year old. After that, the rate of cycler decreases and people are more likely to go by foot. These trends appear for both the female and male groups. The odds ratios are therefore rather similar, too, cf. table 2.7. The other mosaicplots show different dependencies between* **Age** *and* **Vehicle**, *but*

Female				Male			
12.87	0.85	0.88	0.30	15.87	0.55	0.92	0.72
2.79	2.27	0.50	0.41	7.86	3.26	0.53	0.35
0.07	1.50	1.93	1.88	0.03	1.69	1.63	1.06

Table 2.7: *Odds ratios of the Accidents' Victims Data. Each row corresponds to one mosaicplot in figure 2.60.*

still the odds ratios are very alike for both genders. This indicates the absence of a three way interaction between **Age**, **Vehicle** *and* **Gender**.

Alternative Graphical Solution   The basic idea for a graphical solution is, to change from the local odds ratios $\theta_{ij} = \frac{\pi_{ij}\pi_{i+1j+1}}{\pi_{i+1j}\pi_{ij+1}}$ to so called *global-local odds ratios* θ_{ij}^* (Agresti 1984), with

$$\theta_{ij}^* = \frac{\sum_{l_1 \leq i} \pi_{l_1 j} \cdot \sum_{l_2 > i} \pi_{l_2 j+1}}{\sum_{l_1 \leq i} \pi_{l_1 j+1} \cdot \sum_{l_2 > i} \pi_{l_2 j}} \qquad \left(= \frac{\Sigma_a \Sigma_d}{\Sigma_b \Sigma_c} \text{ cf. fig. 2.61} \right).$$

These odds ratios are local in the column variable but "global" in the row variable, since all categories of the column variable are used in each odds ratio. This concept allows the distinction between response and explanatory variables. They can be used to compare pairs of columns with respect to their distribution on an ordinal response.
The advantage of this approach is, that these odds ratios can be handled graphically just the same as θ_{ij} with binary variables in the previous section. As there are very easy-to-check relations between θ_{ij} and the interactions of X and Y in a log-linear model, it is now of interest, in how far the new set of odds ratios allows the same conclusions.

Relationship between θ_{ij} and θ_{ij}^*   Douglas et al. (1992) (Theorem 3.1) showed that in the case of independence the two different sets of odds ratios coincide, i.e. $\forall i < I, j < J$ $\theta_{ij} = 1 = \theta_{ij}^*$. Furthermore, any strict dependence in θ_{ij} implies the same dependence in θ_{ij}^*.

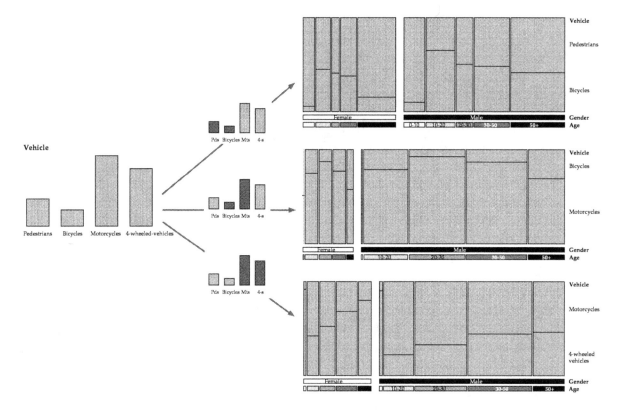

Figure 2.60: *Visualization of the odds ratios between **Vehicle** and **Age** given **Gender** in three steps. The mosaicplots from top to bottom show **Gender**, **Age** and two adjacent categories from the variable **Vehicle**.*

Constant odds ratios $\theta_{ijk} = \lambda_{ij}$ for all levels k of Z imply the absence of a three way interaction between X, Y and Z. The question therefore is: do constant θ_{ijk} imply constant θ_{ijk}^*? - Unfortunately not, as the following example shows.

Example 2.6.21

Let's consider a contingency table from a three-valued variable X and a binary variable Y with cell probabilities as given in the left most table below. The two tables on the right show two examples for probabilities with $\frac{ad}{bc} = \frac{4}{3}$ and $\frac{cf}{de} = \frac{5}{3}$. Figure 2.62 shows the mosaics of these numbers.

	Y_1	Y_2
X_1	a	b
X_2	c	d
X_3	e	f

(1)	Y_1	Y_2
X_1	.58	.42
X_2	.45	.54
X_3	.2	.8

(2)	Y_1	Y_2
X_1	.79	.21
X_2	.69	.31
X_3	.4	.6

The local odds ratios are given by $\theta_{ad} = \frac{ad}{bc}$, $\theta_{af} = \frac{af}{be}$ and $\theta_{cf} = \frac{cf}{ed}$, with $\theta_{ad} \cdot \theta_{cf} = \theta_{af}$.

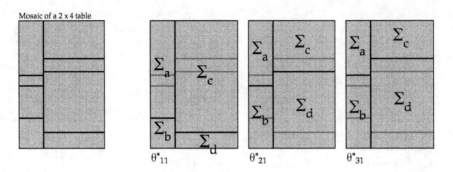

Figure 2.61: *Mosaicplot of a 2 × 4 table, bins separated by a gray line are added up within the particular global-local odds ratio. According to proposition 2.6.18 each difference in the conditional probabilities shows one global-local odds ratio θ^*_{ij}.*

The global-local odds ratio θ^*_{ad} then can be expressed as

$$\theta^*_{ad} = \frac{a(d+f)}{b(c+e)} = \theta_{ad} + \theta_{cf}\frac{e}{c+e}.$$

This expression is not constant for constant θ_{ad} and θ_{cf}, since it also depends on the ratio of e and $c+e$.

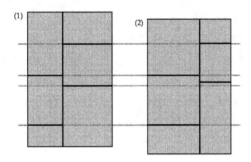

Figure 2.62: *Mosaicplots of 2×3 tables, the differences in the conditional probabilities are approximately the same, the upper difference corresponds to an odds ratio $\theta_1 = 0.6$, the lower to $\theta_2 = 0.3$.*

But *- when the approximation in proposition 2.6.18 holds, i.e when the difference $\frac{c}{e} - \frac{d}{f}$ is small, $\frac{c}{e} \approx \sqrt{\theta_{cf}}$ - and θ^*_{ad} is constant for constant θ_{ad} and θ_{cf}.*

Global-local odds ratios can at least be approximated by local odds ratios as the following proposition shows.

Proposition 2.6.22
Let X and Y be two categorical variables with I resp. J categories. Under the same conditions as in proposition 2.6.22 (i.e. $\frac{\pi_{i1}}{\pi_{i+11}} \approx \frac{\pi_{i+12}}{\pi_{i2}}$ $\forall i$) global-local odds ratios $\{\theta^*_{ij}\}$ can

approximately be written in terms of local odds ratios $\{\theta_{ij}\}$:

$$\theta_{ij}^* \approx \theta_{ij} \cdot \frac{\left(\sum_{l=1}^{i} \prod_{k=l}^{i-1} \sqrt{\theta_{kj}}\right)\left(\sum_{l=i+1}^{I} \prod_{k=i+1}^{l-1} \sqrt{\theta_{kj}}\right)}{\left(\sum_{l=1}^{i} \prod_{k=l}^{i-1} \sqrt{\theta_{kj}^{-1}}\right)\left(\sum_{l=i+1}^{I} \prod_{k=i+1}^{l-1} \sqrt{\theta_{kj}^{-1}}\right)} \forall i, j \qquad (2.9)$$

Proof of Proposition 2.6.22 The number of categories in Y is of no importance, therefore we may set $J := 2$. Since for $J = 2$ $\theta_{ij}, \theta_{ij}^*$ are defined only for $j = 1$, denote $\theta_{i1} =: \theta_i$ and $\theta_{i1}^* =: \theta_i^*$

According to the postulation all differences $\frac{\pi_{i1}}{\pi_{i+11}} - \frac{\pi_{i+12}}{\pi_{i2}}$ are small, i.e. $\forall i$ $\pi_{i1} \approx \pi_{i+11} \cdot \sqrt{\theta_i}$ and $\pi_{i2} \approx \pi_{i+12} \cdot \frac{1}{\sqrt{\theta_i}}$.

These relationships between π_{ij} and π_{i+1j} are now applied iteratively to the sums $\sum_{k \leq i} \pi_{jk}$ and $\sum_{k > i} \pi_{jk}$. For $j = 1, 2$ it holds

$$\sum_{k \leq i} \pi_{jk} = \pi_{j1} + \pi_{j2} + \ldots + \pi_{ji} \approx \left(\sqrt{\theta_1^{\sigma_j}} + 1\right)\pi_{j2} + \ldots + \pi_{ji} \approx$$

$$\approx \left(\left(\sqrt{\theta_1^{\sigma_j}} + 1\right)\sqrt{\theta_2^{\sigma_j}} + 1\right)\pi_{j3} + \ldots + \pi_{ji} \approx$$

$$\approx \pi_{ji} \cdot \left(\sum_{l=1}^{i}\prod_{k=l}^{i-1}\sqrt{\theta_k^{\sigma_j}}\right) \qquad (2.10)$$

similarly,

$$\sum_{k > i} \pi_{jk} \approx \pi_{ji+1} \cdot \left(\sum_{l=i+1}^{I}\prod_{k=i+1}^{l-1}\sqrt{\theta_k^{-\sigma_j}}\right) \qquad (2.11)$$

where $\sigma_j = 1$ for $j = 1$ and $\sigma_j = -1$ for $j = 2$.

Using equations (2.10) and (2.11), θ_i^* can be written as follows.

$$\theta_i^* = \frac{\sum_{k \leq i} \pi_{1k} \cdot \sum_{k > i} \pi_{2k}}{\sum_{k \leq i} \pi_{2k} \cdot \sum_{k > i} \pi_{1k}} \approx$$

$$\approx \frac{\left(\sum_{l=1}^{i} \prod_{k=l}^{i-1} \sqrt{\theta_k}\right)\pi_{1i} \cdot \pi_{2i+1}\left(\sum_{l=i+1}^{I} \prod_{k=i+1}^{l-1} \sqrt{\theta_k}\right)}{\left(\sum_{l=1}^{i} \prod_{k=l}^{i-1} \sqrt{\theta_k^{-1}}\right)\underbrace{\pi_{2i} \cdot \pi_{1i+1}}_{\theta_i}\left(\sum_{l=i+1}^{I} \prod_{k=i+1}^{l-1} \sqrt{\theta_k^{-1}}\right)} \qquad (2.12)$$

This shows statement (2.9). $\qquad\qquad\qquad\qquad\qquad\qquad\qquad\qquad\qquad\qquad\qquad\qquad\qquad$ □

Remark 2.6.23 *One of the consequences of proposition 2.6.22 is, that for constant values of θ_{ijk}, i.e. $\theta_{ijk} = \theta_{ij}$ for all $k = 1, \ldots, K$ levels of a third variable Z, the values θ^*_{ijk} are approximately constant, too. This makes three-way interactions (or their absence) easy to detect in $I \times J \times K$ tables.*

Example 2.6.24 *Detergent Data*
*Figure 2.63 shows two mosaicplots of the variables **Preference, M-User** and **Water Softness** resp. **Preference, Temperature** and **Water Softness**. In the mosaic on the left hand side the differences in the conditional probabilities show up fairly strong - even the visual hints of section 2.6.3 are violated.*
*On the right, the differences in the conditional probabilities are almost the same - suggesting the absence of a three way interaction between **Preference, Temperature** and **Water Softness**.*

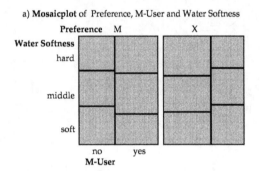
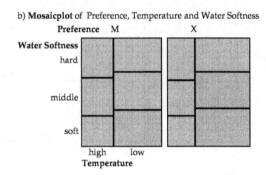

Figure 2.63: *Mosaicplots of the Detergent Data.*
Comparing the differences in the conditional probabilities leads to the conclusion, that there is a three way interaction on the left, no three way interaction on the right.

For tables with more than two columns (i.e. if Y has more than two categories) each two columns with the same values in X have to be compared as described before.

Example 2.6.25 *Accidents' Victims Data*

*Figure 2.64 shows a mosaic plot of **Gender, Age** and **Vehicle**. For a better overview cells corresponding to the same type of **Vehicle** are shaded in the same colour. Obviously, we are dealing with a two way interaction between **Vehicle** and **Age**. Despite the fact, that far less women are involved into accidents than men, the mosaicplots of the genders look very much alike. By comparing corresponding differences in the conditional probabilities more thoroughly, we find the largest deviations at the lower right of the plots between the **Age** groups 30-50 and 50+ and pedestrians and non-pedestrians:*

Women	30 - 50	50+
non-Ped.	12815	8356
Ped.	1863	5827

Men	30 - 50	50+
non-Ped.	38774	21534
Ped.	3401	5910

,

corresponding to global-local odds ratios of $\theta_{women} = 4.80$ and $\theta_{men} = 3.13$. The overall

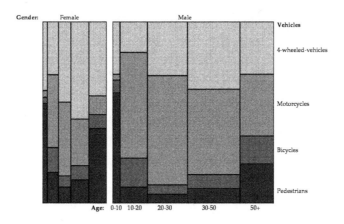

Figure 2.64: *Mosaicplots of **Gender**, **Age** and **Vehicle**.*

*impression hints, though, that the three way interaction between **Age**, **Vehicle** and **Gender** is weak. A G^2 statistic, however, is highly significant: $G^2_{AVG} = 1007.1$ with 12 degrees of freedom due to the large number of observations (180730 accidents in total). On a level of 5% the N value is 3774 - indicating that this three way interaction indeed needs a high support to be significant.*

2.6.4 Generalising Odds Ratios to Higher Dimensions

Motivation

In order to be able to express higher dimensional interaction terms via conditions on the odds ratios, the notion of odds ratios has to be generalised to more than 2 dimensions. In the previous section we already used conditional odds ratios of three variables X, Y and Z for fixed levels of Z.

How can this concept be generalised further? - Let's have a look at the three binary variables X, Y and Z: A two-way interaction λ_{11}^{XY} can be expressed in terms of the log odds , the three way interaction λ_{111}^{XYZ} in terms of the conditional log odds (using zero sum constraints):

$$\lambda_{11}^{XY} = \frac{1}{4} \log \theta_{11},$$

$$\lambda_{111}^{XYZ} = \frac{1}{8} (\log \theta_{11(1)} - \log \theta_{11(2)})$$

Is there a similar expression for rc tables? - using control group constraints, i.e. all effects which have a "1" as one of their indices are set to zero:

$$\lambda_1^X = \lambda_1^Y = \lambda_{i1}^{XY} = \lambda_{1j}^{XY} = 0,$$

we may write the interaction effects of the two dimensional model

$$\log m_{ij} = \mu + \lambda_i^X + \lambda_j^Y + \lambda_{ij}^{XY}$$

as

$$
\begin{aligned}
\mu &= \log m_{11} \\
\lambda_i^X &= \log \frac{m_{i1}}{m_{11}} \\
\lambda_j^Y &= \log \frac{m_{1j}}{m_{11}} \\
\lambda_{ij}^{XY} &= \log \frac{m_{11} m_{ij}}{m_{i1} m_{1j}}.
\end{aligned}
$$

Then λ_{ij}^{XY} can then be expressed as function of the log odds ratios:

$$\lambda_{ij}^{XY} = \log \left(\prod_{k=1}^{i-1} \prod_{l=1}^{j-1} \theta_{kl} \right) = \sum_{k,l} \log \theta_{kl}.$$

In order to deal with higher dimensional effects, we need to extend the concept of odds ratios to more than two variables.

Definition of Odds-Ratios in Higher Dimensions

Definition 2.6.26

Based on the approach by Bhapkar & Koch (1968) we define the odds ratios θ_{ijk} between three variables X, Y and Z with I, J resp. K categories as:

$$\theta_{ijk} := \frac{\theta_{ij(k)}}{\theta_{ij(k+1)}}$$

With this definition the absence of a three way interaction corresponds to $\theta_{ijk} = 1$ for all i, j, k. And for binary variables the three way interaction between the variables can be expressed in terms of the odds ratio (again, using zero sum constraints):

$$\lambda_{111}^{XYZ} = \frac{1}{8} \log \theta_{111}.$$

The interaction effects of a three-dimensional loglinear model of X, Y and Z can, more generally, be given in terms of the odds ratio by using control group constraints:

$$
\begin{aligned}
\lambda_{ijk}^{XYZ} &= \log \left(\frac{m_{ijk} m_{11k}}{m_{i1k} m_{1jk}} \Big/ \frac{m_{ij1} m_{111}}{m_{i11} m_{1j1}} \right) = \\
&= \log \left(\frac{\prod_{a=1}^{i-1} \prod_{b=1}^{j-1} \theta_{ab(k)}}{\prod_{a=1}^{i-1} \prod_{b=1}^{j-1} \theta_{ab(1)}} \right) = \log \left(\prod_{a=1}^{i-1} \prod_{b=1}^{j-1} \prod_{c=1}^{k-1} \theta_{abc} \right) = \sum_{a,b,c} \log \theta_{abc}.
\end{aligned}
$$

Remark 2.6.27 *This definition of odds ratios in three dimensions is easily extendible to higher dimensions: the odds ratios between p variables $X_1, \ldots, X_p$ are given recursively as fraction of the conditional odds ratios in p dimensions, where the conditional odds ratios in p dimensions are calculated as the fraction of $p - 1$ dimensional odds ratios with fixed levels of X_p.*

Definition 2.6.28
The odds ratios between p categorical variables $X_1, \ldots, X_p$ are given recursively for $p \geq 2$:

$$
\begin{aligned}
\theta_{i_1 \ldots i_p} &:= \frac{\theta_{i_1 \ldots i_{p-1}(i_p)}}{\theta_{i_1 \ldots i_{p-1}(i_p+1)}}, \\
\theta_{i_1 \ldots i_{p-1}(i_p)} &= \theta_{i_1 \ldots i_{p-1}} \text{ for fixed level } i_p \text{ of } X_p.
\end{aligned}
$$

This defines odds ratios in any dimension as the ratio of odds of a lower dimension starting with the odds of the counts.
For example four dimensional odds ratios can be written as odds ratios of the odds ratios of the counts.

$$
\theta_{ijkl} := \frac{\theta_{ij(k)(l)} \theta_{ij(k+1)(l+1)}}{\theta_{ij(k+1)(l)} \theta_{ij(k)(l+1)}}
$$

Reformulating the collapsibility condition **Using the control-group-constraints on the interaction effects, the absence of a p dimensional interaction implies, that we are allowed to examine a $p - 1$ dimensional substructure by collapsing over any of the variables.**
Let X_i be the variable, over which we want to collapse the data table. The $p - 1$ dimensional interaction effects in the full data table can be expressed as sums of log odds ratios conditioned in variable X_i. The absence of the p dimensional interaction implies constant conditional $p - 1$ dimensional odds ratios for all categories in X_i, since all p dimensional effects have to be zeroed out, all subsums of log odds ratios are zero, requiring all log odds ratios to be zero. The conditional $p - 1$ dimensional odds ratios coincide with the (unconditioned) $p - 1$ dimensional odds ratios of the data table collapsed over X_i. $\qquad\square$

Assuming hierarchical models, the condition given above is less strict than Fienberg's (cf. theorem 2.6.4), since the absence of a two-dimensional interaction requires the higher interactions to be zero, whereas the absence of a three-dimensional interaction says nothing about the strength of the two-way interaction effects. For a backward selection of (hierarchical) models the collapsibility condition based on the absence of the highest interaction effects will be easier to check and apply.

2.6.5   Summary: Interaction Graphics based on the Counts

One Variable

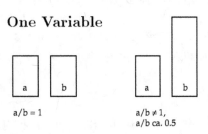

a/b = 1

a/b ≠ 1,
a/b ca. 0.5

Two odds - on the left the odds between the events is 1, on the right the odds is approx. 0.5.

Two Variables

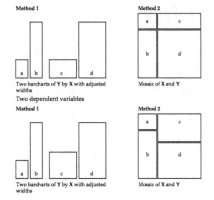

Method 1

Two barcharts of **Y** by **X** with adjusted widths
Two dependent variables

Method 2

Mosaic of **X** and **Y**

Two graphical possibilities for testing for odds ratio 1.

Method 1

Two barcharts of **Y** by **X** with adjusted widths

Method 2

Mosaic of **X** and **Y**

Two graphics for dependent variables **X** and **Y**.

Three Variables

Mosaics of **X** and **Y** by **Z**

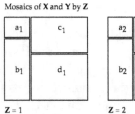 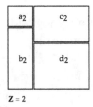

Z = 1   **Z** = 2

No Three Way Interaction
though the odds ratios between X and Y are not 1, they are at least the same for both values of Z, i.e. Z does not affect the association between X and Y, which means that there is no three way interaction. More formally,

$$\theta^{XYZ}_{11(1)} = \theta^{XYZ}_{11(2)} \Rightarrow \theta^{XYZ}_{111} = \frac{\theta^{XYZ}_{11(1)}}{\theta^{XYZ}_{11(2)}} = 1$$

Mosaics of **X** and **Y** by **Z**

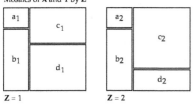

$Z = 1$ $Z = 2$

Three Way Interaction

The association between X and Y is different for different values of Z, i.e. there exists a three way interaction between X, Y and Z.

$$\theta_{11(1)}^{XYZ} \neq \theta_{11(2)}^{XYZ}$$

Four Variables

Mosaics of **X** and **Y** by **Z** and **W**

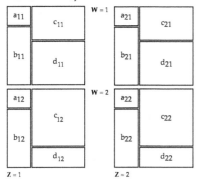

$W = 1$

$W = 2$

$Z = 1$ $Z = 2$

No Four Way Interaction

Though the associations between X and Y are different for the values in W, they change in the same way for the values of Z:

$$\theta_{11(11)}^{XYZW} = \theta_{11(12)}^{XYZW}, \theta_{11(21)}^{XYZW} = \theta_{11(22)}^{XYZW},$$

$$\Rightarrow \theta_{1111}^{XYZW} = \frac{\theta_{11(11)}^{XYZW} \theta_{11(22)}^{XYZW}}{\theta_{11(12)}^{XYZW} \theta_{11(21)}^{XYZW}} = 1.$$

Mosaics of **X** and **Y** by **Z** and **W**

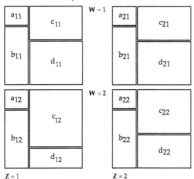

$W = 1$

$W = 2$

$Z = 1$ $Z = 2$

Four Way Interaction

The four way interaction is defined by

$$\lambda_{1111}^{XYZW} = \log \theta_{1111}^{XYZW}.$$

Since the four dimensional odds ratio is a two dimensional odds ratio of the conditional (two dimensional) odds ratios of the counts, i.e.

$$\lambda_{1111}^{XYZW} = \left(\log \theta_{11(11)}^{XYZW} + \log \theta_{11(22)}^{XYZW}\right) -$$
$$- \left(\log \theta_{11(12)}^{XYZW} + \log \theta_{11(21)}^{XYZW}\right).$$

The differences of the conditional probabilities are approx. equal to the corresponding (two dimensional, conditional) log odds ratios. The differences of the conditional probabilities do not sum to the same values, therefore a four way interaction exists in the example.

... p **Variables** ...   High interaction models can, again, be expressed in terms of (local) odds ratios. Finding a p dimensional (sub)structure within odds ratios is equivalent to comparing patterns of $p - 2$ dimensional conditional differences. These patterns get, of course, more and more complex. It is advisable, to not only look at the counts directly but also to look at the mosaic of the odds ratios, the odds' odds ratios, et cetera.

2.6.6   Confidence Intervals and the Strength of an Interaction

Confidence Intervals for the odds ratios

Under the standard random sampling models both $\hat{\theta}$ and $\log \hat{\theta}$ are asymptotically normally distributed around their population values (cf. Agresti (1990) p.17). $\log \hat{\theta}$ tends to converge faster (being additive). The asymptotic standard deviation of $\log \hat{\theta}$ can be estimated by

$$\sigma(\log \hat{\theta}) = \sqrt{\frac{1}{n_{11}} + \frac{1}{n_{12}} + \frac{1}{n_{21}} + \frac{1}{n_{22}}}$$

An approximate $100(1 - p)$ percent confidence interval for $\log \hat{\theta}$ is given by:

$$\log \hat{\theta}_{l/u} = \log \hat{\theta} \pm z_{p/2} \sigma(\log \hat{\theta}).$$

The corresponding confidence interval for $\hat{\theta}$ is given by

$$\left(\exp\left(\log \hat{\theta}_l\right), \exp\left(\log \hat{\theta}_u\right) \right).$$

e.g.

$$\begin{pmatrix} n_{11} & n_{12} \\ n_{21} & n_{22} \end{pmatrix} = \begin{pmatrix} 1198 & 1493 \\ 557 & 1278 \end{pmatrix} \qquad \rightarrow \hat{\theta} = \frac{n_{11}n_{22}}{n_{12}n_{21}} = 1.841$$

A 99% confidence interval for $\hat{\theta}$ is given by $(1.5617, 2.1704)$.
This confidence interval is calculated as follows:
If the margins of the 2×2 table corresponding to an odds ratio θ are fixed to 1, then the frequencies corresponding to the confidence interval of $\hat{\theta}$ can be calculated:
Assume a table of the form

$$\begin{pmatrix} p & (1 - p) \\ (1 - p) & p \end{pmatrix}.$$

This table corresponds to an odds ratio θ of $\frac{p^2}{(1-p)^2}$, i.e. $p = \frac{\sqrt{\theta}}{1+\sqrt{\theta}}$.
From the confidence interval $(\hat{\theta}_l, \hat{\theta}_u)$ for θ we get intervals for $\hat{p}$.

Multiplication of rows and columns with scalars does not affect the odds ratio, therefore the cells can be adjusted to the marginals by multiplying cell ij with $n_{i.}n_{.j}/n$. This is the reason, why we were able to assume the special form of data matrix with fixed margins as above without loss of generality.

The example above gives $(0.555, 0.596)$ as interval for $\hat{p}$. From this, the frequencies can be regained as described, resulting in

$$\begin{pmatrix} 1157.2 & 1533.8 \\ 597.8 & 1237.2 \end{pmatrix} \text{ and } \begin{pmatrix} 1237.8 & 1453.2 \\ 517.2 & 1317.8 \end{pmatrix}.$$

These matrices can, again, be visualised with the help of mosaicplots. Figure 2.65 shows three mosaicplots. The middle one shows the data of the example, the left and right ones correspond to lower and upper boundaries of $\hat{\theta}$. Accordingly, the difference of the conditional probabilities is the smallest on the left and largest on the right.

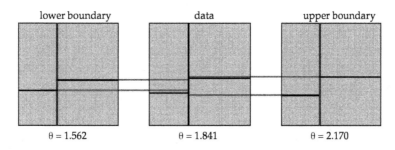

Figure 2.65: *Mosaicplots of the frequencies corresponding to a 99% confidence interval of* $\hat{\theta} = 1.841$.

Goodman (1964) showed that the same confidence intervals for odds ratios can be used for each 2×2 subtable in order to get simultaneous confidence intervals in $r \times c$ tables.

Testing the Significance of an Interaction

Graphical displays support comparisons - therefore, it is easy to decide, whether an interaction is stronger than another, or whether it is exactly zero.

As a measure for the strength of an interaction, the likelihood ratio statistics G^2 can be used. Let M_1 be a hierarchical model and let M_2 be the submodel of M_1 without one of the highest interaction terms λ, then

$$G^2(M_1|M_2) \text{ tests } H_0 : \lambda \neq 0 \text{ vs. } \lambda = 0.$$

This statistic is asymptotically χ^2 distributed with $df_{M_1} - df_{M_2}$ degrees of freedom. For binary variables this difference is 1.

We will write $G^2_\lambda := G^2(M_1|M_2)$ for short.

Example 2.6.29 *Detergent Data*
For convenience we abbreviate each of the variable names with their beginning letter:

P   Preference
M   M-User
W   Water Softness
T   Temperature

Figures 2.44 and 2.63 show several examples of interaction terms within the Detergent Data.
The corresponding statistics are given in the list below:

Page & Figure	Interaction	Test	Likelihood ratio statistic
p. 67, 2.44 left	MP	$G^2(MP|M,P)$	20.5810
p. 67, 2.44 middle	TP	$G^2(TP|T,P)$	4.3616
p. 67, 2.44 right	WP	$G^2(WP|W,P)$	0.3952
p. 88, 2.63 left	MPT	$G^2(MPT|MP,PT,MT)$	5.3382
p. 88, 2.63 right	MPW	$G^2(MPW|MP,PW,MW)$	0.1218

Note: the test makes no statement about the quality of the model's overall fit.

2.6.7   Mosaicplots and the χ^2-test of independence

Another measure of association between two categorical variables is the χ^2 statistic. If the
two variables are independent their χ^2 value is 0. Graphically the independence becomes
apparent from the lattice-like structure of a corresponding mosaic - conversely, the deviation
from a lattice structure can be used as a measure for the amount of dependence between the
variables.

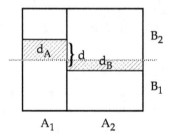

Figure 2.66: *Sketch of a two dimensional mosaicplot in A and B. The hatched line shows,*
how independence between A and B would look like.

Figure 2.66 shows a sketch of a mosaicplot of two binary variables A and B. Recall, that d
denotes the difference in conditional probabilities, $d := P(B_1|A_1) - P(B_1|A_2)$ as in section
2.6.3.

Let d_A resp. d_B be the differences between observed cell probabilities and the product of the marginal probabilities, $d_A = p_{A_1 B_1} - p_{A_1} p_{B_1}$ and $d_B = p_{A_2 B_2} - p_{A_2} p_{B_2}$. Then $d_A = d_B$ and $d = d_A \frac{1}{p_{A_1} p_{A_2}}$.

Proof by simple calculation

$$d_B = p_{A_2 B_2} - p_{A_2} p_{B_2} = -p_{A_2 B_1} + p_{A_2} p_{B_1}$$

This can be used for both statements:

$$d_A - d_B = p_{A_1 B_1} + p_{A_2 B_1} - p_{B_1}(p_{A_1} + p_{A_2}) = 0.$$

and

$$d = \frac{p_{A_1 B_1}}{p_{A_1}} - p_{B_1} - \frac{p_{A_2 B_1}}{p_{A_2}} + p_{B_1} = \frac{d_A}{p_{A_1}} + \frac{d_B}{p_{A_2}} = d_A \frac{1}{p_{A_1} p_{A_2}}$$

$\square$

The χ^2 Test of independence for 2×2 tables

The test statistic in a χ^2 test of independence between two variables is given as $C :=$ $\sum_{ij} \frac{(e_{ij} - o_{ij})^2}{e_{ij}}$. If the variables are binary, C can be written as

$$
\begin{aligned}
C &= \frac{(p_{A_1} p_{B_1} - p_{A_1 B_1})^2}{p_{A_1} p_{B_1}} + \frac{(p_{A_2} p_{B_1} - p_{A_2 B_1})^2}{p_{A_2} p_{B_1}} + \\
&\quad + \frac{(p_{A_1} p_{B_2} - p_{A_1 B_2})^2}{p_{A_1} p_{B_2}} + \frac{(p_{A_2} p_{B_2} - p_{A_2 B_2})^2}{p_{A_2} p_{\bar{B}}} = \\
&= d_A{}^2 \cdot \left(\frac{1}{p_{A_1} p_{B_1}} + \frac{1}{p_{A_2} p_{B_1}} + \frac{1}{p_{A_1} p_{B_2}} + \frac{1}{p_{A_2} p_{B_2}} \right) = \\
&= d_A \frac{1}{p_{A_1} p_{A_2}} \cdot d_B \frac{1}{p_{B_1} p_{B_2}}.
\end{aligned}
$$

Result:

The χ^2 test statistics of independence between two binary variables A and B can be written as a product of two values d_1 and d_2, the differences in conditional probabilities of $B|A$ resp. $A|B$. Each of these differences can be read from a two dimensional mosaicplot of A and B resp. B and A very easily.

By overlaying both mosaicplots as shown in figure 2.67 the value of the χ^2 test statistics becomes visible directly (hatched area). We will call this rectangle the χ^2-*rectangle* of the mosaicplot.

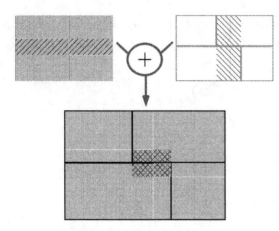

Figure 2.67: *Overlaying the two mosaics of A and B resp. B and A makes the value of a corresponding chi²-test on independence visible (hatched rectangle).*

N-Value, Rectangle of Significance   The χ^2 test of independence is linear in the number of observations. Since a mosaicplot does not regard the underlying number of observations, we therefore can not decide based on the graphical display alone, whether an χ^2-rectangle on a plot is "large" and corresponds to a significant χ^2 value. There are several ways to overcome this problem:

- **The N-value**

  The N-value (Lauer 1997) is defined as the number of observations, which are necessary to let the value χ^2/n become significant on a fixed level of significance α. By rescaling height and width of the χ^2-rectangle with $\sqrt{N}$ makes them comparable for different mosaicplots of the same (screen) size.

- **Rectangle of Significance** Drawing another rectangle, which indicates by its size, how large a χ^2-rectangle has to be to imply a significant deviation of independence, provides us with a visual aid to determine whether an association between the variables is significant and how strong the dependency is.

Figure 2.68 shows the rectangle of significance. The value of χ^2/n is ≈ 0.0625. The value, for which a χ^2 statistic with 1 df becomes significant on a level of 5% is 3.84. N is therefore 60. The number of observations in this example is higher, which makes the rectangle of significance smaller than the χ^2-rectangle (hatched in red).

Extension to $r \times c$ tables

Proposition 2.6.30
The value C of the χ^2 statistics measuring the dependence between two categorical variables

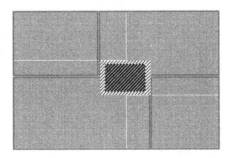

Figure 2.68: 2×2 *mosaicplot with χ^2-rectangle and rectangle of significance (hatched red).*

X and Y with r resp. c categories can be partitioned in the following way:

$$C = \sum_{1 \le i < r, 1 \le j < c} r_{ij} \text{ , where } r_{ij} = d_{ij}^X \cdot d_{ij}^Y$$

and

$$d_{ij}^X = \sum_{k=1}^{j} \left(\frac{p_{ik}}{p_{i\cdot}} - \frac{p_{i+1k}}{p_{i+1\cdot}} \right) \text{ , } d_{ij}^Y = \sum_{s=1}^{i} \left(\frac{p_{sj}}{p_{\cdot j}} - \frac{p_{sj+1}}{p_{\cdot j+1}} \right)$$

Remarks

(i) the r_{ij} may be negative. (see e.g. fig. 2.69)
This implies, that the partitioning of prop. 2.69 is not a partitioning into independent sums of χ^2 distributed variables.

(ii) X and Y are independent $\iff r_{ij} = 0 \; \forall i, j$

Interpretation d_{ij}^X is closely related to the global local odds ratio θ_{ij}^* defined in section 2.6.3 and therefore provides a measurement of "different behaviour" between the ith and $i + 1$th categories of X.

Proof of proposition 2.6.30 Change the order of summation in the statement of of prop. 2.6.30. Then the inner sums collapse over i and j, giving

$$C = \sum_{k,s} \left(\frac{p_{ks}^2}{p_{k\cdot}p_{\cdot s}} - 1 \right),$$

which is the definition of C.   □

Graphical implication   Each r_{ij} in proposition 2.6.30 corresponds to a rectangle derived from overlaying the two mosaicplots of X and Y with structures $S_1 = s_X \otimes s_Y^t$ and $S_2 = s_Y^t \otimes s_X$ as shown for 2×2 tables. These rectangles show the association between adjacent bins (with respect to the probabilities in rows and columns involved). They are therefore strongly dependent on the ordering of categories, re-ordering the categories may help to draw further conclusions.

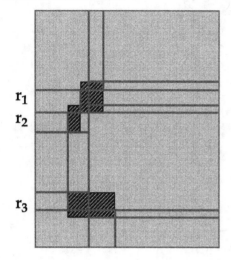

observed data (in %)		χ^2 contributions per cell	
12.32	21.32	0.75	0.30
2.34	7.16	0.05	0.02
7.25	33.87	1.74	0.70
6.73	9.02	1.09	0.44
		total: 5.09	

The rectangles' areas, r_1, r_2, r_3, sum up to the total value of the χ^2-statistics: $r_1 + r_2 + r_3 = 1.58 + 0.79 + 2.72 = 5.09$.

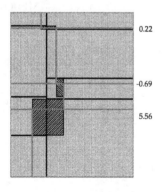 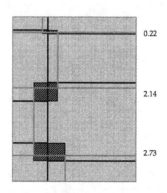 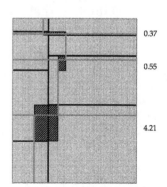

Figure 2.69: *Three mosaicplots of the same data with differently ordered rows - only in the first ordering a negative value occurs.*

Since the overlaid rectangles may represent negative contributions to the χ^2 value, the total

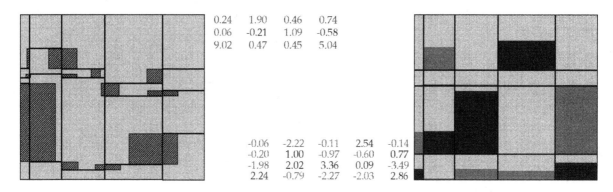

Figure 2.70: *Mosaicplot of a 4×5 table. On the left, the mosaic of the observed values is overlaid with rectangles corresponding to the χ^2 contributions. The mosaicplot on the right shows the table of the expected values. The coloured areas are proportional to the residual value of each cell.*

amount of hatched area is not a very good estimator for the amount of dependency between the variables. In order to overcome this problem, we used differently coloured hatching as shown in fig. 2.70 for positive and negative χ^2 contributions. For comparison, a mosaicplot of the expected values is given on the right hand side of figure 2.70. In this display the coloured areas are proportional to the residuals of each cell. Again, different colours are needed for positive and negative residuals.

One advantage of the overlaying approach still remains: the observed data is shown rather than the model as in fig. 2.70 on the right.

However, overlaying rectangles on mosaicplots made the display and interpretation rather complicated. Therefore we did not pursue this approach to higher dimensions.

2.7 Application to Visual Modelling

2.7.1 Loglinear and Logit models

The reason for concentration on the odds ratios of the data lies, of course, in their close relationship to the effects of a loglinear model, as sketched previously for a model of three variables in section 2.6.4. This is also true for higher dimensions: a p dimensional interaction effect can still be calculated from a sum of p dimensional odds ratios.

The approach to visual modelling for a loglinear model therefore has to be a stepwise examination of all its interaction terms. Detecting and assessing the strength of an interaction is based on highlighting and therefore directed. One variable is distinguished from the others by drawing a barchart of it and selecting its categories one after the other. This is equivalent to treating this variable as a response variable.

To examine all interaction terms of interest each variable of a loglinear model has to be treated as response variable at most once.

Remark 2.7.1

(i) Any logit model can be written as loglinear model (see e.g. Agresti (1990), p. 152).

(ii) The approach to visual modelling simplifies in the case of logit models, since we deal with one true response variable there.

Strategy for Visual Modelling: "Stack or collapse"

Starting with the full loglinear model of all variables, we will examine one interaction effect after the other and exclude the weakest until we reach a sufficiently small model. This procedure is equivalent to a backward selection of models, where the argument for choosing or eliminating an interaction is based on the graphical display. Of course, this can only be done in an exploratory setting, since we are, from a statistical point of view, deep in the problem of multiple testing.

The basic idea for loglinear models is to first choose one of the variables as "response" and highlight one of its categories after the other in a barchart. For loglinear models, the procedure has to be repeated until all possible interactions have been considered (The procedure below has to be repeated for each variable once at most).

A doubledecker plot (see section 2.2) of all of the other variables is used to examine the underlying structure of interaction terms of the marked variable with all of the others.

With the help of the doubledecker plot, compare corresponding differences in the conditional probabilities according to the rules given above. If they indicate the absence of the highest interaction, we may collapse over one of the variables and proceed with the exploration process in a lower dimension.

If an interaction is present, we may stop at this point for a hierarchical model for the variables involved and choose one of the variables, over which the table had been collapsed previously, as response.

Or - in a non-hierarchical setting - we may change the direction of one of the variables, preferably the first one, in the underlying structure. This generates a number of stacked doubledecker plots. The dimension of each of these doubledecker plots is reduced by one. For lower dimensional interaction terms we have to proceed with the analysis for each of them.

Example 2.7.2 *Cancer Knowledge Data*
Goal of the example is to describe graphical methods for modelling the data.

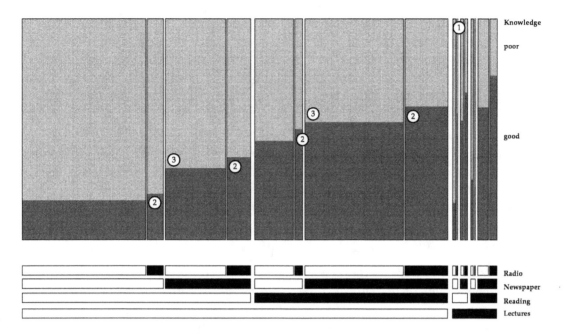

Figure 2.71: *Doubledecker plot with structure* $s_L \otimes s_{Re} \otimes s_N \otimes s_{Ra}$ *of the Cancer Knowledge Data. All combinations of* **Radio, Newspaper, Reading** *and* **Lectures** *are drawn from left to right. From bottom to top the bins are divided according to* **Knowledge** *on Cancer. The heights of the highlighted areas show the conditional probabilities of K given Ra, N, Re and L.*

Figure 2.71 contains a doubledecker plot of the data using the structure $S = s_L \otimes s_{Re} \otimes s_N \otimes s_{Ra}$. *The darker shaded tiles (highlighted cases) show cases of good scores on* **Cancer Knowledge (K)**, *the lighter ones show poor knowledge. The bins are arranged in exactly the same way as the values in table A.2. All combinations of* **Lectures, Reading, Newspaper** *and* **Radio** *are drawn side by side, top and bottom row show the numbers of poor resp. good scores. The exact combination a bin represents can be read from the labels below. Each row corresponds to one variable, the white rectangles stand for "no"s, the blacks for "yes"s. The first bin in fig. 2.71 therefore represents the combination of all "no"s, the second bin contains all "no"s except for* **Radio**, *and so on.*

Figure 2.71 provides several important aspects for the analysis:

- *The variable* **Lectures** *splits the data very unequally, only few people questioned attended lectures at all. This group behaves (with respect to their knowledge on cancer) very differently from the others (circled 1). - Let's therefore first concentrate on persons not attending lectures.*

The full loglinear model between the variables K, Re, Ra and N is

$$\log m_{ijkl} = \quad \lambda_{ijkl}^{KReRaN} + \lambda_{ijk}^{KReRa} + \lambda_{ijl}^{KReN} + \lambda_{ikl}^{KRaN} + \lambda_{jkl}^{ReRaN} +$$
$$+ \quad \lambda_{ij}^{KRe} + \lambda_{ik}^{KRa} + \lambda_{il}^{KN} + \lambda_{jk}^{ReRa} + \lambda_{jl}^{ReN} + \lambda_{kl}^{RaN} +$$
$$+ \quad \lambda_{i}^{N} + \lambda_{j}^{Re} + \lambda_{k}^{Ra} + \lambda_{l}^{N} + \mu$$

The strategy we want to pursue in the sequel is as follows: Starting with the full loglinear model of all variables, we will examine one interaction effect after the other and exclude the weakest until we reach a sufficiently small model. This procedure is equivalent to a backward selection of models, where the argument for choosing or eliminating an interaction is based on the graphical display. Of course, this can only be done in an exploratory setting, since we are, from a statistical point of view, deep in the problem of multiple testing.

- *There are differences in the conditional probabilities of **Knowledge** given **Radio** for all combinations of the variables **Newspaper** and **Reading**, which implies a two way association $K * Ra$. Yet, all of these differences are approximately the same (circled 2). This means, the conditional odds ratios between **Knowledge** and **Radio** are nearly constant ($\theta = 0.82, \theta = 0.81, \theta = 0.81, \theta = 0.75$).*

This has several implications:

- *firstly, there is no four way interaction between these variables. The corresponding four-way interaction effect is very weak. Using the notation from section 2.6.6, the G^2 statistic for this interaction gives:*

$$G_{KNRaRe}^{2} = 0.0114, df = 1$$

- *secondly, there exists neither a three-way interaction between **Knowledge**, **Radio** and **Reading** nor between **Knowledge**, **Radio** and **Newspaper**:*

$$G_{KRaRe}^{2} = 0.1413, df = 1$$
$$G_{KRaN}^{2} = 0.0367, df = 1$$

- *thirdly, since there is no four way interaction, we are allowed to collapse over **Radio** without changing the relationships among the other variables (see the result in figure 2.72).*

- *Figure 2.72 is better suited to detect the three way interaction between **Knowledge**, **Reading** and Newspaper. But this interaction was also already visible in the different conditional probabilities (circled 3) in figure 2.71*

$$G_{KReN}^{2} = 3.715, df = 1.$$

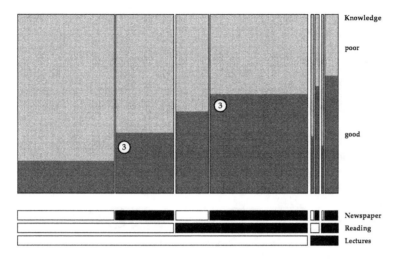

Figure 2.72: *Doubledecker plot of the Cancer Knowledge Data collapsed over* **Radio**.

The only three-way effect not yet examined is $ReNRa$. Figure 2.73 shows a mosaic plot with this interaction (circled 4) - but this interaction is not very strong:

$$G^2_{ReNRa} = 1.838, df = 1.$$

A suggestion for a model based on these graphical conclusions, is (for non-lecture attending persons only!) $M_1 := KRa, KNRe, ReNRa$

$$G^2(M_1) = 0.11169, df = 3.$$

Neither three way interaction was very strong, models without these effects are:

$$
\begin{aligned}
M_2 &= KRa, KNRe, ReN, NRa, RaRe \\
&\quad G^2(M_2) = 1.7928, df = 4 \\
M_3 &= KRa, KN, NRe, KRe, ReNRa \\
&\quad G^2(M_3) = 3.6426, df = 4 \\
M_4 &= KRa, KN, NRe, KRe, NRa, RaRe \\
&\quad G^2(M_4) = 5.5601, df = 5
\end{aligned}
$$

All of these models are acceptable for the group of persons not attending lectures.
Let us now examine the group of persons attending lectures. Figure 2.74 shows a doubledecker plot of the 135 cases, in which the person questioned attended lectures. With the exception of persons without solid book reading but listening to the radio (circled 5a), the association

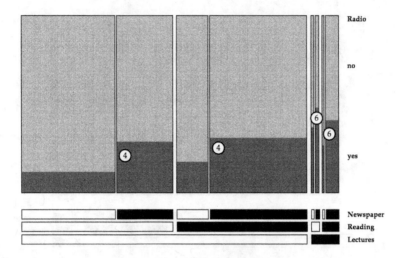

Figure 2.73: *Doubledecker plot of* **N, Re, L** *and* **Ra**.
From left to right the combinations of **Newspaper, Reading** *and* **Lectures** *are drawn. Highlighting shows cases of* **Radio**. *The slightly different differences in conditional probabilities, marked by (4), hint on a (weak) three way interaction between the variables.*

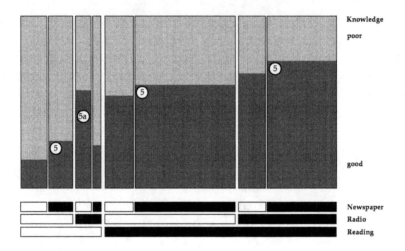

Figure 2.74: *Doubledecker plot of the subtable of the Cancer Knowledge Data: the 135 cases of lecture attending persons.*

between **Newspaper** and **Knowledge** is approximately the same for all combinations of **Radio** and **Reading** (from left to right the odds ratios are 0.53, 4.00, 0.78, 0.70). This exception would be enough for a four way interaction - when there were more cases observed.

As it is, the four way interaction is not very strong:

$$G^2_{KNRaRe} = 1.1974$$

neither are the three way interactions $KNRa$ nor $KNRe$:

$$G^2_{KNRa} = 0.3074,$$
$$G^2_{KNRe} = 0.2943.$$

The three way interaction $NRaRe$, which can be checked graphically (circled 6) with the same doubledecker plot as in figure 2.73 for **Lectures** *"yes", also is not significant:*

$$G^2_{NRaRe} = 0.0415.$$

This means, that a model of all two way interactions is acceptable for lecture-attending persons, too:

$$M'_4 := KRa, KN, NRe, KRe, ReN, NRa, RaRe$$
$$G^2(M'_4) = 2.0430, df = 5$$

For the whole data table, a suggestion for a model based on graphical conclusions is the model, consisting of all three-way interaction of **Lectures** *with all the other variables:*

$$M_5 := L * (M_4 + M'_4) =$$
$$= LKRa, LKN, LNRe, LKRe, LReN, LNRa, LRaRe$$
$$G^2(M_5) = 7.6032, df = 10.$$

By reducing weak high-way interactions to lower dimensional interactions as with model M_1 leads to:

$$M_6 = L K Re, Ra L, Ra K, N K, N Re, N Ra$$

with $G^2(M_6) = 20.1, df = 17$, which coincides with the one proposed by Fienberg (1979), p.88. Stopping one step earlier in the backward selection also gives a very good model

$$M_7 = Re L K, L K N, L Ra, Ra K, N K, N Re, N Ra$$

with $G^2(M_7) = 16.0, df = 16$.

Summary

We have introduced an approach to graphical model selection based on the classical concept of backward selection. Its advantage lies in the graphical display, which allows us to inspect the data directly throughout an analysis and enables us to "see" why a specific model works, what its assumptions are and where it could be improved.

This approach involves graphics in the modelling process. Not only the effects but the fit is visualised - based on the same strict mathematical background as a classical modelling approach.

For the mathematical foundation we have generalised the well-known concept of odds ratios to higher dimensions and given a collapsibility condition we can apply directly in the graphics. Since all of the arguments are based on comparing odds ratios, the method discussed in the paper is applicable to a wider field of models and in particular to association & effect models for ordinal data as discussed in Goodman (1979).

2.7.2   Simple Models for Ordinal Data

When a contingency table has ordered rows or columns, an analysis should take this into account. The models described in this section are - w.r.t. their degree of freedom - all between the mutual independence of two variables X and Y and the model with an interaction between X and Y, which would follow each other immediately in a standard loglinear approach. The basis of an analysis of ordinal data is, that a natural ordering of the categories is given and *scores* can be assigned to the categories, reflecting midpoints of an underlying interval scale, i.e. for variable X we consider the scores $\{u_i\}$ with $u_1 < u_2 < \ldots < u_I$, analogously $\{v_j\}$ with $v_1 < v_2 < \ldots < v_J$ for variable Y.

Most commonly used, though, are the integer scores $u_i = i$ and $v_j = j$.

For these variables, various models regarding dependencies among the categories can be formulated:

(i) **model of independence**

$$\log m_{ij} = \mu + \lambda_i^X + \lambda_j^Y$$

condition for the odds ratio: $\theta_{ij} = 1$

degrees of freedom: $(I-1)(J-1)$

(ii) **model of uniform association**

$$\log m_{ij} = \mu + \lambda_i^X + \lambda_j^Y + \beta(u_i - \bar{u})(v_j - \bar{v})$$

condition for the odds ratio: $\theta_{ij} = \theta$

degrees of freedom: $IJ - J - I$

(iii) **row effect model**

$$\log m_{ij} = \mu + \lambda_i^X + \lambda_j^Y + \beta_{i.}(v_j - \bar{v})$$

condition for the odds ratio: $\theta_{ij} = \theta_{i.}$

degrees of freedom: $(I-1)(J-2)$

(iv) **column effect model**

$$\log m_{ij} = \mu + \lambda_i^X + \lambda_j^Y + \beta_{\cdot j}(u_i - \bar{u})$$

condition for the odds ratio: $\theta_{ij} = \theta_{\cdot j}$

degrees of freedom: $(I-2)(J-1)$

(v) **row-column effect model**

$$\log m_{ij} = \mu + \lambda_i^X + \lambda_j^Y + \beta(u_i - \bar{u})(v_j - \bar{v}) + \tau_{1i}(v_j - \bar{v}) + \tau_{2j}(u_i - \bar{u})$$

condition for the odds ratio: $\theta_{ij} = \theta_{i\cdot}\theta_{\cdot j}$

degrees of freedom: $(I-2)(J-2)$

For a graphical approach we will exploit the conditions on the odds ratios, which we will visualise with the help of mosaicplots as described in sections 2.6.3 to 2.6.3.

Uniform Association

For integer scores $u_i = i$ and $v_j = j$ the additional parameter β coincides with $\log \theta$.

$$\begin{aligned}
\log m_{ij} &= \mu + \lambda_i^X + \lambda_j^Y + \beta(u_i - \bar{u})(v_j - \bar{v}) = \\
&= \mu + \lambda_i^X + \lambda_j^Y + \log \theta \cdot (i - \frac{I+1}{2})(j - \frac{J+1}{2})
\end{aligned}$$

Though a model of uniform association deals with only one parameter, it is graphically easier to check for row and column effects and combine the conclusions. Luckily, the model of uniform association is a special case of both the row-effects model and the column-effects model, since uniform association is equivalent to a row effect model with constant odds ratios for all rows, $\theta_i = \theta \; \forall i$, resp. constant odds ratios for all columns.

Checking on uniform association can be done therefore in two steps - separate checks on row-effects and column effects. These checks are essentially the same, since the problem is symmetrically in rows and columns.

A graphical check whether there is uniform association within a contingency table is based on the condition for the odds ratios to be equal. The following example describes two methods, how this can be performed.

Method 1: Mosaicplots of $s_X \otimes s_Y^t$ resp. $s_Y \otimes s_X^t$

This method is based on proposition 2.6.22 - saying, that global-local odds ratios are close enough to local odds ratios to reflect approximately the same properties. What we therefore look for in a display is, whether the columns show the same differences in corresponding conditional probabilities - this examines row effects. Afterwards we change the order of the variables and check again for row effects (which are the column effects of the previous model, of course).

Example 2.7.3 *Mental Health*

This example has been discussed in Goodman (1979). He showed, that in contrast to a model assumption of independence a model assuming uniform association fitted the data already very well:

model	df	χ^2-statistics
independence	15	45.99
uniform association	14	9.73

In the following we will demonstrate, how we may also see this fact in the displays:

- Checking the effect of Parents' Socioeconomic Status on Mental Health

*Figure 2.75 shows a mosaicplot of the **Parents' Socioeconomic Status** and **Mental Health**. If there was a uniform association between the categories, all of the differences in the conditional probabilities would have to be equal. Though this is not the case exactly,*

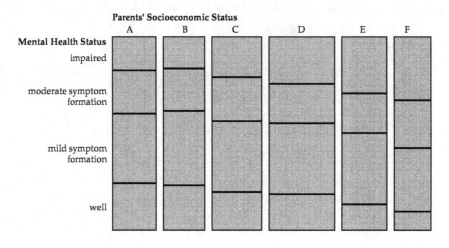

Figure 2.75: *Mosaicplot of the Mental Health Data (cf. section A.7)*

*the deviation from a uniform association is only small. The biggest objection to a model of uniform association is, that the two columns with a parental status of A and B show very similar behaviour with respect to the mental status. Combining these improves the model visibly - compare fig. 2.76. All columns show an overall uniform decrease in **Mental Health** accompanying a lower **Socioeconomic Status** of the parents (see table 2.8).*

- Checking the effect of Mental Health on Parents' Socioeconomic Status

*A mosaicplot of **Mental Health** and the **Parents' Socioeconomic Status** shows the "effect" of mental health on the parents' socioeconomic status (see figure 2.77). There is almost no difference between moderate and mild formation symptoms with respect to the **Parents' Socioeconomic Status**. Combining these, again, improves the overall pattern (see table 2.8).*

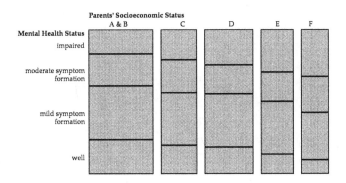

Figure 2.76: *Mosaicplot of the Mental Health Data. Columns with parental socioeconomic status of A and B have been combined.*

model description	df	χ^2-statistics	$\hat{\theta}$
uniform association (see fig. 2.75)	14	9.73	0.913
uniform association (see fig. 2.76) A and B combined	11	7.27	0.898
uniform association mild and moderate combined	9	3.990	0.858
uniform association (see fig. 2.77) A and B combined mild and moderate combined	7	1.795	0.834

Table 2.8: *Overview of the statistics for the models of uniform associations described in figs. 2.75 to 2.77.*

Method 2: Mosaicplot & Hotselection
In contrast to the previous approach, hotselection provides the possibility to look at the local odds ratios directly. To achieve this, a mosaicplot of the variables is necessary (in hotselection mode, i.e. only selected observations are shown in the display). Adjacent categories of one of the variables are highlighted one after the other, resulting in the mosaicplot displaying local odds ratios for each two rows.

Example 2.7.4 *Mental Health*
- Checking the effect of Mental Health on Parents' Socioeconomic Status
*Figure 2.78 shows all three row effects of **Mental Health** on **Parents' Socioeconomic Status** - the corresponding model is given in table 2.9. Both the upper and the lower mosaicplot reveal a fairly strong negative effect of **Mental Health** on **Parents' Socioeconomic Status**, while the mosaic in the middle shows, that mild and moderate symptom formations*

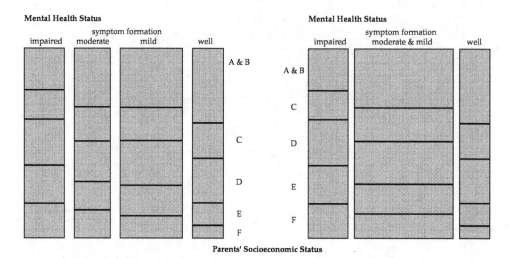

Figure 2.77: *Mosaicplots of **Mental Health** vs. **Socioeconomic Status***.

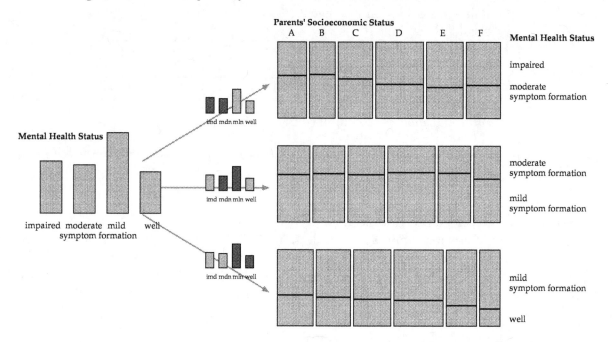

Figure 2.78: *Mosaicplot of **Parents' Socioeconomic Status** and **Mental Health***.
From top to bottom the pairs (impaired, moderate), (moderate, mild) and (mild, well) are highlighted, showing one row effect in each mosaic.

*can not be distinguished with respect to **Parents' Socioeconomic Status**, except for status*
F. The row estimates for θ_i of the corresponding model show the same behaviour,

$$\theta_1 = 0.867 \qquad \theta_2 = 0.982 \qquad \theta_3 = 0.865.$$

- Checking the effect of Parents' Socioeconomic Status on Mental Health
Analogously to the previous procedure, mosaics and barcharts of the variables are set up as
shown in figure 2.79. Each mosaicplot shows one row-effect. All mosaics except the first

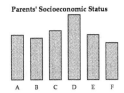

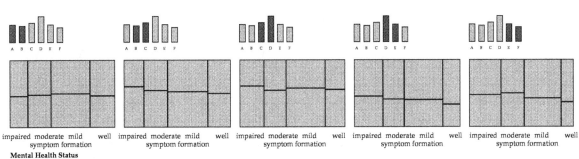

Figure 2.79: *Mosaicplot of **Mental Health** and **Parents' Socioeconomic Status**.*
From left to right the pairs $(A, B), (B, C), (C, D), (D, E)$ and (E, F) are highlighted, showing
one row effect in each mosaic.

show a negative influence of lower socioeconomic status of the parents upon mental health,
more accurately

$$\theta_1 = 1.014 \qquad \theta_2 = 0.882 \qquad \theta_3 = 0.949 \qquad \theta_4 = 0.868 \qquad \theta_5 = 0.870.$$

The first mosaicplot (corresponding to an odds ratio of ≈ 1) again suggests, that categories
A and B of parental status could be combined.

Row or Column Effect Models

Since the model of uniform association is a special case both of a row effect and a column
effect model, the graphical procedure for checking on the later ones is equivalent to one part of
the procedure on checking for uniform association as described in the example of the Mental
Health data of the previous section. Table 2.9 shows the statistics of the corresponding
models following figs. 2.75 to 2.79.

model description	df	χ^2-statistics
row effects (figs. 2.75, 2.78)	12	6.29
column effects (fig. 2.79)	10	6.78
column effects (fig. 2.77, left) *A* and *B* combined	9	3.88
row effects (fig. 2.76) *A* and *B* combined	8	6.42
column effects (fig. 2.77, right) *A* and *B* combined *moderate* and *mild* combined	6	1.79

Table 2.9: *Overview of the statistics for the row and column effect models corresponding to figs. 2.75 to 2.79.*

Row-Column Effects Model

The row-column effects model is given in the form:

$$\log m_{ij} = \mu + \lambda_i^X + \lambda_j^Y + \beta(u_i - \bar{u})(v_j - \bar{v}) + \tau_{1i}(v_j - \bar{v}) + \tau_{2j}(u_i - \bar{u}). \qquad (2.13)$$

For integer scores $u_i = i$ and $v_j = j$ the log odds ratio is modelled as an additive combination of row and column effects:

$$\log \theta_{ij} = \log \frac{m_{ij} m_{i+1j+1}}{m_{i+1j} m_{i+1j}} = \beta + (\tau_{1i} - \tau_{1i+1}) + (\tau_{2j} - \tau_{2j+1})$$

This is no longer easy to see directly in a mosaicplot of the observations - instead, one can use the condition for the odds ratios $\theta_{ij} = \theta_{i.}\theta_{.j}$ and visualise the odds ratios in place of the counts. A mosaicplot of the odds ratios shows in how far the condition for the odds ratios is fulfilled by the deviation from a lattice-like structure. Figure 2.80 gives the mosaicplot of the odds ratios between **Parents' Socioeconomic Status** and **Mental Health** of the Mental Health Data.

A model with row and column effects therefore coincides with the assumption of independence between the data's odds ratios. Starting from this, we may proceed further and look for uniform association among the odds ratios, row or column effects in the odds ratios or visualise row-column effects in the odds ratios with the help of a mosaicplot of the odds ratios' odds ratios.

2.7.3   Association Models in Higher Dimensions

Association models in higher dimensions can be calculated and visualised with the methods introduced in the previous section. We will only give an example here.

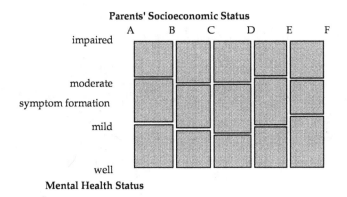

Figure 2.80: *Mosaicplot of the odds ratios between **Parents' Socioeconomic Status** and **Mental Health**.*
The deviation from a lattice is not very strong, since the absolute number is only 13.68. This indicates, that a model with row and column effects fits the data very well.

Example 2.7.5 *College Plans*
*Let us concentrate on the factors, which influence parents to encourage college plans of their children. Figure 2.81 shows two doubledecker plots of **Socio-Economic Status (SES)** and **IQ** vs. **Parental Encouragement (PE)** for female and male pupils. With higher **SES** of the parents as well as with a higher **IQ** of the child the parental encouragement increases. Two other things become obvious: the highlighting heights (percentages of parental encouragement) look very much alike for the two genders. Table 2.10 contains the numbers for both plots. There seems to be a gender-related shift in the percentages: female pupils get less encouragement from their parents than male pupils. A regression of the percentages of parental*

	Socio-economic Status															
	Low				Lower-Middle				Upper-Middle				High			
IQ																
	L	LM	UM	H	L	LM	UM	H	L	LM	UM	H	L	LM	UM	H
F	10	16	20	32	23	35	46	49	39	44	51	68	63	71	84	88
M	18	33	40	54	32	43	59	65	44	59	69	85	65	80	85	95

Table 2.10: *Percentages of parental encouragement classified according to **SES** and **IQ**.*

encouragement for female pupils (F) vs. the percentages of parental encouragement for male pupils (M) confirms both observations: a regression of the form $M = a \cdot F + b$ yields $a = 0.89$ and $b = 0.17$ with $R^2 = 0.93$ (see figure 2.82), i.e. there is indeed a strong relationship between F and M - even a linear one, and boys get overall more encouragement. There is

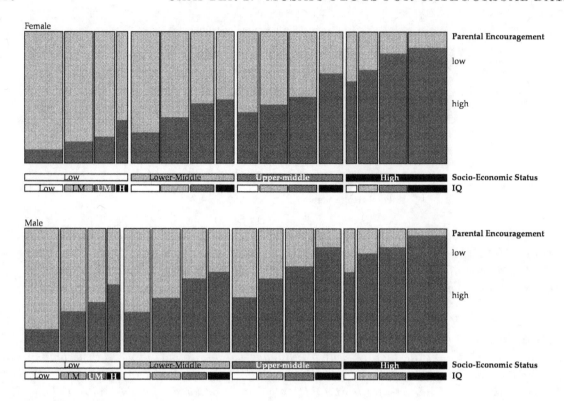

Figure 2.81: *Doubledecker plots of **Socio-Economic Status** and **IQ** vs. **Parental Encouragement** for both genders. The percentages of parental encouragement look very much alike for the genders.*

another interesting effect, though, which becomes apparent from the regression parameters: the difference of parental encouragement between boys and girls is larger for cells with a low percentage of parental encouragement. For higher percentages the difference becomes smaller. Since the percentages of parental encouragement grow with increasing **SES** and **IQ**, this is the hint for a four way interaction between **SES**, **IQ**, **Parental Encouragement** and **Sex**, but a very weak one, since $a = 0.89$, which is rather close to 1. The G^2-statistic of the four way effect is 9.232 with 9 degrees of freedom. We may therefore assume the absence of a four way interaction between the variables and collapse over **Sex**.

Collapsing does not change a lot w.r.t. the linear trends between **IQ** and **Parental Encouragement** for each status, which can already be seen in figure 2.81. These trends are not very different for different statuses - which implies that the three way interaction, also, is rather weak: $G^2_{SES*IQ*PE} = 4.663$ with 3 degrees of freedom.

The two way interactions between **Parental Encouragement** and **SES** resp. **IQ** remain. Figure 2.83 shows doubledecker plots of these effects. The trends are fairly linear for both

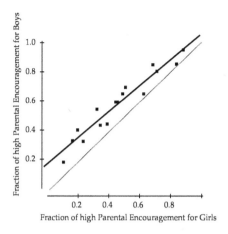

Figure 2.82: *Scatterplot of rates of high parental encouragement for Boys and Girls, cf. table 2.10. The bold line marks the regression line $M = 0.89 \cdot F + 0.17$, the line below is the identity F.*

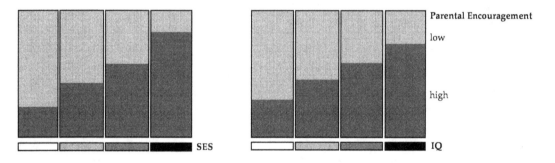

Figure 2.83: *Doubledecker plots of **SES** and **IQ** vs. **Parental Encouragement**. Both plots reveal a strong positive linear trend.*

*variables. Summarising, **PE** is affected linearly by **SES** and **IQ** and has a slight gender-related effect. Table 2.11 shows the output of a logit model **PE~SES + IQ + Sex** from the software R (Gentleman & Ihaka 1995). Again, the uniform growth of the effects of **SES** of approx. 0.8 (0.5 for **IQ**) suggest a linear relationship between these variables. Taking this into account in the model, increases the degrees of freedom by 4 without affecting the residual deviance much.*

*Identifying factors, which affect the **College Plans** of pupils, can be done in the same way. The resulting graphics also look very much alike, for a further analysis see e.g. Fienberg (1979), p. 129-133.*

```
glm(formula = PE ~ SES + IQ + Sex, family = binomial(),
              data = college, weights = number)
```

Coefficients:

	Estimate	Std. Error	z value	$P(>|z|)$
(Intercept)	-1.49441	0.06531	-22.881	<2e-16
SES_{LM}	0.78884	0.06395	12.336	<2e-16
SES_{UM}	1.36193	0.064	21.281	<2e-16
SES_H	2.519	0.07351	34.269	<2e-16
IQ_{LM}	0.53719	0.06329	8.488	<2e-16
IQ_{UM}	0.96435	0.06411	15.041	<2e-16
IQ_H	1.52184	0.06829	22.285	<2e-16
Sex_F	-0.59917	0.04568	-13.117	<2e-16

Table 2.11: *R-output of the logit model* **PE~ SES + IQ + Sex**.

2.8 Extensions of Mosaics

Particular applications - especially non-standard applications - make several extensions for mosaicplots desirable.

So far, only mosaicplots have been shown where all sub-plots had the same kind of display: mixture forms of Same-Bin-Size display, fluctuation diagrams and the default display are also useful. For example, a set of fluctuation diagrams of the last two variables in a structure could be shown given the first variables in default mode (see figure 2.84). The structure at present does not distinguish between different types of display - to allow for mixture forms of the displays, each one-dimensional structure would have to be extended by an index indicating the specific kind of display chosen for this variable - or, to make things even more complex, indices for each category. The dangers of misusage of this extension are, though, manifold. The larger part of mixture forms are difficult to interpret, if they make any sense at all. Before allowing mixture forms one would therefore have to think about sensible restrictions. Another possibility of extension also affects the structure. At each level of a default mosaicplot bins are split according to the *same* variable. Sometimes, though, it is useful to allow more flexibility, see e.g. section 4.2.1. If on the same level splits according to *different* variables are needed, we have to change the underlying structure to a *tree*. Then, however, labelling is essential to be able to interpret the resulting plot. One possibility is, to additionally use a linked tree diagram as shown in figure 4.39, p. 191, another has been proposed by John Hartigan (personal communication, June 1999): each variable is assigned a colour, where different shades represent different categories. Differently coloured labels help to identify the bins. The example in figure 2.85 shows the same tree as figure 4.39, p. 191 in

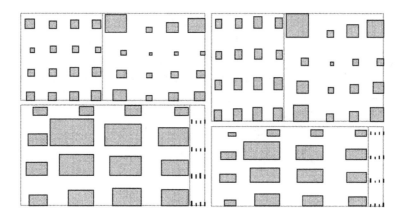

Figure 2.84: *Extension of a mosaicplot: fluctuation diagrams of the last two variables, the first two binary variables are in default mode (sketched with light gray lines).*

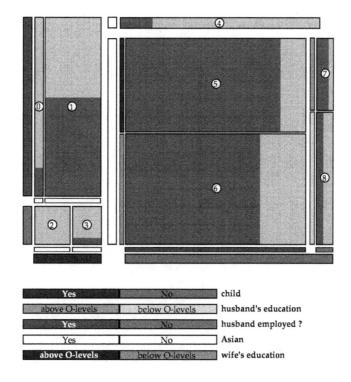

Yes	No	child
above O-levels	below O-levels	husband's education
Yes	No	husband employed ?
Yes	No	Asian
above O-levels	below O-levels	wife's education

Figure 2.85: *Mosaicplot with tree structure. The colouring allows to identify bins.*

section 4.2.1.

The close relationship between mosaicplots with *Trellis displays* (Becker et al. 1994) becomes apparent, if another restriction is loosened. If the last variable does not have to be categorical, i.e. if we regard a continuous response variable, we may plot not a single rectangle for each combination of variables but a dot based plot, such as a dot plot or a boxplot, et cetera. This results in a set of plots, conditioned according to the categorical variables of the mosaicplot - this is the basic idea of a Trellis display. At present, though, the idea of Trellis graphics is merely a static one. An interesting idea would be to allow to set the conditions interactively - and to track the influence of changing them visually.

Chapter 3

Biplots - Merging Categorical and Continuous Data

Compared to mosaicplots, the approach of biplots is a totally different one. Biplots are an example for dot based rather than area based plots.

Biplots are a very promising tool for visualising high-dimensional data, which include both continuous and categorical variables. The strategy of biplots is to choose a linear subspace (usually a 2-dimensional space - in order to be able to plot the result using standard techniques), which is in some respect optimal, and project the high-dimensional data onto this space. One criterion for optimality is, for instance, to minimise the discrepancy between the high- and the two dimensional representations of the data. Biplots show only one projection out of infinitely many. They therefore cannot be exact representations of the data but only approximations.

What gave these plots their prefix "Bi-" ($\beta\iota$ is the greek syllable for "two") is the simultaneous representation of both data points and original axes within the projection space.

The biplot axis of a continuous variable is represented by a straight line (in case of linear models, to which we will restrict ourselves) with unit points marked by small perpendicular lines. One unit of a variable X_i corresponds to one times the standard deviation of X_i. If the data matrix X is centered and standardized, these units are therefore directly comparable for all i, and the length of a unit gives a measure for how well a variable is represented in the chosen projection plane.

The axis of a categorical variable X_j is given by the 1-unit points of the corresponding dummy variables. Each of these points represents one category of X and is therefore called a *category level point, CLP.*

Biplots were first introduced by Gabriel (1971). A recent monograph on biplots by Gower &

121

Hand (1996) summarises different types of biplots and embeds various models in the concept. Possibilities for interactive extensions have been examined in Hofmann (1998).

3.1 PCA, MCA and mixture forms

Biplots are low dimensional representations of high dimensional data. Any dimension reduction technique may therefore build the mathematical basis for the graphical representation. Here, we will have a look at one method in more detail, principal component analysis PCA and its categorical equivalent, multivariate correspondence analysis MCA.
Both techniques are well established and discussed in multivariate statistics. We will therefore give only a very brief overview of the underlying matrix calculations and rather concentrate on their application to biplots.

3.1.1 Basics

Let us assume n observations in a p dimensional space of numerical variables $X_1, \ldots, X_p$. In PCA these variables are regarded as orthonormal vectors e_i^t (row vectors), which form a basis in p dimensional space. The ith observed value $(x_{i1}, x_{i2}, \ldots, x_{ip})$ can then be written as

$$(x_{i1}, x_{i2}, \ldots, x_{ip}) = x_{i1}e_1^t + x_{i2}e_2^t + \ldots + x_{ip}e_p^t = \sum_{k=1}^{p} x_{ik}e_k^t.$$

Denote by X the $n \times p$ matrix of all observations.
The basic idea is to rotate the p-dimensional space such, that the covariance or, more usually, the correlation matrix of these variables is diagonalized. This decomposes the total variance (or correlation) into the sum of eigenvalues. Each eigenvalue may be interpreted as the variance (or correlation) of an eigenvector, a linear combination of the above variables $X_1, \ldots, X_p$. Typically, the eigenvectors for the largest eigenvalues are interpreted as the most important factors, small eigenvalues are regarded as noise. The reduction of dimensionality is based on this conception and, for the representation in a biplot the two eigenvectors corresponding to the largest eigenvalues are taken as basis of the projection plane.
The eigenvectors of the covariance (correlation) matrix of X are called the *principal components of X*.
A measure for the goodness of the representation is the amount of variation, which is represented in the display, i.e. if $\lambda_1, \ldots, \lambda_p$ are the eigenvalues of the covariance (correlation) matrix of X, a measure of the goodness is given by

$$R^2 = \frac{\lambda_{(1)} + \lambda_{(2)}}{\sum_{k=1}^{p} \lambda_k},$$

which for one dimension (i.e. $\varrho = 1$) is equivalent to the R^2 value from linear regression.
In the case of categorical variables, an MCA is calculated instead. MCA and PCA differ only slightly, though.

The basic idea of MCA is to transform a categorical variable to a set of 0-1 coded *dummy variables*, and calculate a PCA from these. The advantage of this approach is, that it allows any mixture of continuous and categorical data.

The re-coding of the variables works as follows: Let X_i be a categorical variable. Each category c_j of X_i is linked with a binary variable Z_j, the kth entry Z_j^k of which is

$$Z_j^k = \begin{cases} 1 & \text{if the } k\text{th entry of } X_i \text{ is } c_j \\ 0 & \text{otherwise.} \end{cases}$$

Because of the linear dependency among the dummy variables of the same (original) variable - their sum gives the vector of 1s (denoted by $\mathbb{I}$) - we have to leave out one of these dummy variables, the last one, usually.

Since (almost) each category is represented as one variable, the dimension of the problem is, at first, increased a lot. Another thing to note is, that dummy variables from the same (original) variable have a covariance of zero by default. This reduces the quality that may be expected from a two dimensional subspace further.

3.1.2 The Biplot Representation

Definition 3.1.1 (Biplot)
A (p, ϱ)-dimensional biplot is defined by

- a matrix X of data points in p dimensions,

- a matrix of distances d_{ij} between observations i and j,

- and a method from multidimensional scaling, which minimises the amount of deviation between the distances d_{ij} and their ϱ-dimensional counterparts δ_{ij}.

Remark 3.1.2
The dimension ϱ usually is 1,2 or 3 for graphical representations. In this section ϱ is set to 2.

The graphical representation of a biplot is dot based. This means for categorical variables, that each combination is shown as one single dot. This, of course, does not allow conclusions about this combination's size any more. One solution to this problem is the use of density estimates. This also covers the problem of over-plotting, which, especially in large data sets, is always present in dot based representations.

The graphical representation of a biplot has two components:

- Data points are projected onto the plane spanned by the first two principal components and visualised as dots. The centre of the plot is given by the projection of the p dimensional mean $(\frac{1}{n}X_1^t \mathbb{I}, \ldots, \frac{1}{n}X_p^t \mathbb{I})$.

- The unit vectors e_i^t corresponding to the (dummy) variables are also projected onto this plane.

  The graphical representation differs for continuous and categorical variables: For continuous variables, an arrow is drawn from plot centre to the projection of the variable, which marks the direction of the original variables. These directions are called the *biplot axes*. The arrowheads mark the unit points on the biplot axes.

  For a categorical variable its projection on the biplot is marked by a square rectangle. These rectangles are called the *category level points (CLP)*.

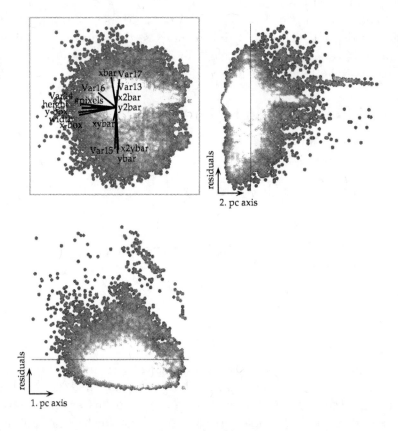

Figure 3.1: *Biplot of the Letter Recognition Data (cf. figure 4.41). Besides the biplot scatterplots of the residuals vs. first and second principal axes are plotted.*

Figures 3.1 and 3.2 show examples of biplots for continuous and categorical variables. Next to the biplot in figure 3.1 scatterplots of the residual values vs. first and second principal component are plotted. The "residual values" in this case are calculated as the length of the residual vector of each observation. The different gray shades of the points in the figure is the effect of a crude graphical density estimate - light areas in the display correspond to a high number of observations.

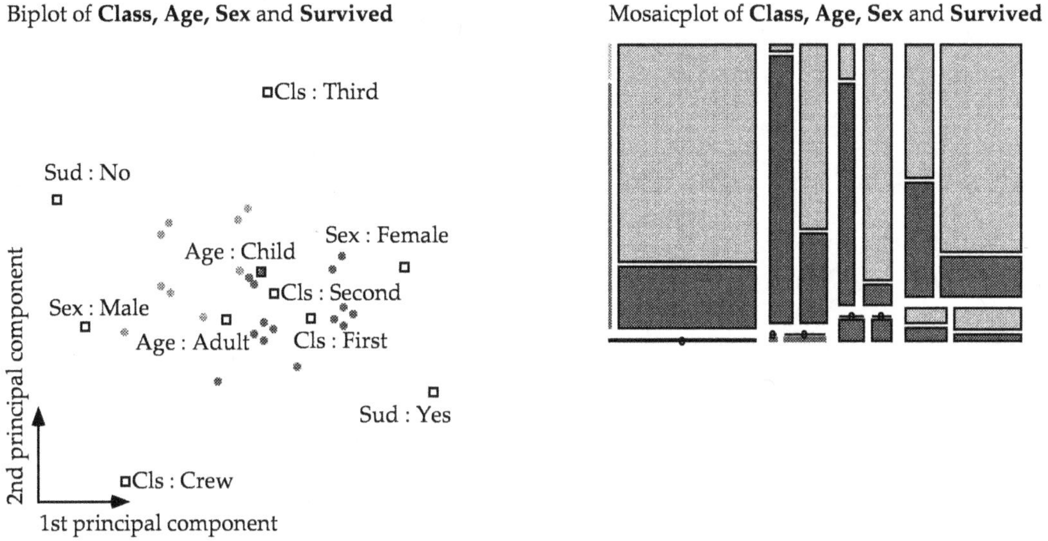

Figure 3.2: *Biplot and corresponding mosaicplot of the Titanic Data. Each dot on the left side corresponds to a cell on the right hand side. Highlighted are survivors.*

Figure 3.2 shows a biplot of categorical variables, based on an MCA. Next to the biplot a mosaicplot of the same variables is drawn additionally.

3.1.3 "Reading" a Biplot

In a biplot the most important source of information lies in the distance objects have from each other. The distance between objects gives a measure of how similar or how closely related objects are.

The distance of a CLP to the plot's centre or the length of a unit on a biplot axis reflect how good the projection of the underlying variable is, i.e. with increasing distance the goodness of fit - and with it the "importance" - of this variable increases.

The meaning of objects lying close to each other varies according to their type:

- **point - point**

  close points reflect high dimensional "neighbours".

- **axis/CLP - axis/CLP**

  axes with a small angle between them indicate a high positive correlation between the variables, angles near 180 indicate a high negative correlation.

  Neighbouring CLPs are also a hint that the corresponding variables are associated, i.e. that these categories frequently occur together in the data.

- **points - axis/CLPs**

  points are assumed to represent the combination of categories to the closest lying CLPs. The axes closest to a point represent the strongest influence for a data point.

3.2 Interactive Methods

Based on the construction and interpretation of a biplot, interactive methods have to be provided for in the display.

The following ideas for interactive features are taken from the diploma thesis of Hofmann (1998) "Interaktive Biplots".

3.2.1 Interactive Querying

Interactive querying is context sensitive - querying different objects provides different information. Examples for several querying results are given in figures 3.3 to 3.5.

3.2.2 Logical Zoom

The difference between logical and "normal" zooming lies in the fact that by logical zooming an object is not only enlarged but more details appear. Logical zooming in biplots has already been shown at the example of the Mushroom data on page 50, figures 2.30 and 2.31. In this example, a part of the data, namely a specific cluster, is selected and an MCA is calculated for these values only. This gives a tool for breaking down large data sets into smaller parts, which are easier to analyse.

Logical zooming has another advantage, it does not only allow a closer inspection of substructure among the data, but it also gives a possibility of excluding outliers from the analysis. This is particularly necessary for the principal component analysis due to its poor behaviour with respect to outliers.

3.3 Univariate Linear Models with Continuous Response

Based on the graphical representation of a biplot and its interactive features, we will try another approach to visualise linear models among the data. The biplot representation

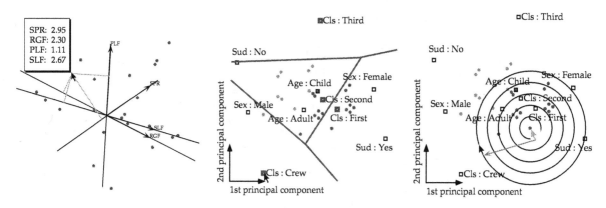

Figure 3.3: *Querying a point or "empty space" of the plot results in drawing perpendicular lines onto the biplot axes. Estimated values of the variables are given for the point in the projection plane.*

Figure 3.4: *Querying a CLP highlights the other CLPs and the prediction regions of the underlying categorical variable.*

Figure 3.5: *Drag-query: dragging from one point of the plot to another draws circles around the starting point as visual aid for estimating distances between objects.*

provides a possibility to draw results from a linear model in such a way, that the goodness of fit as well as the most important explanatory variables become visible in an instant.

Let us assume a situation, where we are dealing with a continuous response variable Y and several independent variables $X_1, \ldots, X_p$. The X_i do not necessarily have to be continuous - but we also do not work with categorical variables directly. Instead, for a categorical variable X_i a set of *dummy variables* is used as before.

Let $X_1, \ldots, X_p$ in the following be a set of independent variables, which has been produced in this way, i.e. a variable is either continuous by default or it is a variable corresponding to a single category.

A *linear regression model* then has the form

$$Y = X\beta + \epsilon, \ \epsilon \sim N(0, \sigma^2 I)$$

where $X = (\mathbb{1}, X_1, \ldots, X_p)$ is the *design matrix* and β the *vector of parameters* β_i.

If some of the variables are dummy variables, we have to use a further condition for the parameters of these variables in order to get a unique result. Let $Z_1, \ldots, Z_I$ be the dummy variables for the categorical variable X and $\beta_1, \ldots, \beta_I$ the corresponding parameters of the linear model, then a commonly used constraint (*null-sum-coding*) on the estimates for these parameters is that they sum to zero, i.e.

$$\sum_{i=1}^{I} \hat{\beta}_i = 0,$$

or one of the categories is used as basis and the parameters of the resulting model show the influence a category has with respect to the basis. The constraint *effect-coding* on the parameters then is

$$\beta_i = 0,$$

if Z_i is the dummy variable corresponding to the basis category.

It is well known, that the *hat matrix* $H := X(X'X)^{-1}X'$ is that projection matrix, which minimizes the least squares problem of $\sum_i \epsilon_i^2$ and gives the predicted values $\hat{Y}$ as

$$\hat{Y} = HY.$$

Accordingly, the LS-estimator for β is

$$\hat{\beta} = (X'X)^{-1}X'Y.$$

One of the favourite methods for examining the structure among the residuals $\epsilon_i = Y_i - \hat{Y}_i$ is to plot residuals versus their predicted values, i.e. the data points are projected into the plane spanned by $\hat{Y}$ and $Y - \hat{Y}$. These vectors indeed are orthogonal to each other, since the scalar product vanishes:

$$(\hat{Y}, Y - \hat{Y}) = (HY, Y - HY) =$$

$$= (Y, H'(HY - Y)) \overset{H'=H;H^2=H}{=} (Y, HY - HY) = 0.$$

3.3.1 Finding the Biplot Axes and Comparing Effects

The biplot axes are constructed in this situation in the same way as for standard biplots of PCA or MCA. The vectors of the p dimensional standard normal basis are projected into the plane spanned by $\hat{Y}$ and $Y - \hat{Y}$. This results in $\hat{\beta}_i$ as the coordinate of $e_i' = (0, \ldots, 0, 1, 0, \ldots, 0) \in \mathbf{R}^p$ in the direction of $\hat{Y}$.

However, while projecting e_i' in the direction of $Y - \hat{Y}$ a problem appears: generally we do not have a value for Y for any given value of X, particularly for e_i'. A direct calculation therefore is not possible. But we do know that the whole X space is orthogonal to the direction of the residuals $Y - \hat{Y}$, since

$$X' \cdot (Y - \hat{Y}) = X'Y - \underbrace{X' \cdot X(X'X)^{-1}}_{=I} X'Y = X'Y - X'Y = 0.$$

Therefore the coordinate of the ith biplot axis in the direction of the residuals is also zero. Figure 3.6 shows the axis of the predicted values $\hat{Y}$ together with the biplot axes for the five variables A, B, C, D and E.

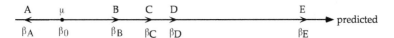

Figure 3.6: *Axis of predicted values together with the five biplot axes of the variables A, B, C, D and E.*

We can re-establish the relation of projected data points and their original values by orthogonal projections of the projected points onto the biplot axes. In the case of an analysis of variance this means, that we get very informative "labels" for the predicted values. Figure 3.7 shows an analysis of variance of the *Barley Data*.

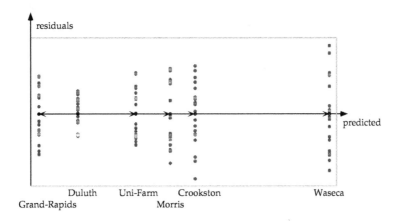

Figure 3.7: *Analysis of variance of the Barley Data. Predicted values are plotted vs. residuals. Six different sites of barley cultivation are drawn as biplot axes. The results of Duluth are used as basis values in the Anova.*

We see not only parallel dot plots of the barley yields, but also a natural ordering of the six categories, even (roughly) their distance or closeness. The last point has a caveat: the lengths of their units are not directly comparable, i.e. an axis with large units is not by default a more important factor, since the "importance" of an axis also depends on the variability of $\hat{\beta}_i$. The standard test of judging, whether the ith parameter is significantly different from 0, i.e. $\beta_i = 0$ vs $\beta_i \neq 0$, uses the estimate's variability. The test statistic $\hat{\beta}_i/SE_{\hat{\beta}_i}$, where $SE^2_{\hat{\beta}_i} = \hat{\sigma}^2 e'_i (X'X)^{-1} e_i$, is approximately t distributed with $n - p - 1$ degrees of freedom.

A second choice of units on the biplot axes therefore is the term $\hat{\beta}_i/SE_{\hat{\beta}_i}$. This re-scales the biplot axes in a way that their lengths are proportional to the values of the t-statistic. More important variables in the regression model now have larger parameters, whereas biplot axes with insignificant parameters remain short. Graphically we can support this by highlighting an interval on the axis of predicted values, which corresponds to the 5% level of a t-test. See figure 3.8: in this example the SE_{β_i} are of the same order of magnitude, and the distances do not change compared to figure 3.7.

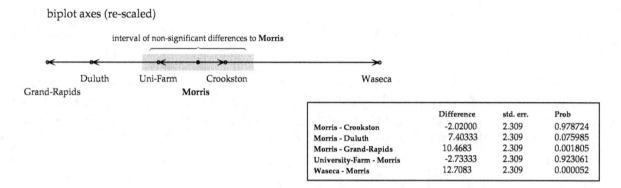

	Difference	std. err.	Prob
Morris - Crookston	-2.02000	2.309	0.978724
Morris - Duluth	7.40333	2.309	0.075985
Morris - Grand-Rapids	10.4683	2.309	0.001805
University-Farm - Morris	-2.73333	2.309	0.923061
Waseca - Morris	12.7083	2.309	0.000052

Figure 3.8: *Comparison of effects: on the left the graphical test via the interval of non-significant values is shown, on the right is a table of the corresponding pairwise tests.*

When setting the origin of this interval the exact coding, which we used for a categorical variable now has a strong influence: if we use effect-coding, the origin of the 5% interval will be placed on the predicted value of the basis. When using a null-sum-coding the origin of the interval is set to the expected value of Y.

Figure 3.8 shows the (re-scaled) biplot axes of the example above. The category *Morris* is set as basis value. Around the parameter value the interval of non-significant values is shown as a gray-shaded rectangle. The categories *Uni-Farm* and *Crookston* fall into this rectangle, indicating that these categories have parameters, which are not significantly different from the parameter of the category *Morris*.

Since the differences between the parameters are not affected by the choice of the coding, we may use these differences for more than one comparison (and with that, multiple tests) in each plot. From a statistical point of view this multiple test situation suggests the use of *Bonferroni- confidence intervals* for each parameter rather than the use of the above significance intervals. The difference between the above intervals and Bonferroni's intervals is essentially a factor, calculated from the level of significance and the number of comparisons made.

The price we have to pay for the re-scaling of the biplot axes with the parameter's variability is that we lose the connection between data points and biplot axes.

In order to avoid re-scaling we may try another approach to visualise the tests between the effects: the software JMP suggests the use of circles of different size around the parameter values. The size of each circle is given by the standard deviation of the parameter times $t_{\alpha/2}$. Whether two parameters are significantly different is decided from whether the angle at the intersection of their circles is less than 90° or not (see figure 3.9). For a more detailed explanation of the underlying statistics see JMP's "Statistics and Graphics Guide", p.94-95. The disadvantage of this approach is that angles have to be compared. This makes the decision between significant and not-significant differences between the parameters rather hard to draw visually.

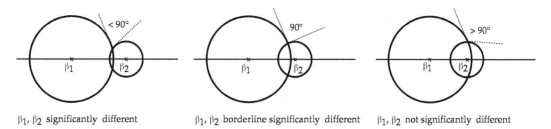

Figure 3.9: *Confidence circles around parameter values. Depending on the angles at the circles' intersections the difference between the parameters is significantly different (left), borderline significantly different (middle) and not significantly different (right).*

3.3.2 Projection of the response variable Y

Since we may write Y as the sum of the projection axes $\hat{Y}$ and $Y - \hat{Y}$,

$$Y = 1 \cdot \hat{Y} + 1 \cdot (Y - \hat{Y}),$$

Y has the coordinates (1,1) in the new coordinate system.

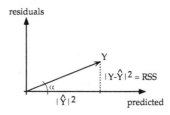

Figure 3.10: *Response variable Y in the projection plane spanned by predicted and residual values.*

The units on the projection axes are given as $|Y - \hat{Y}|$ and $|\hat{Y}|$, where $|Y - \hat{Y}|^2 = \sum_i (Y_i - \hat{Y}_i)'(Y_i - \hat{Y}_i) = RSS$ and $|\hat{Y}|^2 = TSS - RSS$. RSS is the *residual sum of squares* and TSS is the *total sum of squares*.

The coordinate of Y in direction of $Y - \hat{Y}$ shows the square root of the residual sum of squares, $\sqrt{RSS}$; the coordinate in direction of $\hat{Y}$ gives the square root of the difference between the total sum of squares, TSS, and the residual sum. The angle α between Y and $Y - \hat{Y}$ is therefore related to the goodness of fit statistics R^2 of the regression model:

$$\cos^2(\alpha) = \left(\frac{|HY|}{|Y|}\right)^2 = \frac{TSS - RSS}{TSS} = R^2,$$

i.e. the smaller α is, the better is the fit of the regression model. Of course, the angle depends on the aspect ratio of the display. In the following we will fix it in such a way that 1cm will show the same amount on both axes. This will further help to decide on the goodness of fit

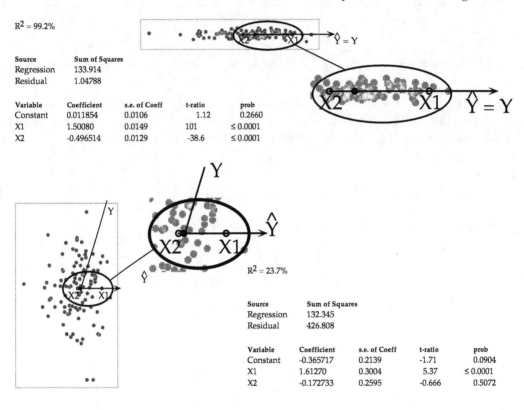

Figure 3.11: *Example of regressions with good fit (above) and bad fit (below). The goodness of fit is emphasized by the shape of the display. The angle between Y and $\hat{Y}$ also corresponds to R^2.*

of a regression. A plot with large width and little height indicates a good fit (the residuals are small with respect to the predicted values), while a quadratic plot or, even worse, a tall and thin plot indicates a very bad fit, see figure 3.11.

Chapter 4

Interactive Graphics vs. KDD Techniques

Methods of Exploratory Data Analysis (EDA) are based on the human factor and the need of a lot of experience. The process of getting to results may be slow and sometimes no essential results will be found at all.

Data Mining (DM) on the other hand works with very computer-intensive methods and uses automated methods from various fields of data analysis. Getting any results is a (comparatively) fast process, yet, checking the results in terms of their usefulness and importance is not quite as straightforward.

To overcome this problem, methods of interactive graphics can be used for visualising and thereby checking results found by DM tools.

We will demonstrate this approach first at the example of association rules. It already has been proposed in DM literature (e.g. Kardaun & Alanko (1999)), to analyse the full $X - Y$ data table, whenever a rule $X \rightarrow Y$ is found. *Mosaicplots* provide analysts with exactly this possibility in a graphical way. Enhanced with standard interactive features they represent a powerful tool to "look at" multidimensional categorical data.

It will be shown in the sequel, how association rules and mosaicplots fit together, and, how these techniques can contribute both to the benefit of EDA and DM.

4.1 Association Rules

Association rules have their origin in market basket analysis, an area which is dominated by researchers with a background in database theory. The concepts, however, are of a statistical nature. They are introduced in section 4.1.1 and "translated" for a better understanding to a more statistical language in section 4.1.1.

When dealing with association rules several problems appear, most of which are due to the sheer mass of rules generated during the mining process. This makes measures for evaluating the quality of rules necessary. Graphical methods are proposed in section 4.1.2 in order to achieve this. In a first approach we deal with the visualization of only one association rule a time. Here, mosaicplot and, in particular, doubledecker plots are helpful tools for inspecting a rule in the context of the corresponding high-dimensional contingency table.

While "mining" associations among variables any standard datamining software produces **all** possible rules - an exponentially explosive undertaking. To filter between "interesting" and less interesting results, several measures of "interestingness" have been introduced in the literature (Srikant & Agrawal (1995), Bayardo & Agrawal (1999)). They find their statistical counterpart in several variations of gaussian and χ^2 tests. Graphically, some of these measures are also visible in the corresponding doubledecker plots.

A second approach of visualization techniques is concerned with the question, whether it is possible to visualise more than one association rule at once - with the goal to visualise both the structure among the variables as well as the structural dependencies of the mined rules.

4.1.1   Definition of Association Rules

Association Rules in Database Terminology

Association rules have been proposed by Agrawal et al. (1993) in the context of market basket analysis. They were invented to provide an automated process, which could find connections among items, that were not known before, especially to answer questions like: "which items are likely to be bought together?".

Typically, the data to be examined consist of customer purchases, i.e. a set of items bought by a customer over a period of time.

The standard way of storing such data is the following: For each customer the transactions are stored with a unique number, the *transaction identification (TID)*.

Beside the TID we have a set of all different *items*, the *itemset* $\mathcal{I} = \{i_1, i_2, \ldots, i_m\}$.

The data or *database D* is a set of purchases (*transactions*), where each transaction T includes a set of items, such that $T \subset \mathcal{I}$.

A transaction T is said to *contain* a set of items X, if X is a subset of T.

Example 4.1.1 *SAS Assocs Data*
A typical data set looks like this:

TID	items
t_1	herring, corned beef, olives, ham, turkey, bourbon, ice cream
t_2	baguette, soda, ham, cracker, heineken, olives, corned beef
t_3	avocado, corned beef, artichoke, heineken, ham, turkey, sardines
...	

Each of the transactions t_1, t_2, t_3 contain the item set $\{ham, corned\ beef\}$.

Definition 4.1.2 (Association Rule, Confidence & Support)

An *association rule* (Agrawal et al. 1993) is defined as an implication of the form $X \rightarrow Y$, where X and Y are mutually exclusive itemsets (i.e. $X, Y \subset \mathcal{I}$ and $X \cap Y = \emptyset$).
An association rule $X \rightarrow Y$ holds with *confidence* $c = c(X \rightarrow Y)$, if $c\%$ of transactions in D that contain X also contain Y. $X \rightarrow Y$ has *support* s in the database D, if $s\%$ of transactions in D contain $X \cup Y$.

The goal is to find (generate) all association rules, that have confidence and support greater than a user-specified minimum support (*minsupp*) and minimum confidence (*minconf*). The algorithmic implementation of association rules was given first in Agrawal & Srikant (1994). Applications of association rules include among others market basket analysis, fraud detection and department store/shelf planning. Bing Liu et al (1998) also showed their usefulness for classification problems.
Presumably the most quoted finding of association rules is the (in)famous and — as recently became known — faked example of supermarket data, in which the beer-diaper analysis concluded, that male customers who buy diapers on Thursday evenings are likely to buy beer also. The following lines are taken from the electronic newsletter KDD Nugget Index of Feb. 12th, 1996:

> Beer and diapers sell well together. Who knew?

> If not for the data-mining power of Oracle7.1, a retailer in a neighborhood populated with young families might never have known that husbands on the way home from work often grab a six-pack of beer as a post-diaper impulse buy.

Example 4.1.3 *SAS Assocs Data*

Output of an association query with minconf= 50 and minsupp= 3. The SAS EnterpriseMiner generated 1000 rules with up to 4 items (47 2-item rules, 394 3-item rules and 559 4-item rules), see table 4.1 for some example rules from the result of this query.
Figure 4.1 shows a rather typical graphic for the visualization of association rules in commercial software packages.
This example is taken from the SAS EnterpriseMiner. It shows 15 rules in a matrix, where each row corresponds to one left-hand-side of a rule and each column corresponds to one right-hand-side. Each rule, which fulfills minsupp and minconf is drawn as a square. The different gray shades of the tiles are assigned by the confidences of the rules - in fig. 4.1 the

# items	conf	supp	count	rule
2	82.62	25.17	252	artichoke → heineken
2	78.93	25.07	251	soda → cracker
2	78.09	22.08	221	turkey → olives
2	75.0	36.56	366	cracker → heineken
...				
3	95.16	5.89	59	soda & artichoke → heineken
3	94.31	19.88	199	avocado & artichoke → heineken
3	93.23	23.38	234	soda & cracker → heineken
3	91.72	14.39	144	cracker & artichoke → heineken
...				
4	100.0	3.1	31	ham & corned beef & apples → olives
4	100.0	3.1	31	ham & corned beef & apples → herring
4	100.0	3.8	38	steak & soda & heineken → cracker
4	100.0	3.8	38	soda & peppers & heineken → cracker
...				

Table 4.1: *Typical output of an association query.*

confidences vary between 99% (light gray) and 100 % (dark gray). The size of the squares is given by the support of the corresponding rule. In fact, the area is proportional to the square of the support - which visually is problematic, since for instance the following two rules (marked by the arrows in fig. 4.1)

turkey & herring & corned beef → olives

ham & corned beef & apples → olives

have support 11.19% and 3.1%, respectively. The factor is approx. 4, whereas the areas differ by a factor of 16. This difference between effect within the data and effect within the visual display has been mentioned a lot in the literature of visualization techniques. Tufte (1983) called it the lie-factor.

We will discuss this and similar approaches to visualization later on in section 4.1.6. For the moment just note that three dimensions (x and y axis plus colour) are used to display two properties of the rules, namely confidence and support.

Another point to note is that only 15 out of a total of 1000 rules are shown in the example - just try to imagine how a plot of all 1000 would look like.

Common to all the standard approaches of visualization is, that they deal with the display of all rules at the same time. This allows neither an estimation of the rules' quality except for support and confidence, of course - we will show that these statistics may lead to quite the wrong conclusions sometimes - nor does it show structures and dependencies among the rules or their items.

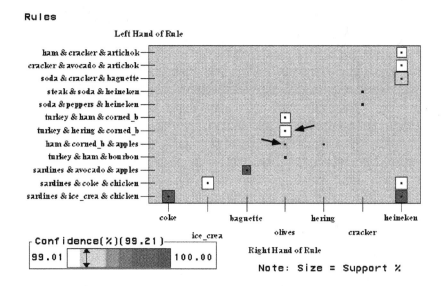

Figure 4.1: *SAS Enterprise Miner: visualization of all 15 association rules with a minimum confidence of 99%.*

Translation to Statistical Terms

Instead of concentrating on each transaction and the items bought in it, the statistical approach usually concentrates on the items themselves: dummy variables are generated for each item, i.e. each item i_j $(1 \leq j \leq m)$ is coded in a binary variable I_j, taking ones and zeroes for "bought" and "not bought" respectively. The kth entry $I_j^{(k)}$ is 1, if item i_j is present in transaction t_k and 0 if not. Since we are dealing with binary data the only values I_j can take are $I_j = 1$ and $I_j = 0$, which we will denote with I_j and $\neg I_j$ for short.

Items bought together can then be expressed as intersections of the corresponding item variables: $I_{j_1} \cap I_{j_2} \cap \ldots \cap I_{j_p}$ - we call this an *event*.

- The *frequency* with which two events X and Y occur together in the data corresponds to the support of rule $X \to Y$,

- the *conditional frequency* of event Y given event X corresponds to the confidence of rule $X \to Y$.

Example 4.1.4 *SAS Assocs Data*

TID	apples	artichoke	avocado	baguette		soda	steak	turkey
t_1	0	0	0	0	...	0	0	1
t_2	0	0	0	1	...	1	0	0
t_3	0	1	1	0	...	0	0	1
t_4	0	0	0	0	...	0	0	1
t_5	1	0	1	0	...	0	1	1
t_6	0	0	0	0	...	0	1	0
t_7	1	0	0	0	...	0	0	1
t_8	0	0	0	1	...	0	0	0

...

Among the transactions visible **turkey** *has a support of 5 (out of 8),* **apple, steak** *and* **avocado** *have each a support of 25%.*

From the frequencies of their intersections we can calculate support and confidence of the association rules:

apples → **turkey** *has a support of 25% and a confidence of 100%. All apple buyers therefore also buy turkey.*

The same is true for the rule **avocado** → **turkey**.

The rule **steak** → **turkey** *has a support of 12.5% and a confidence of 50% and is therefore weaker than the other two rules.*

In classical data analysis the frequency and the conditional frequency are maximum likelihood estimators of the probability of $X \cap Y$ and the conditional probability of Y given X, respectively. The conditions for an association rule given above can therefore be re-formulated as:

$$\text{Let } X \text{ and } Y \text{ be two disjoint events, then}$$

$$X \to Y \iff \left\{ \begin{array}{l} P(X \cap Y) \geq s \\ P(Y \mid X) \geq c \end{array} \right. ,$$

where s and c have the same meaning as before.

4.1.2   Relationship between Association Rules and Mosaics

Mosaics are the graphical analogue of multiway contingency tables. Thus the mosaicplot gives a graphical estimation of the joint distribution of its variables. *Highlighting* as shown in figure 4.2 provides a possibility to link data from different views - in mosaicplots highlighting heights are drawn orthogonal to the direction of the last split. Highlighting proportions therefore show the conditional distribution $Y = y_2 \mid X_1, \ldots, X_k$.

One way to visualise an association rule $X \to Y$ is to combine all variables involved in X as *explanatory* variables and draw them within one mosaicplot. Visualise the *response* Y by highlighting the corresponding categories in a barchart (or a second mosaicplot, if Y consists

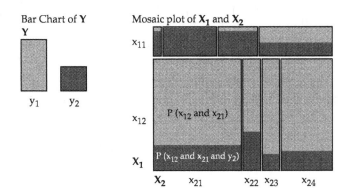

Figure 4.2: *2 dim. Mosaicplot of variables X_1 and X_2.*
The bar chart on the left shows another variable, Y. Observations y_2 have been selected; highlighting shows up in the mosaic as a third dimension.

of more than one variable). Then, the amount of highlighting in a bin in a mosaicplot gives a visual measure for the probability of $X \cap Y$, the support of rule $X \rightarrow Y$. The heights of highlighting relative to the bin's height give the conditional conditional probability of $Y \mid X$, the confidence of rule $X \rightarrow Y$.

Figure 4.2 shows an overview of all possible association rules involving the variables X_1, X_2 and Y. The second bin in the top row ($x_{11} \cap x_{22}$) represents a rule with very high confidence (the highlighting almost fills this bin entirely), whereas the support is relatively small (the bin itself, and therefore the amount of highlighting, is not very large). The first bin in the lower row, ($x_{12} \cap x_{21}$), shows the rule with the highest support (this bin contains the largest amount of highlighting), yet the confidence of the corresponding rule is rather low (highlighting fills this bin to only one fifth, approximately).

In order to be able to compare the proportions of highlighting heights more easily, we will use doubledecker plots (see section 2.2) from now on. This has the advantage that the relationship between the graphical display and an association rule simplifies. The support of a rule then still is given by the area of highlighted values, but the confidence simply corresponds to the height of a highlighted area. Confidences are therefore directly comparable.

The colour code of the bars below the plots is the same for the following examples: white rectangles stand for "0" (not bought) and black rectangles stand for "1" (item bought).

Example 4.1.5 *SAS Assoc Data*
Using a standard method for finding association rules, the following two rules are part of the result set

rule	confidence	support
heineken & coke & chicken → sardines	98.31	11.59
cracker & soda & olives → heineken	96.83	12.18

From these numbers alone it is hard to decide on the quality and validity of the rules. One of the problems is that the support is quite incomparable between rules with different items, especially if the marginal probabilities differ as strongly as P(heineken) = .6 and P(sardines) = .3. Doubledecker plots in figures 4.3 and 4.4 provide us with the additional information we need.

The first rule, heineken & coke & chicken → sardines, proves to be a very strong rule - no other combination of the variables involved shows a similar confidence. Viewing a plot like fig. 4.3 we can be sure, that the correlation between the explanatory variables and the target is high.

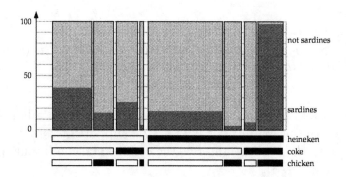

Figure 4.3: *Example of a "good" association rule: the bin **heineken & coke & chicken** is filled almost entirely with highlighting, while none of the other bins is filled to more than a third.*

Figure 4.4 on the other hand exposes the second rule to be rather weak - in a sense, that the rule is not able to grasp and summarise the whole information of this subtable of the data.

Two further combinations of the variables show similar confidences with approx. the same support. The doubledecker plot, however, enables us to draw conclusions even from this starting point: With a minimum confidence of ca. 75% we get the following three rules:

$$\neg \ cracker \ \& \ \neg \ olives \ \& \ \neg \ soda \rightarrow heineken$$
$$cracker \ \& \ \neg \ olives \ \& \ \ \ soda \rightarrow heineken$$
$$cracker \ \& \ \ \ olives \ \& \ \ \ soda \rightarrow heineken$$

*A situation like the one in figure 4.4 is typical if we either deal with several groups within the target or with a too narrowly specified left-hand-side of the rule - also known as **over-fitting**. If we look at the table of rules more closely, we see that we deal with one rule with all negative attributes, i.e. buying neither of the three items above also suggests strongly to buy **heineken**. This means, that we are dealing with at least two different groups of **heineken** purchasers. The remaining two rules can be simplified (with respect to the number of items) using simple Boolean algebra to:*

$$cracker \ \& \ \ \& \ soda \rightarrow heineken,$$

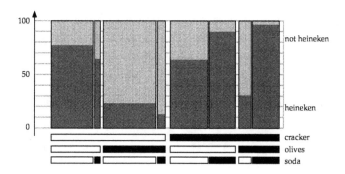

Figure 4.4: *Example of a "bad" association rule. Three combinations of **cracker, soda** and **olives** show high proportions of highlighting (> 75%).*

which results in only one rather strong rule with only three items yielding a confidence of 93% and a support of 23%.

Remark 4.1.6
The doubledecker plot (as well as the mosaic) gives additional insight to all other combinations of the variables $X_1, \ldots, X_k, Y$ not regarded by a rule of the form $X_1 \cap \ldots \cap X_k \to Y$. The plots do not reduce the information except that they do not display the actual numbers - but they prepare the data in such a way, that important features will become prominent. Without formal testing we are able to distinguish between good and weak rules. We are also able to recognize "borderline rules". This is done by basic comparisons of several visual properties, such as support, confidence and behaviour of the target variable in all other combinations of $X_1, \ldots, X_k$. Each of the quality measures can of course be tested and calculated a lot quicker without visualising each rule. But then we do not know beforehand which measure to pick.
Neither mosaics nor doubledecker plots are limited to binary data. Neither are association rules (Brin et al 1999). The applications using more than one item per variable are e.g.

- the analysis of competitive products

- discrimination of different (equivalent) categories: e.g. colors, or different reasons for "no"s in surveys, ...

- approach to include meta-information, such as the taxonomy of items (*is-a* relationships), in the analysis.

4.1.3   Finding "interesting" Rules

The problem is, that depending on what minimum confidence and what support is specified a vast amount of rules may be generated. Among those, however, not only "interesting and new" results - according to the principle of KDD (as defined in the collection of KDD terms by Klösgen & Zytkow (1991)) - are found. In supermarket data for instance most purchases will also contain plastic or paper bags. This leads to some of the following problems of association rules:

1. Association rules tend to prefer frequent events as their response (right hand side of a rule).

$$\text{For all events } Y \quad \exists \, X \subset \mathcal{I}, \text{ such that } P(Y \mid X) \geq P(Y).$$

   This implies that for any large event Y with $P(Y) > minconf$ there will also exist association rules $X \rightarrow Y$, if only the intersection $P(X \cap Y)$ is sufficiently high ($>$ *minsupp*). The importance and meaning of rules generated on this basis, on the other hand, is not reliable at all.

2. When dealing with different association rules which refer to the same response, it is of interest to examine, whether the populations described by the explanatory variables (left hand side of a rule) differ from each other. It could well be one and the same population, and different rules providing only different descriptions for it. - Another goal therefore is, to examine the impact of rules on one another and to find intersections amongst them.

3. Quite often, slight variations of items are listed as different association rules: either the same items alternatively take right and left hand sides of rules, like

$$X_1 \cap X_2 \rightarrow X_3, X_1 \cap X_3 \rightarrow X_2, X_2 \cap X_3 \rightarrow X_1$$

   or sequences occur, such as:

$$X_1 \rightarrow X_j,$$
$$X_1 \cap X_2 \rightarrow X_j,$$
$$X_1 \cap X_2 \cap X_3 \rightarrow X_j, \quad \ldots$$

4. Explicability: besides finding new and interesting results, datamining tools are to find *explicable* results. The interpretation of results therefore should be of great interest - if one can not explain a rule at first, we could use methods of cross-classification in the hope of finding clues within the data, which allow us to decide, whether a result has to be considered as a peculiarity of this particular data set or can be generalized.

There are several possibilities, how to define "interesting" rules - depending on the criterion, which is to be optimized. In the following sections statistics such as "lift", "doc" or "R-interest" of rules are introduced. Each of these values give an order, in which the association rules can be arranged according to one specific criterion. Of course, the most important issue here is to decide, which additional information of the rules to exploit. Section 4.1.3 is based on the facts provided by a single association rule, namely its support and its confidence, together with the number of total cases in the data set. The concepts introduced, however, are of a more general nature, i.e. they basically compare observed and expected features of a rule. The calculation of "expected" values is based upon very weak and universal assumptions in this section.

Section 4.1.3 picks up the same concepts, only that here the notion of what to "expect" from a rule is specified in more detail, in particular, additional and more specific information based on structural dependencies with other rules is included in the evaluation of each of the rules.

Power of an Association

As a remedy to problem (1) on the list, we can think of a measure to decide, whether a rule was found just because its response is a frequent event. This is called the *power of an association*. If we deal with a rule $X \to Y$, which is based only upon the fact that $P(Y)$ is large, then X and Y will be close to being statistically independent:

$$
\begin{aligned}
P(Y \mid X) &\approx P(Y) \\
\Longleftrightarrow P(X \cap Y) &\approx P(X) \cdot P(Y).
\end{aligned}
$$

We will now exploit this fact and introduce two measures, the *lift* and the *doc* of a rule:

1. The *(model-) lift* (Piatetsky-Shapiro & Masand 1991) of a rule $X \to Y$ is defined as

$$
lift(X \to Y) := \frac{conf\ (X \to Y)}{supp\ (Y)}.
$$

   The lift compares a model with the random situation (see figure 4.5). Here, the lift is a measure of the deviation from independence of the two events X and Y, since

$$
lift(X \to Y) = \frac{P(Y \mid X)}{P(Y)} = \frac{P(X \cap Y)}{P(X) \cdot P(Y)}.
$$

2. Alternatively one can measure the **differences of confidences** doc for the rule $X \to Y$ and $\neg X \to Y$:

$$
doc(X \to Y) := conf\ (X \to Y) - conf\ (\neg X \to Y).
$$

   The $doc(X \to Y)$ can be re- expressed as:

$$
doc(X \to Y) = \frac{P(X \cap Y) - P(X) \cdot P(Y)}{P(X) \cdot P(\neg X)}.
$$

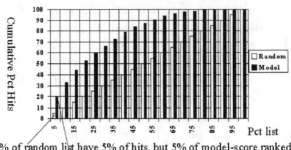

5% of random list have 5% of hits, but 5% of model-score ranked
list have 21% of hits.   Lift(5%) = 21/5 = 4.2

Figure 4.5: *Model vs. a random situation, the lift is calculated as ratio from the bins' heights (picture taken from Piatetsky-Shapiro & Masand (1991)).*

Remark 4.1.7

The product $doc(X \to Y) \cdot doc(Y \to X)$ is approximately χ^2- distributed (see section 2.6.7).

The doc measure can be **seen** directly in a doubledecker plot, as the following sketch shows:

X -> Y

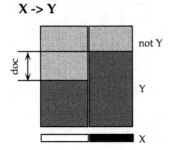

The support of $X \to Y$ is directly proportional to the highlighted rectangle on the right side, its height gives the confidence of $X \to Y$.
Similarly, the height of the highlighted rectangle on the left side shows the confidence of rule $\neg X \to Y$.
The difference of these confidences gives the *doc*.

Example 4.1.8 *SAS Assoc Data*

Figure 4.6 shows an example of the following six association rules:

Rule			support	confidence	lift	doc
heineken	$\to$	*corned beef*	*0.12*	*0.21*	*0.54*	*-0.45*
apples	$\to$	*heineken*	*0.10*	*0.34*	*0.56*	*-0.39*
herring	$\to$	*avocado*	*0.17*	*0.34*	*0.97*	*-0.02*
herring	$\to$	*ham*	*0.16*	*0.32*	*1.09*	*+0.05*
cracker	$\to$	*heineken*	*0.37*	*0.75*	*1.25*	*+0.34*
coke	$\to$	*ice cream*	*0.22*	*0.74*	*2.40*	*+0.61*

The first two rules show rather strong docs - yet, the differences are in the "wrong" direction, i.e. the confidence of $\neg X \to Y$ is a lot higher than $X \to Y$. The two middle rules hardly show any doc at all. This indicates rather weak rules. The last two rules have again strong docs, now in the "right" direction. To decide on the quality of these two rules we can concentrate on support and confidence.

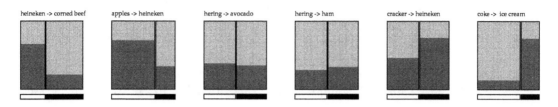

Figure 4.6: *Six selected association rules - sorted according to their lift and docs.*

Since $doc = P(Y \mid X) - P(Y \mid \neg X)$, we can use a standard Gauss test for testing the equality of two binomially distributed probabilities:

Testing the *doc*   Let p be the weighted mean of p_1 and p_2, $P := (n_1 p_1 + n_2 p_2)/(n_1 + n_2)$. A test, whether the *doc* is zero or not, is given by:

$$H_0 : doc = 0 \text{ vs. } H_1 : doc > 0$$

$$doc = p_1 - p_2 \qquad p_1 = P(Y \mid X), \ p_2 = P(Y \mid \neg X)$$
$$n_1 = P(X) \cdot n, \ n_2 = P(\neg X) \cdot n,$$

then $T_1 := \dfrac{p_1 - p_2}{\sqrt{p(1-p)}} \cdot \sqrt{\dfrac{n_1 n_2}{n_1 + n_2}} \sim N(0,1)$,

if n_1 and n_2 are sufficiently large. Since we are dealing with large data sets and n_1 and n_2 reflect the minimal support, the normal approximation will not be violated.

The test statistic T_1 can be transformed to

$$T_1^* = \sqrt{n} \cdot \frac{P(X \cap Y) - P(X)P(Y)}{\sqrt{P(X)(1 - P(X)) \cdot P(Y)(1 - P(Y))}} \sim N(0,1),$$

which coincides with the statistic proposed in Piatetsky-Shapiro (1991). Srikant & Agrawal (1995) claim that only ca. 1% of all the rules found were rejected because of this statistical test. This, however, is strongly dependent both on the specific application and on the choice of minimal confidence and support.

The higher *minconf* and *minsupp* are, the less likely a rule is rejected because of the test. One obvious solution in order to get only rules with a high *doc* is to increase confidence and support. Yet, in most applications we are not interested in the rules with the highest support or confidence - those are quite often known by (data) experts already - but in rules at the borderline, which were not known before.

Comparison between *lift* **and** *doc*

1. • $lift \in [0, \infty)$,

    • symmetric measure, i.e. $X \to Y$ and $Y \to X$ have the same lift, which at least is problematic, since the confidences of these two rules may vary quite a lot,

    • $lift > 1$ indicates a positive correlation between X and Y, i.e. $Y = 1$ is increased given $X = 1$ and vice versa

2. • $doc \in [-1, 1]$,

    • **not** symmetric for $X \to Y$ and $Y \to X$,

    • $doc > 0$ indicates a positive correlation between X and Y.

For the same target Y the *doc* and *lift* of a rule provide results in the same order:

$$doc(X_1 \to Y) > doc(X_2 \to Y) \iff lift(X_1 \to Y) > lift(X_2 \to Y)$$

This gives a consistent possibility for comparing rules with the same targets.

Definition 4.1.9 (Power of a rule)
A rule $X_1 \to Y$ has more *power* than $X_2 \to Y$, iff $lift(X_1 \to Y) > lift(X_2 \to Y)$. (Equivalently, $doc(X_1 \to Y) > doc(X_2 \to Y)$)
$X_1 \to Y$ *dominates* $X_2 \to Y$, if $X_1 \to Y$ has more power.

Setting sensible boundaries for the *lift* is dependent on the specific application. Differently from the *doc* the *lift* is not distributed according to a standard distribution. For setting a boundary value the *elbow-criterion* as known from pruning trees (cf. e.g. Breiman (1984)) is being used instead.
We will pick up both concepts in section 4.1.3 again and extend them further. The lift is generalized to "R-interest" of a rule, the *doc* forms the basis for building two different methods to prune association rules.

Intersection Structure

If we have two association rules that share the same right-hand side, say $X_1 \to Y$ and $X_2 \to Y$, it is very well possible that both rules describe for a large part the same population. In this section, we show how doubledecker plots can be used to discover such an underlying structure. This is done by constructing three plots: one for each of rule, $X_1 \to Y$ and $X_2 \to Y$, and one for their "intersection", i.e. $X_1 \cap X_2 \to Y$.
We are interested in two values particularly:
first of all of course in the **number of transactions** $X_1 \cap X_2$
and second in the **confidence** $P(Y \mid X_1, X_2)$ **of the intersection rule** $X_1 \cap X_2 \to Y$.

Both can be read from a doubledecker plot. The **width** of the rightmost bin in a doubledecker plot of the intersection rule shows $P(X_1 \cap X_2)$, the **height of highlighting** in this bin shows its confidence.

Example 4.1.10 *SAS Assoc Data*
Consider the following two rules:

rule		confidence	support
soda	$\to$ heineken	80.82	25.67
cracker	$\to$ heineken	75.00	36.56

Figure 4.7 shows in the upper row the two doubledecker plots of these rules and in the bottom row their intersection.

What is immediately clear from this last plot is that a very large proportion of the soda-buyers are also cracker-buyers. In fact, by inspecting the numbers, one sees that 25% of all people bought both soda and crackers. In other words, a brief inspection shows that these two rules are far from independent. The confidence of the intersection rule is also fairly high (> 90%),

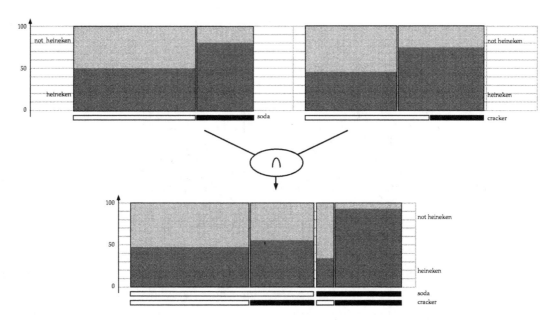

Figure 4.7: *Intersection of two 2-item association rules.*

intersecting the two rules therefore yields a new rule with three items:

rule	confidence	support
soda & cracker $\to$ heineken	93.23	25.07

*Whether we will accept this rule **additionally** to the other two rules or instead **replace** one* *of the others by it, we will be examined more closely using the methods introduced in section 4.1.3.*

A quite different example is given by the following two rules:

rule	confidence	support
corned beef & steak → apples	76.69	10.19
avocado & peppers → apples	76.19	9.59

Figure 4.8 shows doubledecker plots of these rules as well as of their intersection. Here, it

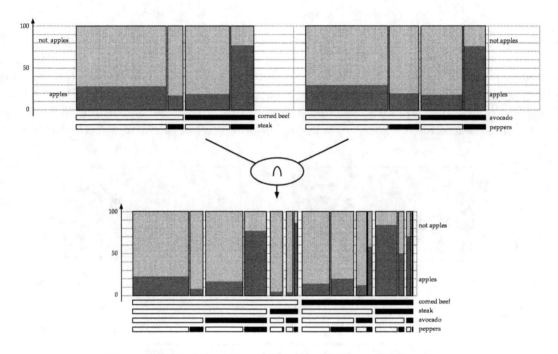

Figure 4.8: *Intersection of two 3-item association rules.*

*is immediately clear that the part of the population that buys **steak, corned beef, avocado**, and **pepper** is very small indeed (0.5%). This means, that we have found two different groups of apple buyers - those, who buy apples, after they have bought steak and corned beef, and those, who buy apples together with avocado and peppers.*

Pruning Sequences

Related Work   There is a large amount of literature in the KDD field involved with the pruning and post analysis of discovered association rules. Among them are:

- **use of templates**

the analyst has to pre-specify, what he/she wants to see (Klemettinen et al 1994).

This approach, however, neither prunes nor summarises the rules but rather selects rules according to the pre-defined scheme - a highly subjective criterion, which also requires a large amount of meta information from the analyst.

- **covers of rules**

  As many "redundant" rules as possible are pruned from the set with the goal to describe a target population. Redundancy of a rule wrt to another rule is defined via the number of cases both rules have in common (their intersection). If the second rule does not describe a significantly different target population it is pruned from the set (Toivonen et al 1995).

  Although this in fact prunes rules from the results, one important property of association rules is being lost: their completeness. This has a strong drawback on the interpretability of the results, since a rule, which we might have interpreted easily may have been pruned with respect to another - statistically better - rule, which is quite inexplicable due to hidden variables for instance.

  This problem originates from pruning rules according to results of arbitrary statistics without regarding the meta information a rule contains.

  The paper by Toivonen et al (1995) discusses another interesting aspect of grouping rules using clustering techniques. This requires the definition of the *distance* between two rules. Toivonen et al exploit for this again the concept of redundancy and the amount of intersection between two rules. We will pick up this idea in more detail in section 4.1.4.

- **pruning with respect to ancestor rules** Srikant & Agrawal (1995) introduced the concept of ancestor relationships among the rules, which we will also exploit for pruning them. They, however, extracted these relations from additional meta-information on the taxonomy of the items. From structures like *jacket "is-a" outerwear "is-a" clothes* they derive expected values for support and confidence of a rule. Rules are pruned according to the result of comparing expected and observed values.

  Bing Liu et al (1999) restricted themselves to rules with the same right-hand-sides only. Again they calculate expected values from an ancestor structure among the rules. And again rules are pruned based on the comparison between expected and observed values.

  The advantage of this approach is that it both involves statistical measurements as well as the structural dependency among the rules.

We want to concentrate on the last approach, since it seems to us to be the most promising one.

Unfortunately, the statistical realization in Bing Liu et al (1999) leaves a lot to be desired. The authors follow an overly complicated mixture of calculating χ^2 statistics together with comparing "directions" of correlations of rules and their ancestors.

We will explain their method in more statistical terms. This, however, reveals, that the method proposed by Bing Liu et al (1999) is improper from a statistical point of view.

Therefore we introduce a slightly different approach to pruning sequences, which additionally to being statistically correct can even be performed visually.

Sequences, Ancestors and Successors   Let us assume, that we are dealing with association rules of the following form:

$$X_1 \to Y$$
$$X_1 \cap X_2 \to Y$$
$$X_1 \cap X_2 \cap X_3 \to Y$$

$$\ldots$$

We will call rules with the same right-hand-side and left-hand-sides, which can be ordered as above a *sequence of association rules for Y*.

Goal of the analysis is to decide, which rules are essential for explaining the data and which rules may be pruned from the set. Since the quality of an association rule is measured by its confidence and support, we may have a closer look at these two statistics first. It is obvious, that each item we add to the left-hand-side of a rule reduces the support of it. What do we gain from that? Our interest is twofold:

- do we lose a lot with respect to support by adding a further item to the left-hand side?

- does a more restricted left-hand side provide us with a "satisfying" gain in confidence?

Definition 4.1.11 (ancestor rule, successor rule)
A rule $X \to Z$ is called *ancestor* of $Y \to Z$, if Y contains X, i.e. the items of X form a subset of the items in Y.
A rule $X \to Z$ is called a *close ancestor* of $Y \to Z$, if Y contains only one additional item besides X.
Accordingly, $Y \to Z$ is called a *successor* of $X \to Z$ and a *close successor*, respectively.

Method 1: Comparing with Ancestor Rules   (Bing Liu et al 1999)
Bing Liu et al (1999) proposed a test to decide in situations like this,

rule	confidence	support
$X \to Z$	c_1	s_1
$X \cap Y \to Z$	c_2	s_2

whether it is "useful" to restrict the left hand side further, i.e. whether s_2 and c_2, the support and confidence of the second rule, can still be regarded as high enough **given its ancestor rule**.

The decision, whether a rule is accepted or not, is now based on expectations founded on information, which has already been mined before - a rule is being judged according to the expectations derived from its ancestor rule. If a rule provides significantly higher values than expected, it will be accepted, since it provides additional information about the data. Otherwise the rule is rejected.

For this, it first has to be defined, what is expected from a rule $X \cap Y \to Z$ given its ancestor $X \to Z$:

Definition 4.1.12 (expected support, expected confidence (Srikant & Agrawal 1995))
Let $X \to Z$ be an ancestor rule of $X \cap Y \to Z$.
The *expected support* of a rule $X \cap Y \to Z$ given $X \to Z$ is defined as

$$supp\ _{X \to Z}(X \cap Y \to Z) = supp\ (X \to Z) \cdot supp\ (Y)$$

the *expected confidence* is defined as

$$conf\ _{X \to Z}(X \cap Y \to Z) = conf\ (X \to Z).$$

From a statistical point of view the above definition of expected confidence and support coincides with the assumption of statistical independence of $X \cap Z$ and Y.
This leads to a first method for testing a rule with respect to its ancestor:

Is the confidence significantly higher than expected? Let us consider the case of the two rules $X \cap Y \to Z$ and $X \to Z$. The ancestor rule provides us with two statistics, its confidence $P(Z \mid X) = p_2$ and its support.
Since we are interested in the new rule only, if its confidence is **increased** with respect to the confidence of the ancestor rule, we deal with a one-sided test situation:

$$p_1 = P(Z \mid X, Y) \qquad\qquad p_2 = P(Z \mid X)$$
$$n_1 = n \cdot P(X \cap Y) \qquad\qquad n_2 = n \cdot P(X)$$
$$H_o : p_1 = p_2 \qquad \text{vs.} \qquad H_1 : p_1 > p_2$$

$$\text{test-statistic: } T_1 = \frac{p_1 - p_2}{\sqrt{p(1-p)}} \sqrt{\frac{n_1 n_2}{n_1 + n_2}},$$

with $p = (n_1 p_1 + n_2 p_2)/(n_1 + n_2)$, again.
If p_1 and p_2 were independent, the above test statistic T_1 would be approximately standard normal distributed in the case of H_o. Unfortunately, p_1 and p_2 are not independent, since a subgroup of the data is being compared to its total.

The problem here is that in practice a situation like this is quite common and often is handled in exactly the same way as described above. What is more, this method proves to provide sensible results in a lot of cases. For a satisfactory solution we therefore have to provide first a statistically proper procedure, which secondly is not inferior to the approach above.

In the following lines we will therefore further discuss the approach above, in order to be able to give an appropriate alternative for it later.

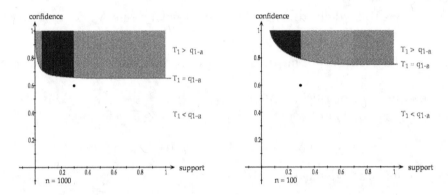

Figure 4.9: *Areas of acceptance (dark gray), based on the results of statistic T_1 and restrictions to the support (support > minsupp).*

Procedure of Pruning according to Method 1:   Accept the association rule, if the alternative is accepted and the support of $X \cap Y \to Z$ is still larger than *minsupp*, i.e. if the null hypothesis is rejected (on a specified level of significance α), the rule is accepted and vice versa.

Of course, we still only accept rules which have a support of at least *minsupp*.

Figure 4.9 shows the areas of acceptance and rejection of rules with respect to one ancestor rule with a support of 0.3 and a confidence of 0.6 (marked by a dot on the plots). Areas where confidence and support have a test statistic $T_1 > 1.29$ (1.29 is the 90% quantile of a standard normal distribution: the value 1.29 corresponds to a 10% level of significance for a one-sided test) are shaded light gray. Since the support of a successor rule can only be as large as the support of its ancestor and the rule must also have the minimal support, we also get vertical restrictions for acceptance. The area of acceptance is shaded dark gray, the light gray areas are irrelevant for the acceptance area. The left plot is based on 1000 transactions, the right plot on only 100.

Alternative: *R***-interestingness**   (Srikant & Agrawal 1995)

The definition of R-interesting rules as in Srikant & Agrawal (1995) is also based on the comparison of expected and observed values.

Definition 4.1.13 (R-interestingness)
An association rule $Y \to Z$ is R-*interesting* with respect to an ancestor rule $X \to Z$, if either observed support or confidence are at least R times as high as expected:

$$\frac{conf\,(Y \to Z)}{conf_{\,X \to Z}(Y \to Z)} \geq R \text{ or } \frac{supp\,(Y \to Z)}{supp_{\,X \to Z}(Y \to Z)} \geq R,$$

for a user-specified value R.

Only rules are accepted, which are R-interesting with respect to their R-interesting ancestors. This procedure, however, has several disadvantages:

Remark 4.1.14

(i) The difference between R-interesting rules and the statistical tests is, that the test-statistic does not only regard the difference of confidences but also the support (n_1 and n_2) and at the same time the absolute values of the confidences. This is important, since an improvement in confidence from 80% of an ancestor to 84% in the successor most often is not as interesting as an improvement from 95% to 99%, whereas the fraction of observed and expected values in the second case is slightly lower.

(ii) Support and confidence of rules have quite different values for the rules - while we are concerned to increase the confidence of a rule, the minimum support is the value of the minimal group of transactions we are still interested in. This may be 5 or 10% percent. Yet, there have to be a lot of good reasons to lower the confidence value to less than 50%.

The R-interestingness, though, does not regard these difference between support and confidence at all.

(iii) Choosing a value for R does not have any statistical foundation and is therefore no improvement on the approach of method 1.

Remark 4.1.15
The R-interestingness coincides with the lift of a rule $X \to Y$, if the most common ancestor of $X \to Y$, namely $\cdot \to Y$, is considered:

$$R_{conf} = \frac{conf\,(X \to Y)}{conf_{\,\cdot \to Y}} = \frac{P(Y \mid X)}{P(Y \mid \cdot)} = \frac{P(X \cap Y)}{P(X) \cdot P(Y)} = lift(X \to Y).$$

No	rule		confidence	support
0		→ bourbon	40.03	40.03
1	olives	→ bourbon	51.80	24.48
2	olives & coke	→ bourbon	73.65	10.89
3	olives & heineken	→ bourbon	65.52	13.29
4	olives & cracker	→ bourbon	70.81	13.09
5	olives & heineken & coke	→ bourbon	61.22	3.00
6	olives & heineken & cracker	→ bourbon	77.86	10.89

Table 4.2: Seven rules from the SAS Assocs Data.

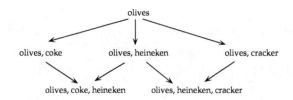

Figure 4.10: *Summary of all the left hand sides of the rules listed above.*

Example 4.1.16 *SAS Assocs Data*
Let us consider the rules from table 4.2.   Figure 4.10 shows a summary of the ancestor structure among the left hand sides of the rules above.
Table 4.3 gives the results from evaluating the rules with respect to their ancestor structures. The numbers given are (in this order)

- *the expected value for the confidence based on the ancestor rule,*

- *the expected value for the support based on the ancestor rule,*

- *the value of test-statistic according to method 1,*

- *the fraction of observed and expected confidence R_{conf},*

- *and the fraction of observed and expected support R_{supp} .*

From the values of R_{conf} and R_{supp} in the table it becomes obvious that it is not an easy task to set an appropriate boundary for R-interest, especially if we do not distinguish between support and confidence. Any value for R below 1.0, though, is not sensible at all, since this does not mean a gain but actually a loss with respect to the expected values. This prunes rule no. 5, olives & heineken & coke → bourbon.
After this, however, it is not at all clear, which lower limit for R to choose; for instance the best rule with respect to R-interest is the rule olives & heineken & cracker → bourbon

id	rule	exptd conf	exptd supp	T_1	R_{conf}	R_{supp}
	test with respect to rule 1					
2	olives & coke $\rightarrow$ bourbon	51.8	7.2	4.69	1.422	1.504
3	olives & heineken $\rightarrow$ bourbon	51.8	14.7	3.29	1.265	0.906
4	olives & cracker $\rightarrow$ bourbon	51.8	11.9	4.42	1.367	1.097
	test with respect to rule 2					
5	olives & heineken & coke $\rightarrow$ bourbon	73.7	6.5	-1.65	0.828	0.460
	test with respect to rule 3					
5	olives & heineken & coke $\rightarrow$ bourbon	65.5	3.9	-0.56	0.871	0.763
6	olives & heineken & cracker $\rightarrow$ bourbon	65.5	6.5	2.46	1.114	1.681
	test with respect to rule 4					
6	olives & heineken & cracker $\rightarrow$ bourbon	70.8	7.9	1.43	1.099	1.388

Table 4.3: *Results of evaluating the rules from table 4.2 according to method 1, method 2 and R-interest.*

because of its unexpectedly high support. - A rather disturbing result, when comparing it with the results of statistic T_1 or viewing the rule in figure 4.16 on page 163.
An overview of the results is given in figure 4.11. Crossed out arrows indicate, that the corresponding rule has been rejected according to T_1 with respect to its ancestor. All rules with a test-statistic $T_1 < 1.65$ have been rejected. This value corresponds to the 95% quantile of a standard normal distribution.

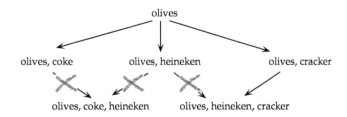

Figure 4.11: *Summary of the left-hand-sides of the rules listed above. Crossed out arrows indicate, that the corresponding rule has been rejected according to T_1 with respect to its ancestor.*

Figure 4.11 leads us to a further property of pruning according to method 1: different ancestors imply different expected values. This opens the way to situations like the one sketched in fig. 4.11, where a rule is pruned with respect to one ancestor but accepted with respect to another (rule 6).

This problem, however, is relatively easy to solve: since we are interested only in rules, which provide some additional information, we may prune any rule, from which we do not gain information with respect to at least one ancestor, as long as this ancestor remains in the set of rules.

Visual Approach   Since two rules are involved in the comparison, we also need two doubledecker plots in order to assess the test result visually. We can either use overlay techniques as shown in figure 4.12, where a rule (on the left, foreground) and its ancestor (on the left, background) are "added" visually (graphic on the right) or use interactive methods, which allow rapid flips between the two different displays. This approach is described later on.

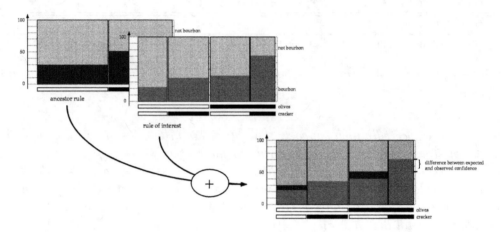

Figure 4.12: *Overlaying doubledecker plots of a rule and its ancestor. The difference of confidences we are examining is marked separately.*

For the overlay technique (see fig. 4.12) the bin to focus on is the last one in all of the plots - since each of the rules $X \to Z$, $X \cap Y \to Z$ and $X \cap Y \cap W \to Z$ corresponds to only one bin of the contingency tables of the variables involved.

Figure 4.13 shows three bins from different doubledecker plots corresponding to the rules 1,3 and 5 from table 4.2. The difference in confidences from the first to the second rule is positive (approx. 50 to 65), whereas the third rule has lower confidence than the second. This rule can definitely be pruned with respect to the second rule: no set of rules containing the second rule can be improved by adding the third rule.

With the help of interactive graphics we may also display expected and observed confidences "together": the special structure of sequences permits transforming the more general ancestor rule into the successor rule by adding further items to it. This has its graphical analogue in adding variables to the doubledecker plot of the ancestor rule and removing them again. If this process is performed fast enough, the observed confidence can be compared with the

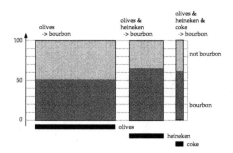

Figure 4.13: *Rectangles from three different doubledecker plots corresponding to the rules number 1, 3 and 5 from table 4.2. The first rule shows approx. 50% of confidence, the second rule has slightly higher confidence, whereas the confidence of the third is lower than that of the second.*

expected, by comparing the actual visible plot with the last one "in mind".
We still have not solved the problem of finding a statistically proper alternative to method 1. The next approach, however, is a step in this direction.

Method 2: Comparing Neighbouring Splits   Instead of testing the confidence of $X \cap Y \to Z$ vs. the confidence of $X \to Z$, another possibility is to test vs. the confidence of $X \cap \neg Y \to Z$. When testing the difference between $P(Z \mid X, Y)$ and $P(Z \mid X, \neg Y)$, we deal with two binomially distributed variables, $Z \mid X, Y$ and $Z \mid X, \neg Y$. Since we can be fairly sure of a high number of cases, this results again in a test statistic, which is $N(0, 1)$ approximately:

$$
\begin{array}{lll}
p_1 = P(Z \mid X, Y) & & p_2 = P(Z \mid X, \neg Y) \\
n_1 = n \cdot P(X \cap Y) & & n_2 = n \cdot P(X \cap \neg Y) \\
H_o : p_1 = p_2 & \text{vs.} & H_1 : p_1 > p_2
\end{array}
$$

$$
\text{test-statistic: } T_2 = \frac{p_1 - p_2}{\sqrt{p(1-p)}} \sqrt{\frac{n_1 n_2}{n_1 + n_2}} \sim N(0, 1),
$$

with $p = P(Z \mid X)(= (n_1 p_1 + n_2 p_2)/(n_1 + n_2))$.
T_2 can be rewritten as

$$
T_2^* = \frac{P(Z \cap Y \mid X) - P(Z \mid X)P(Y \mid X)}{\sqrt{P(Z \mid X)P(\neg Z \mid X) \cdot P(Y \mid X)P(\neg Y \mid X)}} \sqrt{n \cdot P(X)} \sim N(0, 1),
$$

which tests the conditional independence of Y and Z given X.
On the other hand, the square value of the above statistic is asymptotically χ^2 distributed and coincides with the test-statistic of a χ^2 test of independence for a 2×2 table of $Z \mid$

$X, \neg Z \mid X, Y \mid X$ and $\neg Y \mid X$, i.e.

$$T_2 = n \left(\frac{P(Z \cap Y \mid X) - P(Z \mid X)P(Y \mid X)}{\sqrt{P(Z \mid X)P(Y \mid X)}} + \frac{P(Z \cap \neg Y \mid X) - P(Z \mid X)P(\neg Y \mid X)}{\sqrt{P(Z \mid X)P(\neg Y \mid X)}} + \right.$$

$$\left. + \frac{P(\neg Z \cap Y \mid X) - P(\neg Z \mid X)P(Y \mid X)}{\sqrt{P(\neg Z \mid X)P(Y \mid X)}} + \frac{P(\neg Z \cap \neg Y \mid X) - P(\neg Z \mid X)P(\neg Y \mid X)}{\sqrt{P(\neg Z \mid X)P(\neg Y \mid X)}} \right).$$

Proof: simple but lengthy calculation. □

The method for pruning rules is the following: only rules, which show significantly higher confidences than their neighbours are accepted. For the actual performance of this testing procedure we have two possibilities for selecting the neighbours we want to compare with:

a) we can either compare with **all** neighbours - this implies for an accepted rule, that it has a significant maximum confidence among all combinations of its explanatory variables,

b) or we compare only with neighbours of rules given by (accepted) ancestor rules. Figure 4.14 shows the area of acceptance for different confidence and support with respect to one specific ancestor rule (support = 0.3, confidence 0.6).

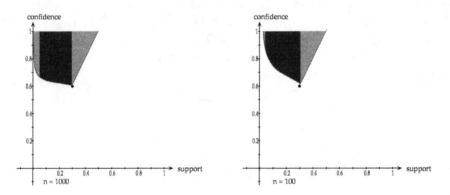

Figure 4.14: *Areas of acceptance (dark gray), based on the results of statistic T_2 and restrictions to the support (support > minsupp).*

These two approaches have, of course, quite different results. Furthermore, they are applicable in different situations with different goals: test statistic a) is a lot stricter than statistic b). There are at least as many tests involved in a) as in b).

Method a) filters out every rule where the explanatory variables split the target variable in more than only one group - an extreme case for this is shown in figure 4.4 on page 143 at the beginning of this section - in the following example several more rules are given. The decision, whether to allow several (different) groups or to mine for only one main group, however, is very restrictive and dependent on the specific application.

The second method is less selective. It is, however, better comparable with the results of method 1. Therefore we will refer to this method if speaking of method 2 and mention 2a explicitly otherwise.

Example 4.1.17 *SAS Assocs Data*
Let us consider again the rules from table 4.2. Comparing neighbouring splits is a less strict test than comparing the confidence of a rule with its ancestor rule. Table 4.4 shows the results

	rule	T_1		T_2 b)		T_2 a)
	test with respect to rule 1					
3	olives & coke → bourbon	*4.690*		*6.418*		
4	olives & cracker → bourbon	*4.420*		*6.633*		
3	olives & heineken → bourbon	*3.290*		*5.179*		*X*
	test with respect to rule 2					
5	olives & heineken & coke → bourbon	*-1.650*	*X*	*-2.417*	*X*	*X*
	test with respect to rule 3					
5	olives & heineken & coke → bourbon	*-0.560*	*X*	*-0.728*	*X*	*-*
6	olives & heineken & cracker → bourbon	*2.460*		*5.513*		*-*
	test with respect to rule 4					
6	olives & heineken & cracker → bourbon	*1.430*	*X*	*3.719*		*X*

Table 4.4: *Test statistics for the rules from table 4.2 based on different ancestor rules. 'X' indicates, that a rule is pruned according to the specified test.*

from testing these rules according to methods 1 and 2. The crosses after some of the test results indicate, that the rule is rejected because of the result on a significance level of 5%, which correspond to a value of the test-statistic of less than 1.65.

T_2 *can not be applied with respect to rule 3, since this rule has already been pruned.*

Visual Approach
Since we are dealing with a special case of intersecting rules in method b), we can use a similar technique as for intersections to visually explore them. For this, we order the left-hand side items according to their appearance in the sequence and start with a doubledecker plot regarding only $X_1 \rightarrow Y$ (see figure 4.15, left most plot). After that, we add the second item, X_2, to the display and look at the effect. In the display, the effect of adding X_2 on the rule $X_1 \rightarrow Y$ has been marked by encircling the difference between $P(Y \mid X_1, X_2)$ and $P(Y \mid X_1, \neg X_2)$ The tile of $X_1 = 1$ is split into two, namely $X_1 \cap X_2$ and $X_1 \cap \neg X_2$. The

support of the resulting rule $X_1 \cap X_2 \to Y$ is still relatively high and, as we had hoped, the split gives us more confidence.

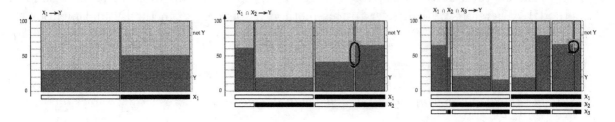

Figure 4.15: *Three doubledecker plots of the rules 1, 3 and 5 of the table.*

Splitting a second time into the combinations $X_1 \cap X_2 \cap X_3$ and $X_1 \cap X_2 \cap \neg X_3$ gives a different result (cf. fig. 4.15, rightmost plot). Here, the support shrinks drastically and at the same time even the confidence is lowered. This allows a clear decision for rejecting the last rule with respect to $X_1 \cap X_2 \to Y$.

Method 2a) is not ancestor based and can therefore be read from any doubledecker plot, independently of the order of the explanatory variables. For an estimate of this method's results we compare the highlighting height of the last bin with the highest highlighting height of all the other bins. If any not too small bin shows higher highlighting proportions, the rule is rejected.

Example 4.1.18 *SAS Assocs Data*
continued from example 4.1.16
Let us again consider the rules from example 4.1.16. Inspecting the left-hand-sides of the rules more closely, several questions arise:

- *Is any of the 3-item rules better (or worse) than the others?*

- *How do the 3-item rules affect the 4-item rules?*

- *Why has the fifth rule less confidence than either of its ancestor rules, rule 2 and rule 3 ?*

For answers to these questions - and to a lot more, which we have not even thought of - have a look at figure 4.16. Here, all doubledecker plots corresponding to the rules of the table are shown.
Plot number 2 and 4 show similar behaviour: rules where both items have been bought together show the highest confidence, while all other rules show relatively low confidences.
Plot number 3 looks more suspicious: here, two combinations have high confidences (above 60%):

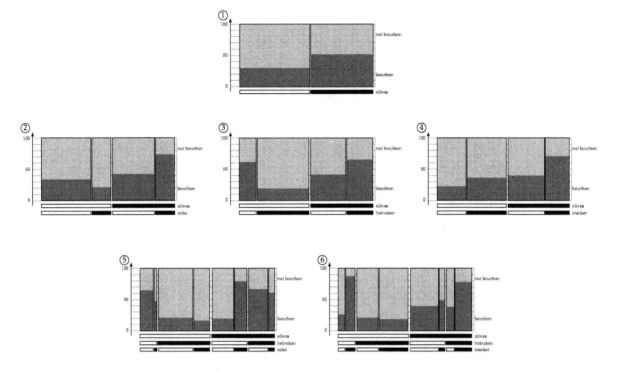

Figure 4.16: *Doubledecker plots corresponding to the rules in table 4.2.*

rule		confidence	support
olives & heineken	$\rightarrow$ *bourbon*	*65.52*	*13.29*
¬ olives & ¬ heineken	$\rightarrow$ *bourbon*	*60.90*	*13.09*

Any left hand side, which includes the same items, will show the same behaviour. This becomes obvious in plot no. 6, a successor of rule 3. Here, again, we deal with two different groups of bourbon-buyers. Two combinations of the variables have very high confidence (≈ 80%). plot no. 5 shows two groups of combinations with relatively high confidences. The important feature here is, however, that the intersection of olives & heineken & coke itself is very small. That means that we again are dealing with two disjoint groups of bourbon buyers: the bourbon & olives & coke buyers and the bourbon & olives & heineken buyers.

Comparing the two Methods

For a comparison of the two methods we consider two different aspects: Above all, of course, the second method is statistically proper. But as we wanted to produce a test which performed equally well as method 1, we have to inspect the two methods more closely. Figure 4.17 shows the areas of acceptance and rejection of the two methods for different threshold values and different numbers of cases.

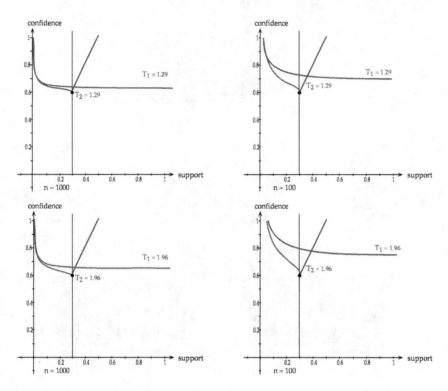

Figure 4.17: *Acceptance/rejection areas of methods 1 and 2 for different threshold values and different numbers of cases.*

Firstly we will compare the statistics T_1 and T_2 behind the tests and secondly, the possibility of visually estimating the value of each statistic.

- The second method is less strict than the first in the sense that on the same level of significance method 1 rejects the null hypothesis earlier than method 2:

  Let us denote the interesting probabilities with $p_1 = P(Z \mid X, Y), p_2 = P(Z \mid X)$ and $p_3 = P(Z \mid X, \neg Y)$. Correspondingly we have $n_1 = nP(X \cap Y), n_2 = nP(X)$ and $n_3 = nP(X \cap \neg Y)$.

  Proof by calculation: square both test statistics and simplify. $\square$

- A clear advantage of the second method is, that it is visually far easier to estimate (in a doubledecker plot e.g.) than the first method.

Where is the first method stricter than the second? From figure 4.17 we can see that T_1, the test statistic of the first method, is a lot larger than T_2, if the difference between the supports of the rules is only small. This effect is intensified, if the number of cases in total is reduced.

Example 4.1.19 *SAS Assoc Data*
*Figure 4.18 shows a scatterplot of the values from test-statistic T_1 against T_2 when pruning all rules with right-hand-side **apples** from the SAS Assoc Data. Each point shows the outcome of T_1 and T_2 of one rule with respect to one of its ancestor rules. The straight line stands for $T_1 = T_2$. What is obvious, is that the absolute values of T_2 are strictly higher than the values of T_1. The occurrence of the line of points together with another cluster well above the*

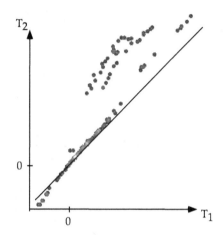

Figure 4.18: *Scatterplot of T_1 vs. T_2. The straight line indicates values, where T_1 and T_2 are equal. The higher strictness of T_1 is obvious.*

line is typical for a plot like this. This has a twofold meaning. The line of points indicates that the second method produces very similar values in comparison to the first method. If we increase the significance level of the second method slightly, it will produce almost identical results.
The reason for the upper cluster of points, however, is of a quite different nature. We will examine this group of points more closely. Highlighting these points reveals, that all of them correspond to rules, where $n_1 = nP(X \cap Y \cap Z)$ is small compared with $n_2 = nP(X \cap \neg Y \cap Z)$ (see figure 4.19).
For a rule $X \cap Y \rightarrow Z$ this means that its ancestor rule $X \rightarrow Z$ has not lost much of its support by splitting the cases according to Y - in other words, we are near the sharp point of the area of acceptance displayed in figure 4.17.
The mosaicplot in figure 4.20 shows a situation like this:
n_1 is relatively large compared with n_2 and at the same time the probabilities $p_1 = P(Z \mid X, Y)$ and $p_2 = P(Z \mid X, \neg Y)$ differ strongly. This large difference in the conditional probabilities

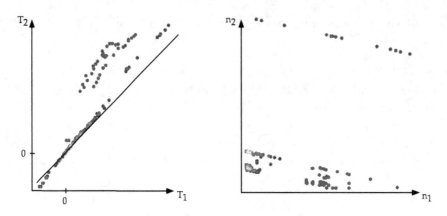

Figure 4.19: *Scatterplots of T_1 vs. T_2 and n_1 vs n_2. Highlighting shows that all points above the straight line of points in the scatterplot on the left correspond to rules with large n_1 and relatively small n_2.*

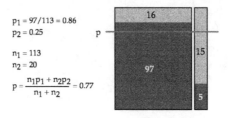

Figure 4.20: *Mosaicplot corresponding to values with very different test statistics T_1 and T_2.*

is the reason, that the test statistic T_2 yields a relatively high value: $T_2 = 5.92$.
On the other hand, T_1 compares the difference between p_1 and the weighted probability p, which is strongly influenced by p_1, since n_1 is large. This difference therefore is quite small, $p_1 - p \approx 0.09$, and T_1 yields a relatively small value, $T_1 = 1.82$.
Hence, the second method tends to wedge off small groups, which differ from the whole. We have to decide, whether we are interested in groups, which are as homogeneous as possible, or whether we want to describe the data with only a few variables.

Examples

The analysis of the data in both examples follows the same scheme:

- we mine all rules first,

- prune them according to their ancestor structure ,

- look at them using doubledecker plots for unusual features (and prune them, if necessary)

- examine the structural dependencies among the rules

- and summarise the results.

The reason for taking the Titanic and the Rochdale Data is that these two data sets are of a size, which still can be handled with analytical methods. So we are able to compare the results from association rules with the ones already known.

The Titanic Data set consists of only four variables and shows some interesting structures, which have been analysed previously e.g. in Friendly (1999), Hofmann (1999) and Theus & Lauer (1999).

Whittaker (1990) analysed the Rochdale data quite thoroughly using loglinear models. However, due to the relatively small number of observations (665) there are a high number of empty cells in the corresponding contingency tables. Whittaker therefore restricted his analysis to two-way interaction models only.

The goal of an analysis with association rules is to find out, whether we come to the same conclusions with this technique and whether more structure is discovered.

Example 4.1.20 *Titanic Data: Mining for Survivors*
Mining for survivors with up to 4 items, a confidence of 50% and a minimum support of 2% results in 9 rules, which are reduced to only 5 after pruning them according to method 1. They are:

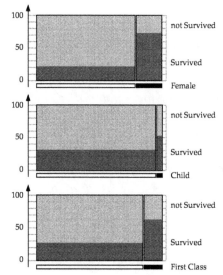

Female → Survival (15.62, 73.19)

Remark: *good rule.*

Child → Survival (2.59, 52.29)

Remark: *little support.*

First Class → Survival   (9.22, 62.46)

Remark: *good rule.*

First Class, Female → Survival
                    (6.40, 97.24)
Remark: *A second combination of the variables also shows high confidence (ca. 60%).*

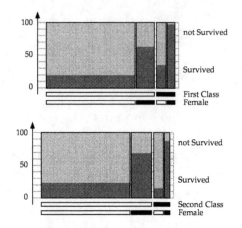

Second Class, Female → Survival
                    (4.22, 87.74)
Remark: *Relatively low support. A second combination of the variables also show a high survival rate (almost 70%).*

Summary:
There are three rules with only one left-hand-side item, one of which has a borderline support of 2.6%. It is not necessary to regard intersections of this rule (Child → Survival) with any of the others, since the support will only be lessened further. The intersection of the other two rules, Female & First Class → Survival appears among the results independently. The remaining intersection contains both the items First and Second Class and is therefore zero by definition.

We therefore deal with three groups of high survival rates: the Children, the Female and the First Class Passengers. The group of the children is rather small, and the two last groups have a high amount of passengers in common (female passengers in the first class represent ca. 7% of all persons on board). From the graphics it also becomes apparent that the rule First & Female → Survival as well as Second & Female → Survival is dominated by the high survival rate of females.

Example 4.1.21 *Mining for (un)employed women in Rochdale*
Whittaker (1990) analysed the Rochdale Data quite thoroughly with log-linear models.
The aim of this analysis was to assess the reasons for the wife's employment. We will concentrate our summary therefore on this point.
*Mining for employed women (**Wife economically active** = yes) with up to 8 items, a confidence of 50% and a minimum support of 3% results in 592 rules, which are reduced to only 12 after pruning them according to method 1.*
*Mining for unemployed women (**Wife economically active** = no) with the same parameters results in 123 rules, which are reduced to only 8 after pruning them according to method 1. For a table of all 20 association rules see A.7.*
*For a better overview of the rules and for better comparability with the results in Whittaker (1990) we will take the same short cuts for the variables as he did. The coding is chosen in such a way that the positive item I has a **positive** correlation with the response, Wife economically active A, and negative items ¬I have a **negative** correlation with A.*

A : *Wife economically active*
B : *Wife older than 38*
C : *Husband employed*
D : *no child, or all children in the household are older than 4*
E : *Wife has at least an O-Level education*
F : *Husband has at least an O-Level education*
G : *Household has **no** Asian origin*
H : *another Household member is working*

Rules with two items all show - with only one exception - relatively high support and a confidence of over 70%. Those of them, which are closely related, are drawn within one doubledecker plot. Reading the second rule can be done by turning the graphic upside down and concentrating on the heights of the non-highlighted parts (shaded in light gray) of the display.

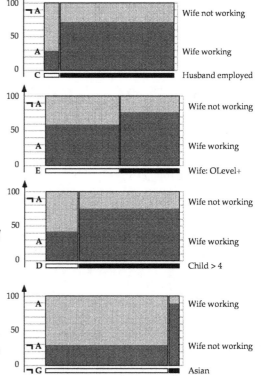

C $\rightarrow$ A   (63.21, 71.84)
$\neg$ C $\rightarrow$ $\neg$ A   (8.41, 70.87)

Remark: *good rules.*

E $\rightarrow$ A   (33.93, 76.61)

Remark: *good rule.*

D $\rightarrow$ A   (56.31, 74.85)
$\neg$ D $\rightarrow$ $\neg$ A   (14.26, 57.93)

Remark: *good rules, the confidence of the second is a bit low.*

$\neg$ G $\rightarrow$ $\neg$ A   (7.21, 88.89)

Remark: *good rule. The support is a bit low, though - this is due to the low numbers of Asian households.*

Summarising, we have three rules, which show a positive effect on the economical activity of women. The number of working women is increased,

- *if their husband is employed,*

- *if there is no child under 4 in the household or*

- *if she has at least an O-Level education.*

Vice versa, there are three negative effects. Women are less likely to be employed,

- *if the husband is not employed,*

- *if there are children under the age of 4 in the household, or*

- *if the household is of Asian origin*

*These altogether four variables of influence to the wife's employment coincide with the significant two-way interactions in Whittaker's all two-way interaction model. He argues against fitting higher interactions than two-way because of too sparse tables. This objection is, of course, relevant for loglinear models, since **all** cells in the corresponding contingency tables have to be estimated. Association rules, however, need fewer parameters, and we may therefore go on with the analysis carefully.*

Rules with three items are:

D,　　E → 　　A　　　(26.88, 84.04)

¬ D, ¬ E → ¬ A　　　(9.01, 73.17)

Remark:　*good rules*

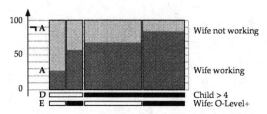

The following rules show a slight, though significant, positive correlation towards economical activity of the wife:

F, H → A (9.01, 80.0)

F, B → A (20.87, 75.96)

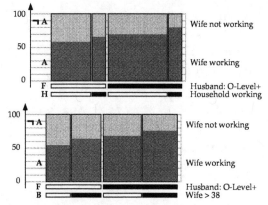

Regarding the two rules above one may also be interested in the intersection of them, F, B, H → A. This rule does not appear among the four-item rules, though it has 7.5% support and 78.1% confidence. Yet, it is pruned from the set of "interesting" rules, since the combination F,H, ¬ B shows an even higher confidence (91.0%).

The following rules have a rather strong negative correlation with economical activity:

¬ C, ¬ D → ¬ A (4.05, 93.10)

Remark: *little support.*

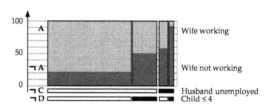

The next three rules only show up, because the rule **not Asian → Wife working** *(G → A) is not significant with respect to its ancestor rule* • → **Wife working**. *Including this one again prunes the others immediately*

G, F → A (40.84, 73.32)

Remark: *very weak rule.*

G, H → A (15.92, 75.18)

Remark: *very weak rule.*

G, B → A (35.59, 73.60)

Remark: *very weak rule.*

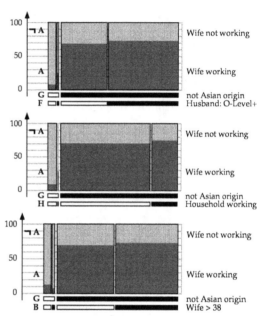

Among the rules with four items we deal with mainly two different groups. The group of rules, which show a positive correlation towards the economical activity of the wife is the group of women aged under 38 without children or children older than 4 years (¬ B ∧ D). The other group, which shows a negative influence on the wife's employment, is the group of women aged under 38 without at least O-Levels education.

All of the rules only show slight tendencies and none of them is very strong. However, we may gain more insight into the structure of the data set, when taking them into account. Rules with positive correlations are:

D, ¬ B, C → A (20.1, 83.2)

Remark: *slight positive correlation*

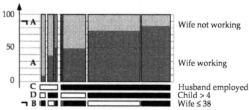

D, ¬ B, F → A (13.7, 85.8)

Remark: *slight positive correlation*

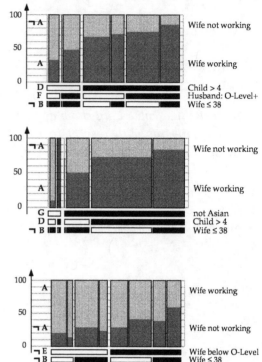

D, ¬ B, G → A (21.0, 83.8)

Remark: *slight positive correlation*

Rules with negative correlations are:

¬ F, ¬ B, ¬ E → ¬ A (7.2, 58.5)

Remark: *slight negative correlation*

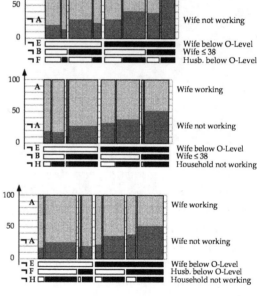

¬ E, ¬ B, ¬ H → ¬ A (10.7, 51.1)

Remark: *slight negative correlation*

¬ H, ¬ E, ¬ F → ¬ A (11.4, 51.4)

Remark: *slight negative correlation*

The group of rules with four items and a negative correlation towards economical activity of the wife comes from combining three items at a time out of a total of the four items {¬F, ¬B, ¬E, ¬H} for the left-hand-sides. Since we have four possible combinations but only three rules, we may look at the missing last rule, ¬F, ¬B, ¬H → ¬A. This rule shows the same slight correlation towards the response as the others. Its confidence, however, is just below the minimum of 50%.

In combination with the positive four-item rules, we see that we deal with two different groups of women, which show also different employment rates:

- *younger women without children have high employment rates, whereas*

- *younger women without an O-Level education show relatively low rates of employment.*

Conclusion: Mining the rules and rating them visually with respect to their quality is made relatively easy by doubledecker plots. The main problem yet to solve is, how to summarise the results. In the next section we describe two kinds of visual summaries.

4.1.4 Summarising Rules

Results can be summarised in different ways according to the different aspects one is interested in. The same is true for association rules. In the following we introduce two different concepts of summarising them. The techniques we use are of a more general nature and can therefore also be extended to other summarising criteria.

The two concepts of summarising are based on two different approaches. The first one (section 4.1.4) is independent from the underlying data set. It only uses the meta-information given by the generated association rules.

The second approach in section 4.1.4 exploits structure, given by the data, based on the amount of intersection between each two rules.

Ancestor Structures

The ancestor relations among rules with the same response correspond to the structure of a directed acyclic graph (*dag*).

Directed acyclic graphs differ from a tree structure insofar, as several nodes may have the same successor.

For a visual display of the ancestor relationships, we will therefore use the means of directed acyclic graphs.

We will visualise the left-hand-side structure of rules with directed graphs according to the following principles:

- each encircled node is the left-hand-side of a rule,

- each rectangularly framed node is an auxiliary node,

- the symbol $\bigcirc$ k describes a set of items, where each k-combination stands for the left hand side of a rule,

- an edge runs from node X to node Y $\iff$ X is an ancestor rule of Y.

Using these graphs, we try to answer questions such as

- do the left-hand-sides build clusters?

- may we separate groups of left-hand-sides?

- are we able to identify important combinations of variables?

- are important combinations missing - and why?

What we can not see is the quality of a single rule - here we depend on the techniques proposed in the previous sections.

Example 4.1.22 *Mining for (un)employed women in Rochdale (cont.)*
The twenty rules from the previous example are summarised in figure 4.21.

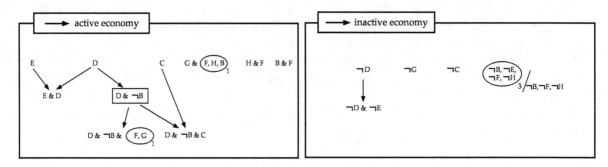

Figure 4.21: *Summary of all association rules from example 4.1.21.*

We are dealing with only a few different groups:

- *We have a strong correlation between* **D**, **E** *and* **A**, *the age of a child (if any) and the level of education of the wife.*

- **D** & ¬ **B** *takes a key position for an active economy. Several combinations with it provide rules. The rule* **D** & ¬ **B** → **A**, *however, does not appear itself - it is pruned with respect to its ancestor* **D** → **A**.

- *Likewise important for an active economy is the fact, whether a household is of Asian origin or not.*

- *The most important factors for an inactive economy is a combination from several social factors: the education of husband and wife, her age and whether another household member is working.*

Example 4.1.23 *SAS Assoc Data*
Figure 4.22 gives an overview of all 20 association rules with right-hand-side **apples***. Three different groups involving altogether only 10 different items can be distinguished. The right-most group consists of one association rule, which on close inspection turns out to be a rather weak rule. The other two groups remain. Using the visualization techniques from the previous section we find out, that these two groups*

- *are almost disjoint, and*

- *describe all apple-buyers.*

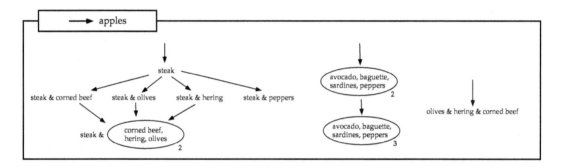

Figure 4.22: *Overview of all association rules with outcome → **apples***.

Data based Dependencies

Toivonen et al (1995) defined the *distance* between two rules with the same right-hand-sides via the number of cases they have in common.

Definition 4.1.24 (Distance between two rules)
The *distance* between two rules $X \to Z$ and $Y \to Z$ is given by (cf. figure 4.23)

$$d(X \to Z, Y \to Z) \quad := \quad n \cdot P\left(((X \cap Z) \cup (Y \cap Z)) \setminus (X \cap Y \cap Z)\right) =$$
$$= \quad nP(X \cap Z) + nP(Y \cap Z) - 2nP(X \cap Y \cap Z).$$

Since we are dealing rules with the same right-hand-side only, we will denote the distance with $d_Z(X, Y)$ for short.

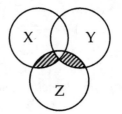

Figure 4.23: *Venn diagram of the basic sets of the rules $X \to Z$ and $Y \to Z$. The hatched area gives the distance as defined by Toivonen et al (1995).*

Lemma 4.1.25

The distance between two rules $d_Z(X, Y)$ fulfills the triangle inequality, i.e.

$$d_Z(U, W) \leq d_Z(U, V) + d_Z(V, W)$$

for all events U, V, W and Z.

Proof: By basic calculation we can transform the left hand side of the above inequality to a form, in which we are able to estimate it versus the right hand side:

$$
\begin{aligned}
\frac{1}{n}\left(d_Z(U, V) + d_Z(V, W)\right) &= P(U \cap Z) + P(V \cap Z) - 2P(U \cap V \cap Z) + \\
&\quad + P(W \cap Z) + P(V \cap Z) - 2P(V \cap W \cap Z) \geq^{(*)} \\
&= P(U \cap Z) + P(W \cap Z) - 2P(U \cap V \cap W \cap Z) \geq \\
&\geq P(U \cap Z) + P(W \cap Z) - 2P(U \cap W \cap Z) = \frac{1}{n} d_Z(U, W).
\end{aligned}
$$

$(*)$ holds, since

$$P(V \cap Z) \geq P(U \cap V \cap Z) + P(V \cap W \cap Z) - P(U \cap V \cap W \cap Z).$$

$\square$

Remark 4.1.26

$d_Z(X, Y)$ defines a distance, since

- $d_Z(X, X) = 0$, the distance is idempotent,

- $d_Z(X, Y) = 0 \iff$ the rules $X \to Z$ and $Y \to Z$ describe **exactly** the same population,

- the triangle inequality holds.

The distance information can then (alternatively) be included in graphs from the previous section using lines with different widths.

We have to note, though, that the width of lines can only be used as a very crude approximation to the actual number, the human eye can distinguish only a few (up to 10 at most) different line widths (Fellner (1988), Lauer (1997)). One problem using this distance is that it is strongly dependent on the support the two rules have.

Alternatively, one could therefore weight the distance with the support a rule has and show proportional intersections among rules. The width of an edge between rules $X \to Z$ and $Y \to Z$ then corresponds to

$$\frac{d_Z(X,Y)}{n\sqrt{P(X \cap Z)P(Y \cap Z)}}. \tag{4.1}$$

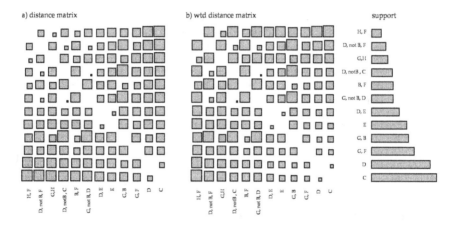

Figure 4.24: *Matrix of the distances among the rules for an active economy (see example 4.1.21). The rules are sorted according to their support.*

Another possibility to visualise distances is to show a square matrix of distances as described in section 2.5. Figure 4.24 shows a matrix of all distances among the rules for an active economy of example 4.1.21. On the left the unweighted distances are shown, on the right the weighted version as proposed in (4.1).

Toivonen et al (1995) performed a cluster analysis of the rules based on the unweighted distances. We have ordered the rules in such a way that clusters among them are easy to see (cf. figure 4.25):

cluster	rules
1	all 4-item rules
2	H & F $\rightarrow$ A, H & G $\rightarrow$ A
3	$\{G, B, F\}_2 \rightarrow$ A
4	E $\rightarrow$ A, D & E $\rightarrow$ A
5	D $\rightarrow$ A, C $\rightarrow$ A

In this representation the difference between the weighted and unweighted version is also better visible. The main differences appear among those rules, where one of them has a relatively small support. In figure 4.25 the largest differences have been highlighted.

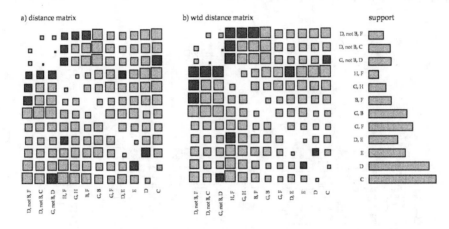

Figure 4.25: *Matrix of the distances among the rules for an active economy, the rules are ordered to make clusters among them visible. Highlighted are rectangles with the largest differences between weighted and unweighted distance.*

4.1.5   Rules and Decision Trees

The concepts of association rules and decision trees are fairly equal. Both are multivariate tools for finding structures among the variables according to a target variable. For association rules, however, the target variable is not specified before the searching process, but we are provided with possible target variables afterwards.

Using the ancestor structure we can impose on sequences of association rules with the same response variable a tree like structure. This enables us to make more precise predictions on expected values of successor rules and we may use this structure for summarising the results. One obvious difference to trees, however, is that one association rule may and usually will have more than one ancestor. We are dealing therefore with an acyclic directed graph (*dag*). We exploit the ancestor/ successor relationship for pruning in the same way as we do with decision trees.

There is one major difference between pruning rules and pruning trees: when snipping a node n from a tree, we prune the whole subtree with root n. With association rules we may prune a single rule and nevertheless keep all of its successor rules. This makes pruning rules easier. As Breiman (1984) pointed out in the context of pruning trees, a major drawback to the intuitive pruning of a tree by stopping its growth at a node, when we do not gain significantly by splitting it, is that a weak split may be followed by a very good split. This problem does not exist for association rules. We could therefore also use pruning or stopping rules for tree growth, such as the AIC (an information criterion) by Akaike (1973) or the more general rule by Breiman (1984):

$$R_\alpha = R + \alpha \cdot size,$$

where besides the test of homogeneity within the nodes of a tree also the number of final nodes (leaves of a tree) is regarded.

In contrast to rules from decision trees different association rules do not describe disjoint populations. This is both a blessing and a curse - the disadvantages are obvious:

- we may describe only parts of the total population, or

- there may be contradictory results for rules with largely the same basis population

On the other hand, we may gain from these disadvantages.

- there may be no answer for a part of the population, and

- different results for similar groups indicate, that a decision with respect to the target is at least problematic.

Secondly, the approach of association rules was to find **all** associations among the variables - in order to avoid the problems from a greedy technique. This of course generates the problem of dealing with a massive output.

4.1.6 Visual Comparison of Several Association Rules

We now proceed with a different approach than before. Now we want to concentrate on association rules only without regarding their high-dimensional background, i.e. only support and confidence.

This has the advantage that we are able to visualise a large number of association rules at the same time.

Matrix of Association Rules

Commercial datamining software such as IBM's Intelligent Miner provides several possibilities to visualise association rules. Figure 4.26 shows two of them for the visualization of 2-item rules (i.e. one item in the body of the rule, one in the head of it). plot a) is similar to the approach of the SAS Enterprise Miner (cf. fig. 4.1). It shows a matrix of association rules with two items each, the color denotes different confidence levels. plot b) shows the same rules. Each association rule is drawn as a bar, starting from a matrix of all combinations of body and head items. The height of each bar denotes the confidence, the color gives the support the rule. Both approaches have in common, that for visualising 2-D and 3-D objects

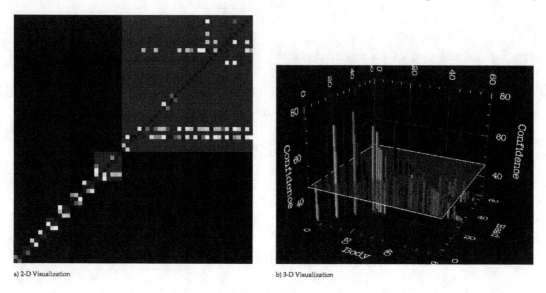

a) 2-D Visualization   b) 3-D Visualization

Figure 4.26: *2 and 3 D Visualization of association rules with two items.*

three and four dimensions are used, respectively (We have to count colour as an additional dimension). This, however, is not necessary. We want to show, how we may use the available dimensions more efficiently.

The basic idea is to visualise a single association rule not as square but as rectangle - this provides us with an additional dimension. After that the use of only one additional colour helps us to gain insight into rules with up to 4-items instead the 2-items as shown above:

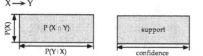

Support and confidence of each rule $X \rightarrow Y$ between two events X and Y can be visualised as a rectangle as follows (see the sketch on the left):

- the *area* of the rectangle is given by $supp(X, Y)$,

- the *height* of the rectangle corresponds to $supp(X)$,

its *width* therefore is $P(X \cap Y)/P(X) = P(Y \mid X)$, the *confidence - visual* of $X \to Y$.

Similar to the visualization techniques introduced above, we plot a matrix of all right hand side items of the rules (response events) vs. the left hand side items (explanatory events). Yet, we want to visualise (by a rectangle as described above) *all* possible combinations between columns and rows. Each column gets the same width, the heights of the rows depend on the corresponding event's probability.

What we are looking for in the plots are relatively large bins (corresponding to a large support) that at the same time have larger widths than heights.

Example 4.1.27 *SAS Assoc Data*
fig. 4.27 shows a matrix of all possible association rules. One of the obvious features (marked

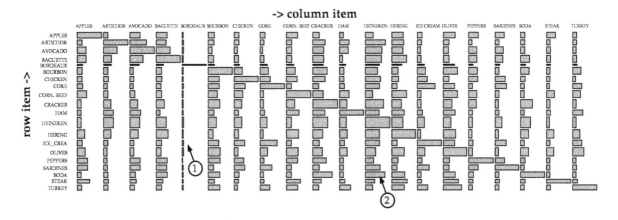

Figure 4.27: *Matrix of all possible association rules (with two items) from the assocs dataset.*

*with a circled 1) of this plot is the empty column of $\cdot \to$ **bordeaux**, indicating, that buying **bordeaux** is not a reaction to buying any of the other items. The rectangle marked with the circled 2 represents the rule **soda** $\to$ **heineken**. The support of it is fairly large, since the bin's area is large. The confidence of the rule corresponds to the width of the bin and is therefore also relatively high.*

Additional Highlighting
With the means of highlighting we get access to association rules with a higher number of items.

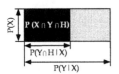

Using two different aspects of the highlighting proportions we are able to look at two different rules at the same time. Let H be some highlighted transactions, then:

1. $X \rightarrow Y \cap H$

   The *absolute width* of highlighting gives $P(Y \cap H \mid X)$, which is the confidence of rule $X \rightarrow Y \cap H$.

2. $X \cap Y \rightarrow H$

   The *proportion* of highlighted area and total area of a bin is

   $$\frac{P(X \cap Y \cap H)}{P(X \cap Y)} = P(H \mid X \cap Y), \text{ the confidence of rule } X \cap Y \rightarrow H$$

Example 4.1.28 *SAS Assocs Data*

Let's consider the following two association rules from the Assocs Data,

rule	conf	supp
sardines → chicken	45.61	12.26
sardines → coke	49.66	14.69

which are visible as rectangles in figure 4.28.

Figure 4.28: *Rectangles of the association rules sardines → chicken and sardines → coke. Highlighted are transactions including coke & ice cream.*

All transactions including the items **coke & ice cream** *are highlighted. As described above, we can either concentrate on the absolute number of highlighted cases or on the proportion of highlighted cases vs the total cases in each of the bins. Each of the views provides us with two more association rules:*

1. *absolute number of highlighted cases:*

rule $(X \rightarrow Y \cap H)$	conf	supp
sardines → chicken & coke & ice cream	39.39	11.59
sardines → coke & ice cream	44.59	13.19

2. *proportions of highlighting*

rule $(X \cap Y \rightarrow H)$	conf	supp
sardines & chicken → coke & ice cream	85.93	11.59
sardines & coke → ice cream	78.91	13.19

Remark 4.1.29

(i) What becomes obvious from the example is, that the two different methods for gaining association rules can be applied in different situations:

The first method provides rules, which are weaker both with respect to the confidence and support - yet, the statement the new rule makes is stronger than its parent rule ("people buy **also** H").

Rules derived by using the second method also lose with respect to the support, yet, here the hope is to gain confidence by intensifying the conditions ("people buy Y **after** buying X **and** H").

(ii) Note the difference between the rules used in the example: the first rule, *sardines → chicken*, is independent from the highlighted values (*coke & ice cream*), whereas highlighting and the second rule, *sardines → coke*, have one item in common. This, of course, determines, which rules are gained from method 1 and 2.

In the example $X = sardines$, $Y = coke$ and $H = coke \ \& \ ice \ cream$.

The rule from method 1 then is
$$sardines \ \to \ coke \ \& \ (coke \ \& \ ice \ cream) \quad \equiv$$
$$sardines \ \to \ coke \ \& \ ice \ cream.$$

Method 2 supplies us with rule
$$sardines \ \& \ coke \ \to \ coke \ \& \ ice \ cream \quad \equiv$$
$$sardines \ \& \ coke \ \to \ ice \ cream.$$

Example 4.1.30 *SAS Assoc Data*
Figure 4.29 shows the matrix of all possible association rules with two items. Highlighted are all transactions that include **coke & ice cream**. *By viewing cells with a large area*

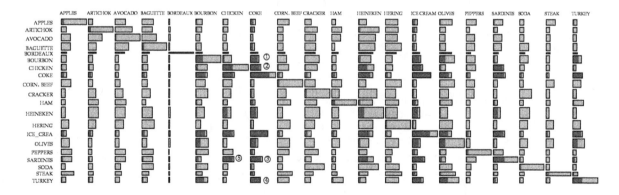

Figure 4.29: *Matrix of all (2-item) association rules with additional highlighting. Highlighted is the combination* **coke & ice cream**.

($\propto$ support) of highlighting, we regard rules of the form $X \to Y \cap H$, this results e.g. in

No	rule	supp	conf
1	bourbon → coke & ice cream	117	$117/403 \approx 0.29$
2	chicken → coke & ice cream	123	$123/315 \approx 0.39$
3	sardines → coke & ice cream	132	$132/296 \approx 0.45$
4	turkey → coke & ice cream	106	$106/283 \approx 0.37$
5	sardines → chicken & coke & ice cream	116	$116/296 \approx 0.59$

Rules according to the second pattern, where we regard proportions of highlighting in cells are:

No	rule	supp	conf
1	bourbon & coke → ice cream	117	$117/140 \approx 0.84$
2	chicken & coke → ice cream	123	$123/139 \approx 0.88$
3	sardines & coke → ice cream	132	$132/147 \approx 0.90$
4	turkey & coke → ice cream	106	$106/119 \approx 0.89$
5	sardines & chicken → coke & ice cream	116	$116/135 \approx 0.86$

Besides the 3- and 4-item association rules we also get insight into the structure among the variables - and we are able to identify (not necessarily disjoint) clusters of variables with this technique:

*Highlighting the combination **coke & ice cream** shows for instance their link to the variables **bourbon, chicken, heineken, olives, sardines & turkey**. More specifically:*

Highlighting	Linked variables
coke & ice cream	bourbon, chicken, heineken, olives, sardines, turkey
artichoke & apples	baguette, peppers, sardines
artichoke & avocado	baguette, cracker, ham, heineken, herring
artichoke & baguette	avocado, heineken, herring

Matrix of rules and power of rules

To visualise an association rule together with its *doc* we introduce the concept of a *Flag-plot* (see fig. 4.30). Beyond the rectangle of the association rule $X \to Y$, another rectangle is drawn corresponding to the rule $\neg X \to Y$. The difference in the widths then represents the difference of confidences $P(Y \mid X) - P(Y \mid \neg X) = doc(X \to Y)$ (cf. section 4.1.3).

Example 4.1.31 *SAS Assoc Data*
Figure 4.31 shows an example of the following six association rules:

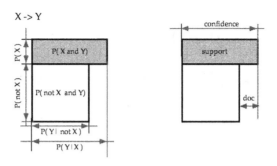

Figure 4.30: *Schematic Flag plot.*

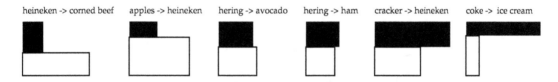

Figure 4.31: *Six selected association rules - sorted according to doc and lift.*

	Rule		support	confidence	lift	doc
heineken	$\rightarrow$	*corned beef*	*0.12*	*0.21*	*0.54*	*-0.45*
apples	$\rightarrow$	*heineken*	*0.10*	*0.34*	*0.56*	*-0.39*
herring	$\rightarrow$	*avocado*	*0.17*	*0.34*	*0.97*	*-0.02*
herring	$\rightarrow$	*ham*	*0.16*	*0.32*	*1.09*	*+0.05*
cracker	$\rightarrow$	*heineken*	*0.37*	*0.75*	*1.25*	*+0.34*
coke	$\rightarrow$	*ice cream*	*0.22*	*0.74*	*2.40*	*+0.61*

Figure 4.34 shows a graphical variation of the matrix in fig. 4.27. Together with the rectangle corresponding to the association rule between an explanatory item and its response also the **negative** *rule is shown. From the difference in the rectangles' heights the rule's doc can be seen.*

Plotting confidence vs. support

A scatterplot of confidence vs. support lets the data appear on straight lines (see fig. 4.32). The reason for this is simple. Let $X \rightarrow Y$ be an association rule, then

$$\frac{conf\ (X \rightarrow Y)}{supp\ (X \rightarrow Y)} = \frac{P(Y \mid X)}{P(X \cap Y)} = \frac{1}{P(X)},$$

i.e. for each left hand side X, there is a straight line, on which all data points $X \rightarrow Y$ appear with increasing confidences (starting from the origin). The line of points with 100%

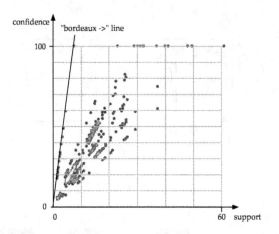

Figure 4.32: *Confidence vs. support of all 2 item rules in the Assocs Data.*

confidence shows rules of the form $X \to X$ - the single items therefore are sorted according to their sizes (smallest is bordeaux on the very left, largest single item is heineken - on the very right side). Direct comparisons between rules, which lie on vertical or horizontal lines

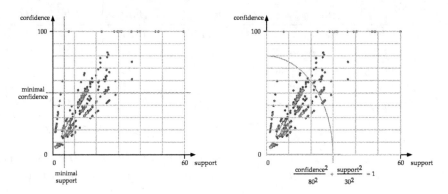

Figure 4.33: *Two different principles of accepting rules. On the left, the traditional area of acceptance with specified minimal confidence and minimal support. On the right a possible alternative.*

are now possible: if two rules have the same confidence, the one with the higher support is better (the same is true for two rules with the same support).

Accepted rules therefore (see sketch 4.33, left side) fall in a rectangle bounded by *minconf* and *minsupp*. Alternatively, one can also think of a different criterion for accepting rules. The right hand side of sketch 4.33 shows an area of acceptance, where a low support can be balanced by a high confidence and vice versa. Using interactive selection methods and

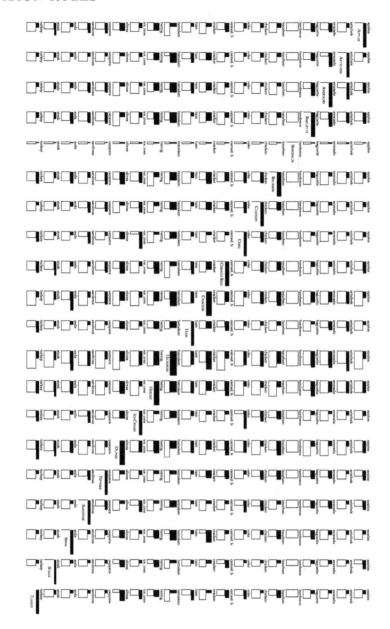

Figure 4.34: *Association rules of the Assocs data and corresponding docs.*

linking we have a lot more choices for criteria of acceptance, all of which may be sensible in the background of a specific application.

4.2   Classification Trees

4.2.1   Visualising Trees

There are several possibilities to visualise trees. The most important decision for visualising a tree structure is the **aspect**, which is to be emphasised.
In the sequel three different concepts are introduced:

- Visualization of the hierarchy:

  show all nodes and splits generated during the tree growing.

- Visualization of the variables' space (measurement space)

  each bin corresponds to one leaf in the tree graph.

- Visualization of the relationship between the data points and the tree model.

The most common display, of course, is the standard tree graph (see figure 4.35), consisting of root and derived nodes.

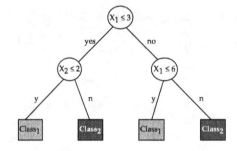

Figure 4.35: *Standard visualization of a classification tree. Leaves are labelled with the category they represent.*

An alternative is shown in figure 4.36 a). This display has already been proposed in Breiman (1984):

> *"An equivalent way of looking at this tree is that it divides the unit square as shown in Figure 2.9. From this geometric viewpoint, the tree procedure recursively partitions X into rectangles such that the populations within each rectangle become more and more class homogeneous."*   p.31

Sometimes also dots are added to it to give an approximation of the size of each leaf. If we deal with only two continuous variables, we are even able to draw the corresponding scatterplot within the measurement space (see figure 4.36 b).

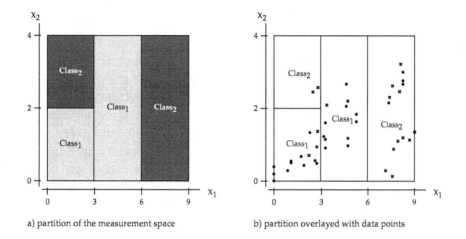

a) partition of the measurement space

b) partition overlayed with data points

Figure 4.36: *Hierarchical partition of the measurement space. On the right, the data points are displayed additionally.*

Instead of considering the measurement space we also can concentrate on the number of data points within each leaf and show a similar recursive partitioning of the data space (see figure 4.37 a). The size of each rectangle now corresponds to the number of cases within the leaf. This is exactly the concept of a mosaicplot. The hierarchy of a tree is more general than that of a mosaic, since nodes of the same level may be split according to different variables.

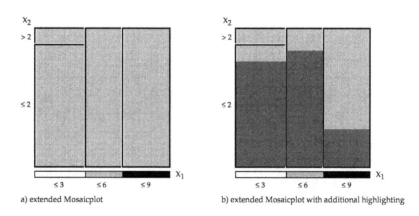

a) extended Mosaicplot

b) extended Mosaicplot with additional highlighting

Figure 4.37: *Two extended mosaicplots displaying the tree of figure 4.35. On the right, values of Class 1 are highlighted additionally.*

Extended Mosaicplots (cf. section 2.8) are powerful enough to visualise a tree.
Highlighting proportions (see figure 4.37 b) show additionally the assignment of each leaf to target class 1 or 2 (if the proportion of area with highlighting is higher than the unhighlighted

area a node is assigned to class 1, otherwise to class 2) as well as the leaf's misclassification rate.

Figure 4.38 shows two further aspects of the classification above. Extensions of doubledecker plots are used to display the tree data. Now, it is possible to compare highlighting heights between nodes on different levels. On the right of figure 4.38 the bins are sorted according to the highlighting heights. This gives a way to distinguish nodes in those, where the classification is "clear" - on either side of the plot, and those, where the tree does not separate the classes clearly - nodes with approx. 50% highlighting, in the middle of the plot.

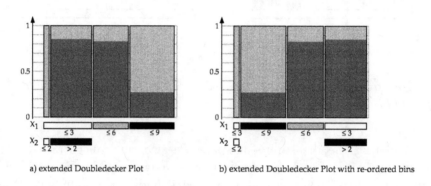

a) extended Doubledecker Plot

b) extended Doubledecker Plot with re-ordered bins

Figure 4.38: *Extended doubledecker plots of the tree in figure 4.35. On the right, the bins are ordered according to highlighting heights.*

Different views emphasise different aspects. The tree graph reflects the hierarchy of the splits and the structure of the classification model, the partition of the measurement shows the placement of each leaf in the measurement space, while the (extended) mosaicplot concentrates on the data and shows the number of cases in the leaves. Together with additional highlighting mosaics also give an estimate of the classification and misclassification within each leaf.

Example 4.2.1 *Rochdale Data*
Figure 4.39 shows a classification tree together with the corresponding mosaicplot. Goal of the classification was to describe households, where the wife was economically active.

Figure 4.40 shows two spineplots of the nine leaves. The bottom row displays the same bins sorted according to highlighting proportions. On either side of this display "unproblematic" bins are collected, i.e. those branches of the tree, where the classification works fine. The bins in the middle are those, where the entropy is high (less class homogeneous).

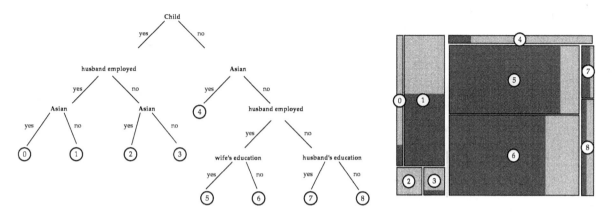

Figure 4.39: *Tree and accompanying mosaicplot*
Target of the classification are households, where the wife is economically active.

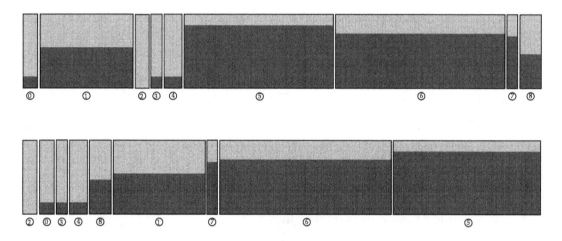

Figure 4.40: *Spineplots of the leaves in the classification tree in figure 4.39.*
Households, where the wife is economically active, are highlighted.

4.2.2 Growing a Tree

Let the target be binary (c_1 or c_2). For each of the explanatory variables $X_1, \ldots, X_p$ do the following:

Define a *split value* for variable X_i (starting with the variable's minimal value). Set up the following table:

	target	
	c_1	c_2
$X_i \leq$ split value	n_{11}	n_{12}
$X_i >$ split value	n_{21}	n_{22}

These are the sufficient statistics for several splitting criteria, such as CHAID, entropy or the Gini index.

Split the node according to the best split value and variable.

There are mainly three families of different splitting criteria.

1. The CART family (CART , IND CART , Splus CART , etc.)

2. The ML family (ID3, C4.5, C5 and other derivatives, etc.)

3. The AID family (THAID, CHAID, XAID, TREEDISC, etc.)

Where are the differences between these tree classifiers - what do they have in common? The main difference between them lies in the splitting criterion they use: Breiman (1984) defined for each node a measure of *impurity*.

Definition 4.2.2 (impurity of a node)

Let $c_1, \ldots, c_K$ be the values of the target variable and $P(c_i \mid n), i = 1, \ldots, K$, the (estimated) probability of class c_i in node n (then $\sum_{i=1}^{K} P(c_i \mid n) = 1$).

The *impurity* of a node n is a nonnegative function $i(n)$ such that

- $i(n)$ has its only maximum for $P(c_1 \mid n) = \ldots = P(c_K \mid n) = \frac{1}{K}$, i.e. the node is as "impure" as possible.

- $i(n)$ is minimal if $\exists i \in 1, \ldots, K$ such that $P(c_i \mid n) = 1$, i.e. the node contains only cases, which have the same target value.

Some very common splitting criteria based upon impurity measures are:

- Entropy

$$i(n) = - \sum_{j=1}^{K} P(j|n) \log P(j|n).$$

- the Gini index of diversity

$$i(n) = \sum_{i \neq j} P(i|n) P(j|n).$$

Another splitting rule, which is not based on an impurity measure, is the *twoing rule*: A node n is split into a left and a right node n_L and n_R such that

$$\frac{P(n_L)P(n_R)}{4} \left(\sum_{j=1}^{K} |P(j \mid n_L) - P(j \mid n_R)| \right)^2$$

is maximised. For binary targets this rule coincides with the CHAID criterion, which calculates the χ^2 value of a 2×2 table.

Breiman (1984), p. 38, concluded that

> within a wide range of splitting criteria the properties of the final tree selected are surprisingly insensitive to the choice of splitting rule

Hand (1997) p. 69, however, mentioned several problems concerning impurity functions for splitting nodes, for instance

> It [the Gini index] has a tendency to produce offspring nodes that are of equal size.

Unfortunately, there is no such thing as an optimal splitting criterion. "Optimal" splits very strongly depend on the specific application. Visualization techniques are asked for to ease the decision, which criterion to choose.

Linking between the nodes of different trees, for instance, helps to figure out, whether some values are notoriously classified badly - which could be a hint, that an important explanatory variable is still missing - or if a mixture of several trees would help to gain an overall better classification.

In the sequel we will discuss some approaches to these questions by means of interactive graphics.

4.2.3 Adding Basic Interactive Features

- selection of nodes (linking)

- interactive querying

- warnings

- changing the hierarchy

- changing the display

Example 4.2.3 *Letter Recognition*
The goal of this data set is to identify a set of pixels as one of the letters 'A' to 'Z'. Not the pixels themselves are recorded but several statistics of them, such as mean number of black pixels in x and y direction, number of black pixels in total, width and height of the black area, . . .

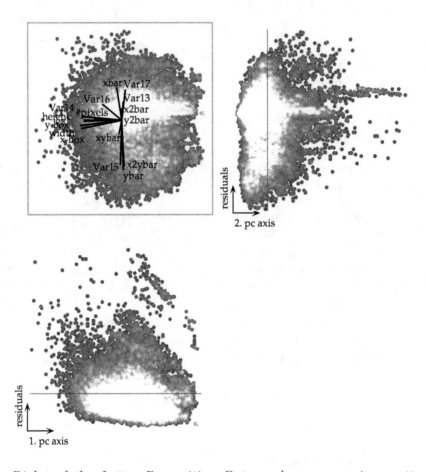

Figure 4.41: *Biplot of the Letter Recognition Data and accompanying scatterplots of the residuals. The residuals show patterns and some outliers.*

Figure 4.41 shows a biplot of all 17 pixel statistics together with two scatterplots of the residual values. The residual plots show some patterns as well as outliers - the first two principal components cover only 43.2 % of the correlation, which in total makes a principal component analysis not a satisfying solution. But — together with highlighting, the graphic reveals several nice properties of the data: highlighting in the biplots of figure 4.42 shows letters 'A', 'K', 'L' and 'O' one after the other. It becomes clear that each letter appears

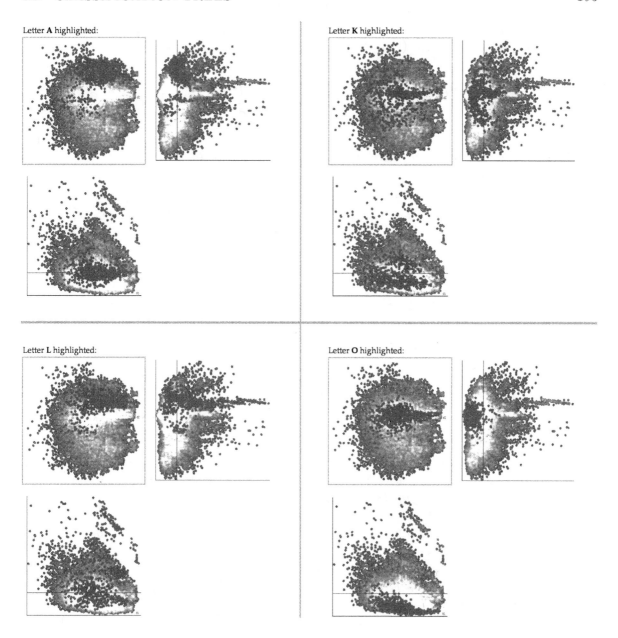

Figure 4.42: *Biplots with highlighting: highlighted are (from left to right) the letters 'A', 'K', 'L' and 'O'.*

only in a small partition of the measurement space - the goal of trees will be to describe this partition in terms of the variables. Since the letters in the data set were generated from different fonts, we may gain an additional piece of information from the biplot display: an estimate of the number of different groups a letter has in the measurement space. The letters 'L', 'L' and 'L' look different and will be described by different pixel-statistics.

The lower residual plot of letter 'L' shows an interesting structure among the highlighted values. Three different clusters appear, indicating that there exist at least three different groups among the 'L's.

A classification tree of 'L', see figure 4.43 gives the same result. Using the linking structure we find that, indeed, the same three groups are involved in both plots.

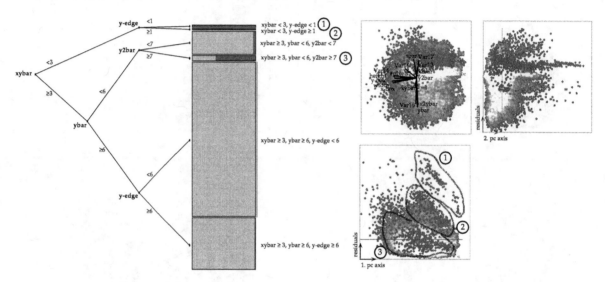

Figure 4.43: *Classification tree and biplot of the Letter Recognition Data. Response of the tree is the letter 'L'. Mainly three different groups among the 'L's appear in the tree. These three groups are also visible in the lower residual plot.*

*The mosaicplot of **xbar** and **ybar** in figure 4.44 shows basically the same three groups of 'L's. The third group, though, is only visible from the red frames around the rectangles. This indicates that there are some highlighted values in the rectangles but too few to visualise them compared with the total numbers in the rectangles. These values can not be distinguished from the other values in the rectangles, which means that all values of group 3 are misclassified in this mosaicplot.*

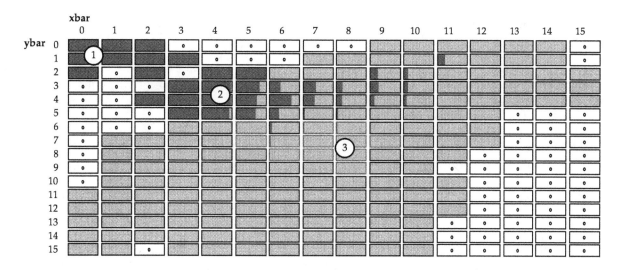

Figure 4.44: *Mosaicplot of **xbar** and **ybar**. Values corresponding to the letter 'L' are highlighted. Again, the same three groups as in fig. 4.43 are visible. The third group, though, is only visible in a "negative" form: the red framed rectangles contain some highlighted values, but to few to visualise them compared to the total numbers within.*

Summary   This section sketches briefly the possibilities for working with classification trees in an interactive setting. Identifying groups and verifying a proposed classification by means of other displays and different methods allows a basic form of graphical cross classification. The approach of doubledecker plots is suitable for comparing and combining several trees.

4.3   Bayesian Networks

Bayesian networks are a tool widely used for the analysis of relationships among a set of variables based upon the structure of conditional (in)dependencies. Crucial for an analysis is the model selection, i.e. a way to decide, how well a network structure fits the prior knowledge and the data. Several techniques have been proposed in the literature including the optimization of different criteria or averaging over a number of models.

The drawbacks are obvious: single numbers are certainly not very well suited for reflecting complex structures, while model averaging may be very computer intensive.

In the sequel we want to propose an approach, which in other areas of data analysis has already been very well established: we want to provide facilities to look at both the data and the results graphically. Though there exist various methods for visualising multivariate data, it is by far not explored as well, how to visualise conditional dependencies. We will develop easy to use methods from interactive statistical graphics which tackle this problem.

Features of interest are

- a measure for the strength of a dependency,

- a more detailed description of the dependencies among a clique of variables,

- as well as conclusions on higher-dimensional associations.

We will show through a set of examples, how these questions can be answered using basic tools of interactive statistical graphics.

4.3.1 Preliminaries

A Bayesian network for a set of variables X is an encoding of the joint probability distribution for X. It consists of a set of local probability distributions associated with each variable combined with a set of assertions of conditional independence that allow one to construct the joint distribution from local distributions.

A Bayesian network structure is a *directed acyclic graph* (dag) with the following properties:

- each variable in X corresponds to a node. For notational convenience we will equate a node with its variable,

- $\Pi_i := \Pi(X_i)$ is the set of parents of X_i,

- $\forall X_i \in \mathcal{X}$ holds $p(X_i|\mathcal{X}\backslash X_i) = p(X_i|\Pi_i)$.

The structure of a *dag* ensures, that a variable X_i is conditionally independent of all the variables in $\mathcal{X}$ given its parents (based on the decomposition condition by Lauritzen (1996)). Nodes can be classified according to their number of parents and children into three types:

- **explanatory:** number of parents is zero, arbitrary number of children,

- **response:** these nodes do not have any children, but may have any number of parents

- and **intermediate** nodes: these nodes have both children and parents.

One problem, though, with the classification of nodes results from the possibility that edges may be reversed sometimes without changing the underlying distribution.

Equivalence of Graphs

Definition 4.3.1

(i) The *skeleton* of a dag is the undirected graph resulting from ignoring the directionality of every edge.

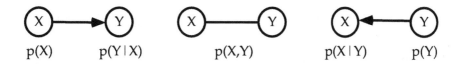

Figure 4.45: *Three equivalent graphical models of X and Y.*

(ii)   An edge $X \to Y$ is **covered**, if the parent sets of X and Y coincide: $\Pi(X) \cup X = \Pi(Y)$.

(iii) Two nodes X and Y are **adjacent** in a dag S, if either $X \to Y \in S$ or $Y \to X \in S$.

(iv)   A v-structure in a dag is an ordered triple of nodes (X, Y, Z), such that the dag contains $X \to Y$ and $Z \to Y$ and X and Z are not adjacent.

(v)   Two dags are **equivalent**, if the sets of distributions that can be represented are identical.

The following statements are quoted, since they are basic tools for working with Bayesian networks. Proofs can be found in any standard literature on Bayesian networks, e.g. in Heckerman et al. (1994) or Barlow & Pereira (1992).

Theorem 4.3.2
Two dags are equivalent, iff they have the same skeleton and v-structure.

Lemma 4.3.3
An edge can be reversed in a dag with respect to the equivalence structure, iff it is covered.

Theorem 4.3.4
Any two equivalent dags can be transformed into each other by several reversions of covered edges.

4.3.2   Using Interactive Graphics

What are features of interest?

- **Strength of a dependency**

  the strength corresponds essentially to a number between 0 and 1 and often has already (very crudely, see Lauer (1997)) been encoded within a Bayesian network via the thickness of an edge,

- a more detailed **description of the relationship** between a clique of variables,

- conclusions on **three-way dependencies** (and higher).

We will show approaches to solve these problems in the following example.

Example 4.3.5 *Rochdale*
Figure 4.46 shows a Bayesian network of the Rochdale Data using uninformative priors: None of the edges is reversible without adding further edges to the network. **Husband's Education** *is spotted as the only explanatory variable,* **Asian** *and* **household member working (household** *for short) are classified as response. This network, of course, can only suggest (data driven) the dependencies among the variables, since - using uninformative priors - no prior information has been given to the system, which explains the somewhat awkward classification into explanatory and response variables.*

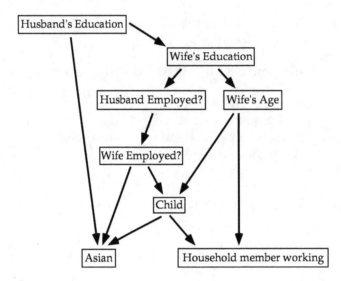

Figure 4.46: *Bayesian network of the Rochdale Data.*

Wife's Age *and* **Child** *are given as parents of* **household.** *Figure 4.47 shows two mosaicplots, which allow a closer inspection of the dependencies between* **household** *and* **Wife's Age** *resp.* **Child.** *It becomes visible that the probability of a working household member is a lot higher, if either the wife is older than 38 (about five times higher) or no child under four is in the household (almost seven times higher).*
Neither figure 4.46 nor 4.47 allow conclusions on higher dimensional dependencies between the variables, such as e.g., whether it is the same households, where there is a child under four and the wife under 38. Figure 4.46 at least shows that a dependency between **Wife's Age** *and* **Child** *exists. But it is not clear at all, in what way* **household** *is affected by this, since this would be a three way relationship - and Bayesian networks can not deal with those. Figure 4.48 shows two mosaicplots of* **Wife's Age** *and* **Child.** *The dependency between those two variables is fairly strong: there are e.g. only very few households with small children where the wife is older than 38.*

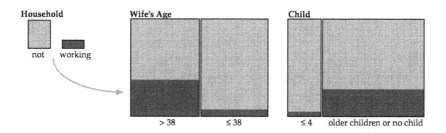

Figure 4.47: *Mosaicplots of **Wife's Age** and **Child**.*
*Highlighted are **households**, where at least one member - besides husband or wife - is working.*

*The mosaic on the right of fig. 4.48 shows an additional dimension (included via highlighting). There are several interesting things to notice: first, there are no households with a small child and the wife older than 38, where at the same time a further household member is working. Secondly, the odds ratio on the top, i.e. the odds ratio between **Wife's Age** and **household** given no child, is quite different from the odds ratio on the bottom (≈ 6.7) suggesting the existence of a three-way interaction between the variables.*

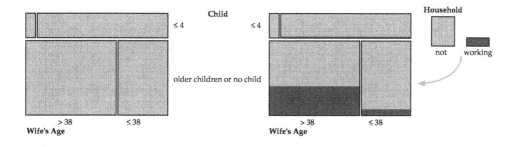

Figure 4.48: *Mosaics of **Wife's Age** and **Child**. In the mosaic on the right a third dimension is added via highlighting showing the dependency with **household**.*

*The theory of Bayesian networks states, that a variable is conditional independent from all other variables given its parents. Conditional independence of variables can easily be checked in mosaicplots (cf. section 2.1.4). Figure 4.49 shows five four-dimensional mosaicplots of **household** and another variable, given **Child** and **Wife's Age**. These mosaics reveal, that **household** is indeed conditionally independent from any of the variables in the Rochdale Data given its parents.*
*Figure 4.50 is based on the same idea as the previous one, only this time the relationship between "**wife economically active?**" and the other variables is regarded. "**wife economically active?**" is the actual variable of interest in this data set - the others are*

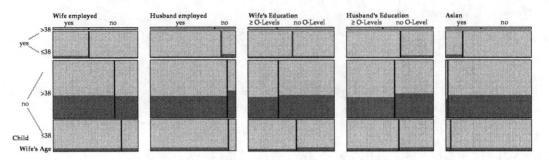

Figure 4.49: *Four-dimensional mosaicplots of the Rochdale Data.*
*Each of the mosaics shows **household** (highlighting) and another variable given **Child** and* **Wife's Age**. *The similar heights of highlighting in each row indicate conditional independence of* **household** *from every other variable.*

collected as explanatory variables for this one. The deviation from independence is largest for **Asian**, *followed by* **Child** *and* **Wife's Education**.

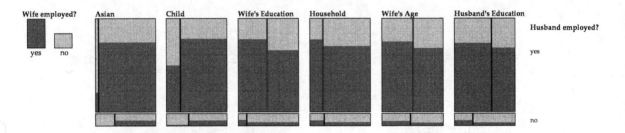

Figure 4.50: *Three-dimensional mosaicplots of the Rochdale Data.*
*Each of the mosaics shows "**wife economically active?**" (highlighting) and another variable given "**Husband employed?**". The mosaics are ordered according to the strength of conditional dependence they reveal.*

*By adding edges to the network (in order to get covered edges) the edges between "**wife economically active?**" and* **Child** *resp* **Asian** *can be reversed (cf. fig.4.51). "**wife economically active?**" results in being a response variable with five parent variables:* **Husband employed** *(as before),*
Asian *and* **Child**, *which had been children,*
and additionally **Husband's Education** *and* **Wife's Age**.
*Figure 4.52 gives two seven dimensional mosaicplots, showing the variable "**wife economically active?**" (as highlighting) and all its parents as well as* **household** *(left mosaic) and* **Wife's Education** *(right mosaic).*
The highlighting heights on the left hand side are approximately the same in each row, which

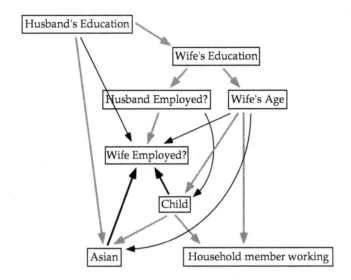

Figure 4.51: *Bayesian network of the Rochdale Data.*
"wife economically active?" has been set to a response variable by adding several edges and reversing others.

indicates conditional independence of "wife economically active?" and household given the parents of "wife economically active?" (in contrast to fig. 4.50).
The highlighting heights on the right hand side, however, still do not coincide - all of the rows show, that a woman is more likely to be economically active, if she has at least O-levels.

Summary   Though Bayesian networks are propagated as data mining technique, their use in large data sets with many variables is rather doubtful, as they very soon become very unclear. An automatic ordering technique for nodes is essential - perhaps an ordering as used for figure 4.46 from explanatory to response nodes.

Small networks, though, profit a lot by adding interactive techniques, such as linked mosaic-plots to examine the strength of single nodes. Bayesian networks regard two dimensional dependencies among variables at most - how we may deal with higher dimensional interactions by means of mosaicplots has been shown in detail in section 2.6.

For large networks linking with alternative approaches would be promising. Wills (1997) introduced the concept of interaction networks for visualising large networks. Especially the layout of the nodes has to be carefully designed in order to get as little overplotting of lines and as much overview as possible in a sensible amount of time.

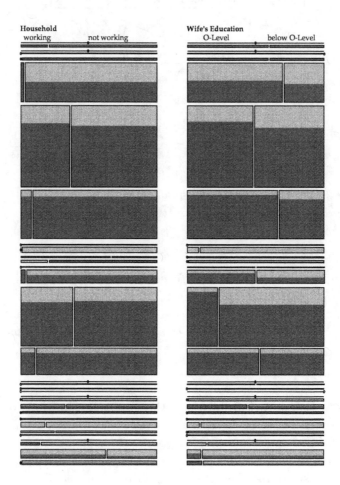

Figure 4.52: *Two seven dimensional mosaicplot of the Rochdale Data. Highlighting shows households, where the wife is economically active.*

Chapter 5

Conclusions and Future Work

In the present work we emphasised the formalization of graphics and mosaicplots in particular. This is a further step towards the goal of formal deduction based on graphics as outlined by Friendly: "With a powerful conceptual model, a graph can also become a tool for thinking" Friendly (1995), p.160. Exemplary applications of interactive graphics are given. Extensions appear in a natural way. In the field of datamining the application of mosaicplots to association rules has yielded the most promising results. Far more KDD Techniques exist; it would be very interesting to examine in how far the proposed methods of interactive graphics contribute to understanding and interpretability of the results from decision rules and neural networks.

In my opinion the approaches to visual modelling have the greatest theoretical impact. The concept is a rather old one: to combine statistical modelling with visualization by calculating a model and visualise its "results". But "results" of models are not necessarily results. In fact, statistical modelling is a continuous process, whereas static displays are a one way road. Interactive methods are the natural solution.

The mathematical foundation is important to enable us to distinguish between real facts and mere features, so that we can rely on what we "see". The applications are numerous. Graphical methods for loglinear models, several association models and univariate linear models are discussed. Many more are within reach.

Appendix A

Data Sets

A.1 Accidents' Victims

In 1958 the French ministry of transport published data on the numbers of accidents in France during this year, classified according to a number of categorical factors.

For each accident additional information was recorded: **Vehicle** (Pedestrian, Bicycles, Motorcycles, 4-wheeled Vehicles), **Age** (0-10. 10-20, 20-30, 30-50, 50+), **Gender** and **Consequence** (Dead, Injured).

Table A.1 shows a cross classification of these variables.

Age	Cons.	Pedestrian M	Pedestrian F	Bicycles M	Bicycles F	Motorcycles M	Motorcycles F	4-wheeled Vehicles M	4-wheeled Vehicles F
	D	704	378	396	56	742	78	513	253
50	I	5206	5449	3863	1030	8597	1387	7423	5552
	D	223	49	146	24	889	98	720	199
30	I	3178	1814	3024	1118	18909	3664	15086	7712
	D	78	24	55	10	660	82	353	107
20	I	1521	864	1565	609	18558	4010	9084	4361
	D	70	28	76	31	362	54	150	61
10	I	1827	1495	3407	1218	12311	3587	2543	2593
	D	150	89	26	5	6	6	70	65
	I	3341	1967	378	126	181	131	1593	1362

Table A.1: *Accidents' Victims Data, the numbers are taken from Bertin (1967), p. 30.*

A.2   Cancer Knowledge

This data set results from an observational study by Lombard & Doering (1947). 1729 individuals were cross-classified according to five binary variables **Lectures (L), Reading (Re), Newspaper (N)** and **Radio (Ra)**. Each of them was allotted either a good or a poor score on cancer knowledge. Table A.2 shows the data. These data have been analysed several times, among others by Fienberg (1979), Goodman (1970) and Dyke & Patterson (1952).

Lectures	No								Yes							
Solid Reading	No				Yes				No				Yes			
Newspaper	No		Yes		No		Yes		No		Yes		No		Yes	
Radio	N	Y	N	Y	N	Y	N	Y	N	Y	N	Y	N	Y	N	Y
Knowledge:																
Poor	393	50	156	56	83	16	177	67	10	3	6	4	8	3	18	8
Good	84	13	75	35	67	16	201	102	2	4	7	8	3	1	27	23

Table A.2: *Cancer Knowledge Data, the numbers are taken from Fienberg (1979), p. 85.*

A.3   College Plans Data

Sewell & Shah (1968) performed a study on 10318 randomly selected Wisconsin high school seniors asking for their college plans. The individuals were cross-classified according to the five variables **Socio-economic Status (SES)** (low, lower-middle, upper-middle, high), **IQ** (low, lower-middle, upper-middle, high) measured by the Hemmon-Nelson Test of Mental Ability, **Sex**, **Parental Encouragement (PE** (low, high) and **College Plans** (yes, no). Table A.3 gives the contingency table.

A.4   Detergent Data

Double blind study on consumer behaviour (Ries & Smith 1963). Table A.4 contains a contingency table of the data. The data come from an experiment in which a sample of 1008 individuals was asked to compare two detergents, a new product X and a standard product M, placed with members of the sample. In addition to assessing brand preferences (X or M) the experimenters inquired about whether sample members had used brand M previously (yes or no), about the degree of softness of the water they used (soft, medium, hard), and about the temperature of the laundry water used (high, low) (Fienberg (1979), p. 71).

College Plans	Sex	PE	SES	IQ H	L	LM	UM	Total
No	F	High	H	98	58	76	81	313
			L	24	44	47	35	150
			LM	50	61	88	85	284
			UM	77	72	90	100	339
		Low	H	49	50	70	48	217
			L	96	454	312	216	1078
			LM	113	285	236	164	798
			UM	81	163	193	174	611
	M	High	H	54	57	90	65	266
			L	43	64	72	54	233
			LM	59	84	95	92	330
			UM	73	91	110	100	374
		Low	H	17	48	47	41	153
			L	67	349	207	126	749
			LM	79	232	201	115	627
			UM	42	166	120	92	420
Yes	F	High	H	360	36	110	230	736
			L	28	9	14	20	71
			LM	72	29	47	62	210
			UM	142	36	75	91	344
		Low	H	13	6	5	12	36
			L	13	5	5	8	31
			LM	15	11	19	12	57
			UM	20	7	13	12	52
	M	High	H	414	39	123	224	800
			L	49	13	33	38	133
			LM	119	27	64	93	303
			UM	198	47	74	148	467
		Low	H	8	4	5	9	26
			L	10	4	9	12	35
			LM	17	2	7	12	38
			UM	6	8	6	17	37
Total				2506	2561	2663	2588	10318

Table A.3: *College Plans Data, numbers are taken from Fienberg (1979), p.130.*

A.5 Letter Image Recognition

This is one of the datasets from the UCI repository of machine-learning-databases

| Water Softness | Preference | M-User | | non M-User | |
		High Temp.	Low Temp.	High Temp.	Low Temp.
Soft	X	19	57	29	63
	M	29	49	27	53
Medium	X	23	47	33	66
	M	47	55	23	50
Hard	X	24	37	42	68
	M	43	52	30	42

Table A.4: *Detergent Data, numbers are taken from Fienberg (1979), p. 71.*

http://www.ics.uci.edu/̃mlearn/MLRepository.html.

It has been donated by Frey & Slate (1991)

The objective is to identify each of a large number of black-and-white rectangular pixel displays as one of the 26 capital letters in the English alphabet. The character images were based on 20 different fonts and each letter within these 20 fonts was randomly distorted to produce a file of 20,000 unique stimuli. Each stimulus was converted into 16 primitive numerical attributes (statistical moments and edge counts) which were then scaled to fit into a range of integer values from 0 through 15.

Number of observations: 20000

Variables:

1.	lettr	capital letter (26 values from A to Z)
2.	x-box	horizontal position of box
3.	y-box	vertical position of box
4.	width	width of box
5.	high	height of box
6.	onpix	total # on pixels
7.	x-bar	mean x of on pixels in box
8.	y-bar	mean y of on pixels in box
9.	x2bar	mean x variance
10.	y2bar	mean y variance
11.	xybar	mean xy correlation
12.	x2ybr	mean of $x \cdot x \cdot y$
13.	xy2br	mean of $x \cdot y \cdot y$
14.	x-edge	mean edge count left to right
15.	xedgvy	correlation of x-edge with y
16.	y-edge	mean edge count bottom to top
17.	yedgvx	correlation of y-edge with x

A.6 Mammals' Milk

In his monograph "Clustering algorithms" Hartigan (1975) gave the following example for a clsering data set. Percentages of ingredients (Water, Fat, Protein, Lactose and Ash) of milk for 25 mammals are listed in the table A.5.

Mammal	Water	Protein	Fat	Lactose	Ash
BISON	86.9	4.8	1.7	5.7	0.90
BUFFALO	82.1	5.9	7.9	4.7	0.78
CAMEL	87.7	3.5	3.4	4.8	0.71
CAT	81.6	10.1	6.3	4.4	0.75
DEER	65.9	10.4	19.7	2.6	1.40
DOG	76.3	9.3	9.5	3.0	1.20
DOLPHIN	44.9	10.6	34.9	0.9	0.53
DONKEY	90.3	1.7	1.4	6.2	0.40
ELEPHANT	70.7	3.6	17.6	5.6	0.63
FOX	81.6	6.6	5.9	4.9	0.93
GUINEA PIG	81.9	7.4	7.2	2.7	0.85
HIPPO	90.4	0.6	4.5	4.4	0.10
HORSE	90.1	2.6	1.0	6.9	0.35
LLAMA	86.5	3.9	3.2	5.6	0.80
MONKEY	88.4	2.2	2.7	6.4	0.18
MULE	90.0	2.0	1.8	5.5	0.47
ORANGUTAN	88.5	1.4	3.5	6.0	0.24
PIG	82.8	7.1	5.1	3.7	1.10
RABBIT	71.3	12.3	13.1	1.9	2.30
RAT	72.5	9.2	12.6	3.3	1.40
REINDEER	64.8	10.7	20.3	2.5	1.40
SEAL	46.4	9.7	42.0	0.0	0.85
SHEEP	82.0	5.6	6.4	4.7	0.91
WHALE	64.8	11.1	21.2	1.6	1.70
ZEBRA	86.2	3.0	4.8	5.3	0.70

Table A.5: *Mammals Milk Data, numbers taken from Hartigan (1975), p. 6.*

A.7 Mental Health

Table A.6 contains data on the relationship between mental health and socioeconomic status of the parents. This data is taken from Goodman (1979) and has been studied previously by

Srole et al. (1962).

Mental Health Status	Parents' Socio-Economic Status						Total
	A	B	C	D	E	F	
impaired	46	40	60	94	78	71	389
moderate symptom formation	58	54	65	77	54	54	362
mild symptom formation	94	94	105	141	97	71	602
well	64	57	57	72	36	21	307
Total	262	245	287	384	265	217	1660

Table A.6: *Mental Health Data, numbers taken from Goodman (1979), p. 537.*

A.8   Mushroom Data

Among the machine learning community this data set is one of the standard data sets for testing classification problems; it is freely available from the UCI repository of machine-learning-databases (http://www.ics.uci.edu/mlearn/MLRepository.html).

This data set includes descriptions of hypothetical samples corresponding to 23 species of gilled mushrooms in the Agaricus and Lepiota Family (Lincoff (ed.) (1981), pp. 500-525). Each species is identified as definitely edible, definitely poisonous, or of unknown edibility and not recommended. This latter class was combined with the poisonous one. The Guide clearly states that there is no simple rule for determining the edibility of a mushroom; no rule like "leaflets three, let it be" for Poisonous Oak and Ivy.

Number of mushrooms: 8124

Number of variables: 22 (all nominally valued)

Variables:

classes:	edible=e, poisonous=p
cap-shape:	bell=b, conical=c, convex=x, flat=f, knobbed=k, sunken=s
cap-surface:	fibrous=f, grooves=g, scaly=y, smooth=s
cap-color:	brown=n, buff=b, cinnamon=c, gray=g, green=r, pink=p, purple=u, red=e, white=w, yellow=y
bruises?:	bruises=t, no=f
odor:	almond=a, anise=l, creosote=c, fishy=y, foul=f, musty=m, none=n, pungent=p, spicy=s
gill-attachment:	attached=a, descending=d, free=f, notched=n
gill-spacing:	close=c, crowded=w, distant=d
gill-size:	broad=b, narrow=n

gill-color: black=k, brown=n, buff=b, chocolate=h, gray=g, green=r, orange=o, pink=p, purple=u, red=e, white=w, yellow=y
stalk-shape: enlarging=e, tapering=t
stalk-root: bulbous=b, club=c, cup=u, equal=e, rhizomorphs=z, rooted=r, missing=?
stalk-surface-above-ring: fibrous=f, scaly=y, silky=k, smooth=s
stalk-surface-below-ring: fibrous=f, scaly=y, silky=k, smooth=s
stalk-color-above-ring: brown=n, buff=b, cinnamon=c, gray=g, orange=o, pink=p, red=e, white=w, yellow=y
stalk-color-below-ring: brown=n, buff=b, cinnamon=c, gray=g, orange=o, pink=p, red=e, white=w, yellow=y
veil-type: partial=p, universal=u
veil-color: brown=n, orange=o, white=w, yellow=y
ring-number: none=n, one=o, two=t
ring-type: cobwebby=c, evanescent=e, flaring=f, large=l, none=n, pendant=p, sheath-ing=s, zone=z
spore-print-color: black=k, brown=n, buff=b, chocolate=h, green=r, orange=o, purple=u, white=w, yellow=y
population: abundant=a, clustered=c, numerous=n, scattered=s, several=v, solitary=y
habitat: grasses=g, leaves=l, meadows=m, paths=p, urban=u, waste=w, woods=d

A.9 Rochdale Data

(Whittaker 1990) The data contain information on 665 households of Rochdale, Lancashire, UK. Goal of the study was to identify factors which influence, whether a wife is economically active or not. 7 additional binary variables were recorded for each household:

	variable's name	value	explanation
A	**Wife employed?**	no/yes	yes, if wife is economically active
B	**Wife's Age**	$\leq 38/ > 38$	
C	**Husband Employed**	no/yes	
D	**Child**	no/yes	yes, if there's a child of age < 4 in the household
E	**Wife's Education**	O-level+/not	
F	**Husband's Education**	O-level+/not	
G	**Asian Origin**	no/yes	
H	**Household Working**	no/yes	yes, if any other member (than wife or husband) of the household is working

One of the main problems when working with this data set is the large number of empty combinations - only 91 out of a total of 256 combination contain any observation.

Table A.7 shows all twenty association rules.

rules for active economy				supp	conf
C			→ A	63.21	71.84
E			→ A	33.93	76.61
D			→ A	56.31	74.85
D	E		→ A	26.88	84.04
H	F		→ A	9.01	80.00
B	F		→ A	20.87	75.96
G	F		→ A	40.84	73.32
G	H		→ A	15.92	75.18
G	B		→ A	35.59	73.60
D	¬ B	C	→ A	20.12	83.23
D	¬ B	F	→ A	13.66	85.85
G	¬ B	D	→ A	21.02	83.83

rules for inactive economy				supp	conf
¬ D			→ ¬ A	14.26	57.93
¬ G			→ ¬ A	7.21	88.89
¬ C			→ ¬ A	8.41	70.89
¬ C	¬ D		→ ¬ A	4.05	93.10
¬ E	¬ D		→ ¬ A	9.01	73.17
¬ F	¬ B	¬ E	→ ¬ A	7.21	58.54
¬ H	¬ B	¬ E	→ ¬ A	10.66	51.08
¬ H	¬ E	¬ F	→ ¬ A	11.41	51.35

Table A.7: *List of all association rules with response* A *or* ¬ A *after pruning according to method 1.*

A.10   SAS Assocs Data

One of the example data sets of the SAS EnterpriseMiner called `ASSOCS.DAT`. The data consists of 1001 customers, of whom each bought exactly 7 items out of a total of 20 items. The items are:

apples, artichoke, avocado, baguette, bordeaux, bourbon, chicken, coke, corned beef, cracker, ham, heineken, herring, ice cream, olives, peppers, sardines, soda, steak, turkey

A.11   Titanic Data

For each person on board the fatal maiden voyage of the ocean liner SS Titanic, this dataset records Sex, Age (child/adult), Class (Crew, 1st, 2nd, 3rd Class) and whether or not the person survived.

The lines listed below are taken out of the final report of the British Board of Trade enquiring the loss of the ship (Great Britain Parliament 1998).

1st Class
Adult males	57	out of 175, or 32.57 percent.
Adult females	140	out of 144, or 97.22 percent.
Male children	5	All saved.
Female children	1	All saved.
Total	203	out of 325, or 62.46 percent.

2nd Class
Adult males	14	out of 168, or 8.33 percent.
Adult females	80	out of 93, or 86.02 percent.
Male children	11	All saved.
Female children	13	All saved.
Total	118	out of 285, or 41.40 percent.

3rd Class
Adult males	75	out of 462, or 16.23 percent.
Adult females	76	out of 165, or 46.06 percent.
Male children	13	out of 48, or 27.08 percent.
Female children	14	out of 31, or 45.16 percent.
Total	178	out of 706, or 25.21 percent.

Crew saved
Deck Department	43	out of 66, or 65.15 percent.
Engine Room Department	72	out of 325, or 22.15 percent.
Victualling Department	97	out of 494, or 19.63 percent.
		(including 20 women out of 23)
Total	212	out of 885, or 23.95 percent.

Table A.8: *"Numbers saved" from the Report on the Loss of the "S.S. Titanic", 1912, by Mersey, Wreck Commissioner.*

The data set has been used previously by Dawson (1995).
Theus & Lauer (1999), Friendly (1999) and Hofmann (1999) used the Titanic data set for illustration of mosaicplots, which was commented by Andreas Buja (1999), the editor of the JCGS, with:

"The Titanic survival data seem to become to categorical data analysis what Fishers Iris data are to discriminant analysis."   p.32

Appendix B

Algorithm for Fitting Association Models

Darroch& Ratcliff (1972) proposed the iterative proportional fitting algorithm for fitting loglinear models. This algorithm can also be used for fitting association models iteratively by setting specific constraints (cf. Agresti (1984), chapter 5).

Let the set $\{m_{ij}\}$ be the set of expected values for a contingency table of the two variables X and Y with I and J categories. Depending on the model assumption, different constraints for the m_{ij} are given, leading to the following iterations:

B.1 Uniform association model

$$m_{ij}^{(t+1)} = \frac{n_{i.}}{m_{i.}^{(t)}} m_{ij}^{(t)}$$

$$m_{ij}^{(t+2)} = \frac{n_{.j}}{m_{.j}^{(t+1)}} m_{ij}^{(t+1)}$$

$$m_{ij}^{(t+3)} = m_{ij}^{(t+2)} \left(\frac{\sum\sum u_a v_b n_{ab}}{\sum\sum u_a v_b m_{ab}^{(t+2)}} \right)^{u_i v_i} \left(\frac{\sum\sum (1 - u_a v_b) n_{ab}}{\sum\sum (1 - u_a v_b) m_{ab}^{(t+2)}} \right)^{1 - u_i v_j}$$

where $0 \le u_i \le 1$ and $0 \le v_j \le 1$.

initial estimates $\left\{ m_{ij}^{(0)} \right\} \equiv 1$

B.2   Row effects model

$$
m_{ij}^{(t+1)} = \frac{n_{i.}}{m_{i.}^{(t)}} m_{ij}^{(t)}
$$

$$
m_{ij}^{(t+2)} = \frac{n_{.j}}{m_{.j}^{(t+1)}} m_{ij}^{(t+1)}
$$

$$
m_{ij}^{(t+3)} = m_{ij}^{(t+2)} \left(\frac{\sum v_b n_{ib}}{\sum v_b m_{ib}^{(t+2)}} \right)^{v_j} \left(\frac{\sum (1-v_b) n_{ib}}{\sum (1-v_b) m_{ib}^{(t+2)}} \right)^{1-v_j}
$$

where $0 \leq u_i \leq 1$ and $0 \leq v_j \leq 1$.
initial estimates $\left\{ m_{ij}^{(0)} \right\} \equiv 1$

B.3   Row and Column effects model

$$
m_{ij}^{(t+1)} = \frac{n_{i.}}{m_{i.}^{(t)}} m_{ij}^{(t)}
$$

$$
m_{ij}^{(t+2)} = \frac{n_{.j}}{m_{.j}^{(t+1)}} m_{ij}^{(t+1)}
$$

$$
m_{ij}^{(t+3)} = m_{ij}^{(t+2)} \left(\frac{\sum v_b n_{ib}}{\sum v_b m_{ib}^{(t+2)}} \right)^{v_j} \left(\frac{\sum (1-v_b) n_{ib}}{\sum (1-v_b) m_{ib}^{(t+2)}} \right)^{1-v_j}
$$

$$
m_{ij}^{(t+4)} = m_{ij}^{(t+3)} \left(\frac{\sum u_a n_{aj}}{\sum u_a m_{aj}^{(t+2)}} \right)^{u_i} \left(\frac{\sum (1-u_a) n_{aj}}{\sum (1-u_a) m_{aj}^{(t+3)}} \right)^{1-u_i}
$$

$$
m_{ij}^{(t+5)} = m_{ij}^{(t+4)} \left(\frac{\sum \sum u_a v_b n_{ab}}{\sum \sum u_a v_b m_{ab}^{(t+4)}} \right)^{u_i v_i} \left(\frac{\sum \sum (1-u_a v_b) n_{ab}}{\sum \sum (1-u_a v_b) m_{ab}^{(t+4)}} \right)^{1-u_i v_j}
$$

where $0 \leq u_i \leq 1$ and $0 \leq v_j \leq 1$.
initial estimates $\left\{ m_{ij}^{(0)} \right\} \equiv 1$

Appendix C

Heuristics for an Optimal Linear Ordering

Preliminaries

(i)   Let Π be the set of all prime implicants.

(ii) For $m \in \Pi$ let $\mathcal{X}(m)$ be the set of variables, which occur in m.

(iii) Let A be a variable and m some variables with a specified order, denote with $\mathcal{P}(A \mid m)$ the set of all prime implicants, which appear in the order (m, A) but do not occur in m alone:

$$\mathcal{P}(A \mid m) = \{ p \in \Pi \mid \mathcal{X}(p) \not\subset \mathcal{X}(m), \mathcal{X}(p) \subset \mathcal{X}(m) \cup \{A\} \}$$

(iv) Denote with $\mathcal{P}_d(A \mid m)$ the result from transforming the set of prime implicants $\mathcal{P}(A \mid m)$ into a set of mutually exclusive implicants.

The transformation works as follows: For each two implicants p_1 and p_2 with a non-empty intersection include three implicants instead of the two, namely $p_1 \cap \neg p_2$, $\neg p_1 \cap p_2$ and $p_1 \cap p_2$. Proceed until the implicants are mutually exclusive.

(v)   Denote with v_{mA} the number of visible target cells. Then the number of newly visible cells after adding variable A is calculated from the number of prime implicants, which contain only A and variables in $\mathcal{X}(m)$, and their length:

$$v_{mA} - v_m = \sum_{p \in \mathcal{P}_d(A|m)} \prod_{X \in \mathcal{X}_{m \setminus p}} |c(X)|,$$

219

where $\mathcal{X}_{m\backslash p} := \mathcal{X}(m)\backslash\{\mathcal{X}(p) \cup \mathcal{X}(p\cap\mathcal{P}(m))$ and $|c(X)|$ is the number of categories of variable X.

Remark C.0.1

For any variable B the set $\mathcal{P}(A \mid m)$ is a subset of $\mathcal{P}(A \mid mB)$.

Proof   From the definition,

$$\mathcal{P}(A \mid mB) = \{q \in \Pi \mid \mathcal{X}(q) \not\subset \mathcal{X}(mB), \mathcal{X}(q) \subset \mathcal{X}(mB) \cup \{A\}\}.$$

For any prime implicant $q \in \mathcal{P}(A \mid m)$:

(i) $\mathcal{X}(q) \subset \mathcal{X}(m) \cup \{A\}$

$$\Rightarrow \mathcal{X}(q) \subset \mathcal{X}(m) \cup \{A\} \cup \{B\} = \mathcal{X}(mB) \cup \{A\}.$$

(ii) $\mathcal{X}(q) \not\subset \mathcal{X}(m)$ and $B \notin \mathcal{X}(q)$, since $B \notin \mathcal{X}(m), B \neq A$

$$\Rightarrow \mathcal{X}(q) \not\subset \mathcal{X}(m) \cup \{B\}.$$

Combining (i) and (ii) gives us the above statement, $p \in \mathcal{P}(A \mid mB)$. $\square$

The difference of these sets, $\mathcal{P}(A \mid mB)\backslash\mathcal{P}(A \mid m)$, is independent from the order, in which A and B occur, since

$$\mathcal{P}(A \mid mB)\backslash\mathcal{P}(A \mid m) =$$
$$= \{p \in \Pi \mid A, B \in \mathcal{X}(p), \mathcal{X}(p) \subset \mathcal{X}(m) \cup \{A\} \cup \{B\}\}.$$

Therefore we get the same result for the difference $\mathcal{P}(B \mid mA)\backslash\mathcal{P}(B \mid m)$.

Remark C.0.2

The transformation of $\mathcal{P}(A \mid B)$ into $\mathcal{P}_d(A \mid B)$ is unique. The above remark can therefore be extended to

$$\mathcal{P}_d(A \mid m) \subset \mathcal{P}_d(A \mid mB) \text{ for any variable } B$$

and

$$\mathcal{P}_d(A \mid mB)\backslash\mathcal{P}_d(A \mid m) = \{\mathcal{P}(A \mid mB)\backslash\mathcal{P}(A \mid m)\}_d.$$

If we now regard the difference $v_{mBA} - v_{mB}$, we get the following:

$$
\begin{aligned}
v_{mBA} - v_{mB} &= \sum_{p \in \mathcal{P}_d(A|mB)} \prod_{X \in \mathcal{X}_{mB \backslash p}} |c(X)| = \\
&= \sum_{p \in \mathcal{P}_d(A|m)} \prod_{X \in \mathcal{X}_{m \backslash p}} |c(X)| \cdot |c(B)| \\
&\quad + \sum_{p \in \mathcal{P}_d(A|mB) \backslash \mathcal{P}(A|m)} \prod_{X \in \mathcal{X}_{m \backslash p}} |c(X)| = \\
&= |c(B)|(v_{mA} - v_m) + x,
\end{aligned}
\tag{C.1}
$$

where $x := \sum_{p \in \mathcal{P}(A|mB) \backslash \mathcal{P}(A|m)} \prod_{X \in \mathcal{X}_{m \backslash p}} |c(X)|$ is independent from the order of A and B. Analogously we have

$$
v_{mAB} - v_{mA} = |c(A)|(v_{mB} - v_m) + x
\tag{C.2}
$$

Combining equations (C.1) and (C.2) yields

$$
\begin{aligned}
v_{mBA} &- v_{mAB} \\
&- v_{mB}(1 - |c(A)|) \\
&+ v_{mA}(1 - |c(B)|) \\
&+ v_m(|c(B)| - |c(A)|) = 0.
\end{aligned}
\tag{C.3}
$$

At this stage we are able to decide on the basis of v_m, v_{mA}, v_{mB} and the number of categories of A and B, which variable to choose to minimize the number of visible cells in the end.

Moreover, we are able to prove the heuristic of the algorithm for the special case of variables with equal category numbers.

While comparing the visible cells of order (A, B, C) with that of order (B, A, C) we find out that the number of newly visible cells after adding variable C is not affected by the order of A and B:

$$
v_{mABC} - v_{mAB} = v_{mBAC} - v_{mBA} \text{ for any variable } C,
\tag{C.4}
$$

since

$$
\begin{aligned}
v_{mABC} - v_{mAB} &= \sum_{p \in \mathcal{P}_d(C|mAB)} \prod_{X \in \mathcal{X}_{mAB \backslash p}} = \\
&= \sum_{p \in \mathcal{P}_d(C|mBA)} \prod_{X \in \mathcal{X}_{mBA \backslash p}} = v_{mBAC} - v_{mBA}.
\end{aligned}
$$

A basic property of an order, which is minimal with respect to the number of visible cells it produces, is that all subsequences are also minimal among the group of variables they regard:

$$v_m \text{ is minimal in } \mathcal{X}(m) \Rightarrow$$
$$v_n \text{ is minimal in } \mathcal{X}(n) \text{ for all } n \text{ with } m = nr.$$

Proof   by contradiction

Assume that there exists a beginning u of m, which is not minimal in X(u), i.e. there exists an order u' such that $v_{u'} < v_u$.

Let r be the tail of the sequence with $m = ur$, then $v_m = v_{ur}$. From equation (C.4) we get $v_m > v_{u'r}$, which contradicts the assumption that v_m is minimal.   □

On the other hand, the above property is sufficient for an order to be minimal (proof is clear, set $r = 0$).

Order of variables with equal category sizes   If A and B have the same number of categories $|c(a)| = |c(B)| =: c$, equation (C.3) simplifies to

$$v_{mBA} - v_{mAB} = (1 - c)(v_{mB} - v_{mA}). \qquad \text{(C.5)}$$

This proves remark 2.3.4, which may be summarised to "try to get as many target cells as early in the hierarchy as possible".

The following consideration has a major impact on the algorithm:

It is a very interesting feature, that we may draw conclusions about the two dimensional structure from the one dimensional situation among the target cells:

$$v_{mY} > v_{mX} \Rightarrow v_{mYX} < v_{mXY}.$$

This follows directly from equation (C.5), since $v_{mXY} - v_{mXY} = (1 - c)(v_{mX} - v_{mY})$.

It would be even nicer, if we could conjecture a statement of the following form:

$$v_{mY} > v_{mX} \Rightarrow v_{mYB_1...B_kX} < v_{mXB_1...B_kY} \text{ for any sequence of variables } B_1 \ldots B_k \qquad \text{(C.6)}$$

Unfortunately, the following transformation shows the impossibility of it:

$$v_{mYB_1...B_kX} - v_{mXB_1...B_kY} =$$

$$= \quad v_{mYB_1...B_kX} - v_{mYB_1...B_{k-1}XB_k}$$
$$+ v_{mYB_1...B_{k-1}XB_k} - v_{mXB_1...B_{k-1}YB_k}$$
$$+ v_{mXB_1...B_{k-1}YB_k} - v_{mXB_1...B_kY} =$$

$$\overset{eqn(C.5),eqn(C.4)}{=} \quad (1-c)(v_{mYB_1...B_k} - v_{mYB_1...B_{k-1}X})$$
$$+ v_{mYB_1...B_{k-1}X} - v_{mXB_1...B_{k-1}Y}$$
$$+ (1-c)(v_{mXB_1...B_{k-1}Y} - v_{mXB_1...B_k}) =$$

$$= \quad c(v_{mYB_1...B_{k-1}X} - v_{mXB_1...B_{k-1}Y})$$
$$+ (1-c)(v_{mYB_1...B_{k-1}} - v_{mXB_1...B_{k-1}}) = \ldots$$

$$= \quad c^k(v_{mYX} - v_{mXY}) + (1-c)\sum_{i=1}^{k-1} c^{k-1-i}(v_{mYB_1...B_i} - v_{mXB_1...B_i}).$$

The first part of this sum, $v_{mYX} - v_{mXY}$, is negative by supposition; about the sign of the other summands, though, no general statement can be made.

This is due to the fact, that we can not make any statements about the i dimensional structures between Y and $B_1, \ldots, B_{i-1}$ (X and $B_1, \ldots, B_{i-1}$, respectively) from the one dimensional situation.

Remark C.0.3
The above considerations are equally valid, if Y is a set of variables or a single one.

Supposing that equation (C.6) holds, it is shown in the sequel, that the algorithm leads to an optimal ordering of the variables. If we have a closer look at the postulation of (C.6), we find, that it is basically the same which an optimization in several steps makes. Equation (C.6) is the supposition of a (greedy) One-Step optimization algorithm. Higher dimensional structures are ignored or supposed to be "well-behaved". Taking higher dimensional structures into account (by letting Y be a set of variables), we can step by step achieve eliminate all possible counter examples to the optimality of the results. Of course, the price to pay, is an exponential increase in time.
In the sequel we will assume eqn. (C.6) to be true:

Proposition C.0.4
Let m be an order of the variables, which is constructed as follows: for any head sequence n of m the subsequent variable A fulfills

$$v_{nA} \geq v_{nX} \forall X \in \mathcal{X} \backslash \mathcal{X}(n).$$

Then m is minimal with respect to the number of visible cells v_m.

Proof by contradiction

Let us assume that m is not minimal, i.e. there exists an order m' in X(m), such that $v_{m'} < v_m$.

Let us further assume that we may write m and m' as

$$m = nAXr \text{ and } m' = nAYu'Xv',$$

for an arbitrary head sequence n of m and arbitrary sequences r, u', v', i.e. the assumption is, that m and m' coincide at the beginning.

By construction of m:

$$v_{nAX} > v_{nAZ} \text{ for all } Z \in \mathcal{X}\backslash\mathcal{X}(nA),$$

and, in particular, $v_{nAX} > v_{nAY}$.

From assumption (C.6) we get that

$$v_{nAX} > v_{nAY} \Rightarrow v_{nAXu'Y} < v_{nAYu'X}.$$

This means that the beginning sequence $nAYu'X$ of m' is not minimal in X(nAYu'X). m' therefore can not be minimal. This holds for every order m' with $v_m < v_m$.

$\Rightarrow m$ is minimal. $\square$

Unfortunately, if the variables have different numbers of categories, the visible cells alone are not enough to decide on the order of the variables.

Therefore we introduce a second concept to describe different orders, the **cover of an order**.

Definition C.0.5

Let c_m denote the number of cells, which are **covered** by the implicants in m, i.e.

$$c_m := \sum_{p \in \mathcal{P}_d(\,)m} \prod_{X \in \mathcal{X}\backslash\mathcal{X}(p)} |c(X)|.$$

Remark C.0.6

The following statements hold:

(i)

$$c_{mA} - c_m = (v_{mA} - v_m) \prod_{X \in \mathcal{X}\backslash\mathcal{X}(mA)} |c(X)|,$$

(ii) $c_{mAB} = c_{mBA}$ for all variables A and B.

Let us assume that the covers of the orders mA and mB are different and $c_{mA} < c_{mB}$. What does this imply on the number of visible cells?

It can be shown that the following statement holds:

$$c_{mA} - c_{mB} = \prod_{X \in \mathcal{X}\backslash\mathcal{X}(mAB)} |c(X)|(v_{mBA} - v_{mAB} + v_{mA} - v_{mB}) \qquad (C.7)$$

Proof The cover only depends on the variables but not on their order, therefore $c_{mAB} = c_{mBA}$ for all variables A and B. This fact provides us with a connection between the cover and the number of visible cells:

$$0 \quad = \quad c_{mAB} - c_{mBA} =$$

$$\overset{\text{by dfn}}{=} \quad c_{mA}$$

$$+(v_{mAB} - v_{mA}) \prod_{X \in \mathcal{X} \setminus \mathcal{X}(mAB)} |c(X)| + c_{mB}(v_{mBA} - v_{mB}) \prod_{X \in \mathcal{X} \setminus \mathcal{X}(mAB)} |c(X)|,$$

$$\Rightarrow v_{mBA} - v_{mAB} = \frac{c_{mA} - c_{mB}}{\prod_{X \in \mathcal{X} \setminus \mathcal{X}(mAB)} |c(X)|} + v_{mB} - v_{mA}.$$

$\square$

This leaves us with the possibility to choose an optimal order of the variables, if

$$c_{mA} = max_{X \in \mathcal{X} \setminus \mathcal{X}(m)} c_{mX} \text{ and } v_{mA} = min_{X \in \mathcal{X} \setminus \mathcal{X}(m)} v_{mX}.$$

List of Figures

Bibliography

Akaike H.: *Information theory and an extension of the maximum likelihood principle.* In B.N. Petrov and F. Csaki, editors, Proc. 2nd Int. Symp. Information Theory, Budapest, pp. 267-281, 1973.

Agrawal R., Imielinski T. & Swami A.: *Mining Associations between Sets of Items in Massive Databases.* Proc. of the ACM-SIGMOD 1993 Int'l Conference on Management of Data, Washington D.C., pp. 207 - 216, 1993.

Agrawal R. & Srikant R.: *Fast Algorithms for Mining Association Rules.* IBM Research Report RJ9839, 1994.

Agresti A.: *Analysis of Ordinal Data.* John Wiley & Sons, New York, 1984.

Agresti A.: *Categorical Data Analysis.* John Wiley & Sons, New York, 1990.

Becker R.A., Cleveland W.S. & Wilks A.: *Dynamic Graphics For Data Analysis.* In: Cleveland & McGill (eds) (1988), pp.1-50, 1987.

Becker R.A., Cleveland W.S. & Shyu, M.: *Trellis Displays: Questions and Answers.* AT&T Bell Laboratories Statistics Research Report No 9/94.

Bertin J.: *Semiologie Graphique.* Editions Gauthier-Villars, Paris, 1967.

Bhapkar V. & Koch G.: *Hypotheses of 'No interaction In Multidimensional Contingency Tables* Technometrics, New York, vol. 10, 2, pp. 107-123, 1968.

Bayardo R. & Agrawal R.: *Mining the Most Interesting Rules.* In Proc. of the 5th ACM SIGKDD Int'l Conf. on Knowledge Discovery and Data Mining, pp. 145-154, 1999.

Barlow R.E & Pereira C.: *Conditional Independence and Probabilistic Influence Diagrams* IMS Lecture Notes-Monograph series Vol. 16, in Topics in Statistical Dependence, pp.19-34 , 1992.

237

Bing Liu, Wynne Hsu & Yiming Ma: *Pruning and Summarizing the Discovered Association Rules*. In Proc. of the 5th ACM SIGKDD Conference: KDD99, pp.125-134, 1999.

Bing Liu, Wynne Hsu & Yiming Ma: *Integrating Classification and Association Rule Mining*. In Proc. of the 4th ACM SIGKDD Conference: KDD98, pp.80-86, 1998.

Bishop Y.V.V., Fienberg S.E. & Holland P.W.: *Discrete Multivariate Analysis*. MIT Press, Cambridge MA, 1975.

Breiman L.: *Classification and regression trees*. The Wadsworth statistics, probability series, Belmont CA, 1984.

Brin S., Motwani R. & Silverstein C.: *Beyond Market Baskets: Generalizing Association Rules to Correlations*. Data Mining and Knowledge Discovery 2(1), pp. 39-68, 1998.

Buja A.: *A word from the editor of JCGS*. Statistical Computing & Graphics Newsletter **10** (1), pp.32-33, 1999.

Chickering D.M.: *Learning Bayesian Networks from Data* Technical Report R-245, Cognitive Systems Laboratory, University of California, Los Angeles CA, 1996.

Cleveland W. & McGill R.: *Dynamic Graphics for Statistics*. Pacific Grove, CA: Wadsworth & Brooks, Inc., 1988.

Cleveland W. & McGill R.: *Graphical Perception: Theory, Experimentation and Application to the Development of Graphical Methods*. Journal of the American Statistical Association, 79(387), pp. 531-554, 1984.

Darroch J.N. & Ratcliff D.: *Generalized Iterative Scaling for Log-Linear Models*. The Annals of Mathematical Statistics,43(5), pp. 1470-1480, 1972.

Dawson R. J. M.: *The "unusual episode" data revisited*. Journal of Statistics Education, 3(3).

Douglas R., Fienberg S.E., Lee M.-L.T., Sampson A.R. & Whitaker L.R.: *Positive Dependence Concepts for Ordinal Contingency Tables*. IMS Lecture Notes-Monograph series Vol. 16, in Topics in Statistical Dependence, pp. 189-202, 1992.

Dyke G.V. & Patterson H.D.: *Analysis of factorial arrangements when the data are proportions*. Biometrics, 8, pp. 1-12, 1952.

Eick S.G. & Wills G.J.: *Navigating Large Networks with Hierarchies* In Visualization '93 Conference Proceedings,San Jose CA, pp. 204-210, 1993.

Falguerolles A., Friedrich F. & Sawitzky G.: *A Tribute to J. Bertin's Graphical Data Analysis.* In: W. Bandilla, F. Faulbaum (eds.) Advances in Statistical Software 6, Lucius & Lucius Stuttgart, pp. 11-20, 1997.

Fellner W.D.: *Computergrafik.* BI-Wis.-Verl., Mannheim, 1988.

Fienberg S.E.: *The analysis of cross-classified categorical data.* MIT Press, Cambridge MA, 1975.

Fisherkeller M., Friedman J. & Tukey J.: *PRIM-9: An Interactive Multidimensional Data Display and Analysis System.* In: Cleveland & McGill (eds) (1988), pp. 91-110, 1971.

Frey P. & Slate D.: *Letter Recognition Using Holland-Style Adaptive Classifiers.* Machine Learning, *6*, 2, pp. 161-182, 1991.

Friendly M.: *Mosaic displays for loglinear models.* In: ASA: Proceedings of the statistical graphics section, pp. 61-68, 1992.

Friendly M.: Mosaic Displays for Multi-Way Contingency Tables, Journal of the American Statistical Association (89), pp.190-200, 1994.

Friendly M.: *A fourfold display for 2 by 2 by k tables.* Tech. Rep. No. 217, York University, Psychology Dept., 1994.

Friendly M.: *Conceptual and visual models for categorical data.* Amer. Statistician, 49, pp. 153-160, 1995.

Friendly M.: *Extending Mosaic Displays: Marginal, Conditional, and Partial Views of Categorical Data.* Journal of Computational & Graphical Statistics **8** (3), pp. 373-395, 1999.

Gabriel K.R.: *The biplot-graphic display of matrices with application to principal component analysis*, Biometrika, **58**, pp. 453-467, 1971.

Gentleman R. & Ihaka R.: *The R Home Page.* http://www.stat.auckland.ac.nz/rproj.html, Department of Statistics, University of Auckland, 1995.

Goodman L.A.: *Simultaneous Confidence Limits for Cross-Product Ratios in Contingency Tables.* Journal of the Royal Statistical Society, B(26), pp. 86-102, 1964.

Goodman L.A.: *The Multivariate Analysis of Qualitative Data: Interactions Among Multiple Classifications.* Journal of the American Statistical Association, 65, pp. 226-256, 1970.

Goodman L.A.: *Simple models for the Analysis of Association in Cross-Classifications Having Ordered Categories.* Journal of the American Statistical Association, 74, pp. 537-552, 1979.

Gower J.C. & Hand D.J.: *Biplots*, Chapman & Hall Ltd, London, 1996.

Great Britain Parliament: *Report on the Loss of the S.S. Titanic - The official government enquiry*, Picador, USA, 1998 .

Greenacre M.: *Theory and Application of Correspondence Analysis*, Academic Press Inc., London, 1984 .

Hand D.: *Construction and Assessment of Classification Rules.* John Wiley & Sons, Chichester, 1997.

Hartigan J.A. & Kleiner B.: *Mosaics for Contingency Tables.* Computer Science and Statistics: Proceedings of the 13th Symposium on the Interface. New York, Springer Verlag, pp.268-273, 1981.

Hartigan J.A.: *Clustering algorithms.* Wiley Series in probability and mathematical statistics, John Wiley & Sons, 1975.

Heckerman D.: *A Tutorial on Learning Bayesian Networks* Technical Report MSR-TR-95-06, Microsoft Research, Redmond WA, 1995.

Heckerman D., Geiger D. & Chickering D.M.: *Learning Bayesian Networks: The Combination of Knowledge and Statistical Data* Proc.10th Conf. Uncertainty in Artificial Intelligence, Morgan Kaufmann Publishers, San Francisco, CA, pp. 293-301,1994.

Hoaglin D.C., Mosteller F. & Tukey J.W.: *Fundamentals of Exploratory Analysis of Variance.* John Wiley & Sons, New York, 1991.

Hofmann H.: *Simpson on Borad the Titanic? Interactive Methods for Dealing with Multivariate Categorical Data.* Statistical Computing & Graphics Newsletter **9** 2, pp. 16-19, 1999.

Hofmann H. (1998) *Exploring categorical data: interactive mosaic plots*, Metrika **51** 1, pp. 11-26, 2000.

Hofmann H. (1998) *Interaktive Biplots - Eine Verbindung zwischen multivariater Statistik und Interaktiver Statistischer Graphik*, Diplomarbeit im Studiengang Mathematik am Institut fr Mathematik der Universitt Augsburg, February 1998.

Huber P.: Comment to Dynamic Graphics For Data Analysis. In: W.S. Cleveland, M.E. McGill, (eds) Dynamic Graphics For Statistics. Pacific Grove, CA: Wadsworth & Brooks, Inc., pp. 51, 1988.

Hummel J.: Linked Bar Charts: Analysing Categorical Data Graphically. Journal of Computational Statistics, pp. 23-33, 1996 (11).

Kardaun J., v.d. Waeteren-de Hoog B., Kaper E., Laaksonen S., Alanko T., Lehtinen H., Mattsson C., v.d. Heyde C., Potamias G., Dounias G. & Moustakis V.: *KESO - User's Evaluation Report.* Centraal Bureau voor de Statistiek, Research paper no. 9925, 1999.

Kardaun J. & Alanko T.: *Exploratory Data Analysis and Data Mining in the setting of National Statistical Institutes.* in Kardaun et al, 1999.

Klemettinen M., Mannila H., Ronkainen P., Toivonen H. & Verkamo I.: *Finding interesting rules from large sets of discovered association rules.* In Proceedings of the Third International Conference on Information and Knowledge Management (CIKM'94), ACM Press, pp. 401-407, 1994.

Klösgen W. & Zytkow J.: *Knowledge Discovery in Databases Terminology.* In Knowledge Discovery in Databases, eds. Piatetsky-Shapiro G. & Frawley W., pp. 573-592, 1991.

Lancaster H.O.: *Complex Contingency Tables Treated by the Partition of χ^2.* Journal of the Royal Statistics Society, B(13), pp. 242 - 249,1951.

Lauer S.: *Graphische Modelle* Diplomarbeit im Studiengang Diplom-Wirtschaftsmathematik am Institut fr Mathematik der Universitt Augsburg, July 1997.

Lauritzen S.L.: *Graphical Models* Oxford statistical science series 17, Oxford U.P., 1996.

Lincoff G.H (ed.): *The Audubon Society Field Guide to North American Mushrooms.* New York: Alfred A. Knopf, 1981.

Lombard H.L. & Doering C.R.: *Treatment of the four-fold table by partial correlations as it relates to public helath problems.* Biometrics, 3, pp. 123-128, 1947.

Piatetsky-Shapiro G.: *Discovery, Analysis and Presentation of Strong Rules.* In Knowledge Discovery in Databases, eds. Piatetsky-Shapiro G. & Frawley W., pp. 229-248, 1991.

Piatetsky-Shapiro G. & Masand B.: *Estimating Campaign Benefits and Modeling Lift.* In Proc. of the 5th ACM SIGKDD Int'l Conf. on Knowledge Discovery and Data Mining, pp. 185-193, 1999.

Playfair W.: *The Commerical and Political Atlas.* London, 1786.

Quine Willard V. O.: *A way to simplify truth functions.* American Mathematical Society, *62*, 627-631, 1955.

Quinlan R.: *Data Mining Tools See5 and C5.0 - Homepage.* http://www.rulequest.com/see5-info.html, 2000.

Quinlan R.: *Bagging, Boosting, and C4.5.* AAAI/IAAI, *1*, pp.725-730, 1996.

Riedwyl H. & Schuepbach M.: Parquet diagram to plot contingency tables, Softstat '93: Advances in Statistical Software, pp.293-299, 1994.

Ries P.N. & Smith H.: *The use of chi-square for preference testing in multidimensional problems.* Chemical Engineering Progress, 59, pp. 39-43,1963.

Sewell W. & Shah V.: *Social class, parental encouragement, and educational aspirations.* Amer. J. Sociol., **73**, pp. 559-572, 1968.

Simpson E.H.: *The interpretation of interaction in contingency tables.* Journal of the Royal Statistics Society, B(13), pp. 238 - 241,1951.

Srikant R. & Agrawal R.: *Mining Generalized Association Rules.* Proc. of the 21st Int'l Conference on Very Large Databases, Zürich, Switzerland, 1995.

Srole L., Langner T.S, Michael S.T., Opler M.K. & Rennie T.A.C.: *Mental Health in the Metropolis: The Midtown Manhattan Study.* McGraw-Hill, New York, 1962.

Swayne D. & Klinke S.: Introduction to the special issue on interactive graphical data analysis: what is interaction?. Journal of Computational Statistics, pp. 1-6, 1999 (1).

Theus M.: *Theorie und Anwendung Interaktiver Statistischer Graphik.* Augsburger mathematisch-naturwissenschaftliche Schriften, **14**, Wißner Verlag, Ausgburg, 1996.

Theus M. & Lauer S.: *Visualizing Loglinear Models.* Journal of Computational and Graphical Statistics **8** 3, pp. 396 - 412, 1999.

Theus M., Wilhelm A.F.X. (1996) *Analysing the Structure of Categorical Data using Interactive Mosaic Plots and the Minimisation of Boolean Functions*, Proceedings in Computational Statistics '96, 119-120.

Toivonen H., Klemettinen M., Ronkainen P., Hätönen K. & Mannila H.: *Pruning and grouping discovered association rules.* In MLnet Workshop on Statistics, Machine Learning, and Discovery in Databases, 47-52, Heraklion, Crete, Greece, 1995.

Tufte E.: *The Visual Display of Quantitative Information.* Graphics Press, Chesire Connecticut, 1983.

Unwin A., Theus M., Hofmann H. & Siegl B.: *MANET - Extensions to Interactive Statistical Graphics for Missing Values,* New Techniques and Technologies for Statistics II, IOS-Press, Amsterdam, pp.247-259, 1997.

Unwin A. & Wills G.: *Exploring TIme Series Graphically.* Statistical Computing and Graphical Newsletter, 2, pp.13-15, 1999.

Unwin A.: *Requirements for Interactive Graphics Software for Exploratory Data Analysis.* Journal of Computational Statistics, *1*, pp. 7-22, 1999.

Unwin A. & Unwin D.J.: *Exploratory Spatial Data Analysis with Local Statistics.* The Statistician, *47*, 3, pp. 415-421, 1998.

Unwin A., Hawkins G. Hofmann H. & Siegl B.: *Interactive Graphics for Data Sets with Missing Values - MANET.* Journal of Computational and Graphical Statistics, 5, 2, pp. 113 - 122, 1996.

Unwin A.: *REGARDing Geographic Data.* Journal of Computational Statistics, Physica Verlag, pp.315-326, 1994.

Velleman P.: *Data Desk 5.0, Data Description.* Ithaka, New York, 1995.

Whittaker, J.: *Graphical Models on Applied Multivariate Statistics.* John Wiley & Sons, New York, 1990.

Wilhelm A.: *Interactive Statistical Graphics: The Paradigm of Linked Views.* Habilitationsschrift, Universität Augsburg, 2000.

Wilkinson L.: *The Grammar of Graphics.* Springer-Verlag, New York, 1999.

Wills G. & Eick S.: *High Interaction Graphics.* European Journal of Operational Research, pp. 445-459, 1995.

Wills G.J.: *NicheWorks - Interactive Visualisation of Very Large Graphs* In Graph Drawing '97 Conference Proceedings, Rome, Italy, Springer-Verlag, 1997.

Yule, G.U.: *Notes on the theory of associations of attributes in statistics.* Biometrika (2), pp. 121-134, 1903.

Index